THE CLASSICAL HERITAGE IN ISLAM

THE CLASSICAL HERITAGE IN ISLAM

S M Hasan

MD PUBLICATIONS PVT LTD
NEW DELHI
www.mdppl.com

Published by :

MD Publications Pvt Ltd
"MD House", 11, Darya Ganj,
New Delhi - 110 002
Phone : +91-11-45355555
E-mail : contact@mdppl.com
Website: www.mdppl.com

ISBN: 978-81-7533-274-4

Published and Printed by Mr. Pranav Gupta on behalf of **MD Publications Pvt Ltd** at Mohit Enterprises, Delhi.

PREFACE

There is much misunderstanding in the West about the nature of Islam; there is also much ignorance about the debt our own culture and civilisation owe to the Islamic world. It is a failure, which stems, I think, from the straight-jacket of history, which we have inherited. The medieval Islamic world, from central Asia to the shores of the Atlantic, was a world where scholars and men of learning flourished. But because we have tended to see Islam as the enemy of the West, as an alien culture, society, and system of belief, we have tended to ignore or erase its great relevance to our own history."

Few places throughout the world have remained untouched by the extraordinary, multi-faceted heritage of Islam. For more than 1000 years the unique and unsurpassed achievements of Islamic culture illuminated the known world, building a civilization that in it formed one of the greatest epics of human history.

From the 7th to the 18th centuries - more than an entire millennium - Islam permeated society with a profound cultural fabric whose influence is still being revealed even in today's postmodern age.

Inspired in new and revolutionary ways by the teachings of the Prophet Muhammad, as well as by his Companions and later followers, Muslim artists, architects, scholars and scientists carried the intellectual and creative concepts of Islam from present-day Saudi Arabia across the lands now known as Morocco, Spain, France and Sicily, as well as eastward throughout ancient Persia (now Iran) to India and the Far East.

Over time as Islam spread, many lands and many peoples also flowed into the faith, resulting in a diverse global community where all believers became brothers and sisters in spirit, united by their faith in the one God. Thus, diversity developed within unity, expressed in an astonishing breadth and flowering of culture which had a deep and permanent effect on life, art and science throughout societies even beyond Muslim borders. Sadly, however, this noble and living heritage, together with the importance of its worldwide influence is too little known today among both Muslims and non-Muslims.

I am very grateful to Mr. Pranav Gupta, Director of MD Publications Pvt Ltd, New Delhi, for his kind cooperation and support for this book.

S M Hasan

CONTENTS

1

Historical Significance of the Muslim Classical Heritage

The formation of the Arab-Islamic culture is connected with the birth and strengthening of the Arabic Caliphate, which under the aegis of a new religion (Islam), proclaimed by the prophet Muhammad, has spread over an extensive area, from the Middle Volga in the north down to Madagascar in the south, from the Atlantic coast of Africa in the west to the Pacific coast of Asia in the east. Having united the Hellenic Mediterranean with the Indo-Iranian world for the first time after Alexander the Great, the Caliphate turned it into a new center of interaction and mutual enrichment for different cultural traditions.

The "Golden Age" of its civilization grew during the 9th to 12th centuries and defined the level of both its material and the scientific-philosophical world culture. Alongside Christianity and Judaism, Islam represents the family of "Abrahamic religions," which, first of all, are characterized by Monotheism—faith in one God who is Life and Love, All-knowing, Omnipotent, and the Creator of the world. At the same time, Islamic Tawhid claims greater severity and sequence in contrast to Christianity and Judaism. According to Islam, such dogmas as the Trinity and the Incarnation are deviations from the true Monism and blot its essential purity.

The Islamic religion shares some of biblical traditions, such as the world being created within six days, the creation of man in God's image (the Sacred Scripture of Muslims, the Quran, underlines, the animation of man by the Spirit of God), Adam and Eve as their ancestors, their falling into sin, and their withdrawal from the original Paradise, as well as other events of sacred history connected both with Old Testament names of Noah, Abraham, Jacob and Joseph, Moses, David, and Solomon and the New Testament names of Zechariah, John the Baptist, Mary, and Jesus Christ. But Islam does not recognize the crucifixion of Christ.

According to the Quran another man was crucified instead of Christ, who was taken alive to Heaven. The denial of Christ's martyrdom is explained partially by the fact that according to the Quran, God forgave the Primogenitors their offense and, consequently, their original sin. Thus the original sin is deprived of its hereditary character and does not require any expiation by divine self-sacrifice. The Quran teaches the end of the world, the Day of Judgment, Paradise, and Hell as does the Bible. But in contrast to medieval Christianity, the Quran did not instill apocalyptic feelings in its adherents, and did not keep them in constant expectation of the Day of Judgment.

As Muhammad said, the believer should prepare himself for his future life as if he would die the next day, but he must work in the present life as if he would live forever. For Quranic eschatology it typically presents in a concrete, sensual form not only infernal sufferings, but the pleasures of Paradise as well. But for the inhabitants of Islamic Paradise (as with the Christian Paradise) the highest happiness is the spiritual bliss of seeing God. Like Christianity and Judaism, Islam is a religion revealed by God, who himself reveals to the people his essence and will, granting to them the Holy Scriptures and messenger-prophets. But in Islam prophecy (prophetism) plays such an important role that theocentrism in Islamic history takes the form of prophetcentrism. According to the Islamic prophetology, God grants at least one prophet to each nation. The total number of God's messengers reaches 124.000. The first one was Adam, and the last was Muhammad. There are about 30 prophets mentioned in the Quran, including those noted above.

Islam teaches not only the universality of prophecy, but also its unity: All prophets propagate the same faith (dogma); only the laws that regulate the moral-legal and cult-ritual sides of the adherents' lives, can be varied. Thus, not only Muhammad but also all God's messengers before him were Muslims, adherents of Islam, because "Islam," in a broad sense of the word, means Monotheism. As a rule, God sent His revelation to the prophets with the archangel Djibril (Gabriel in the Bible) in "Scriptures" or "Books." God sent 100 commandments: to Adam—21; to Seth—29; to Enoch (Arab. Idris)—30; to Abraham—10; to Moses—10. Four books were presented: to Moses—the Torah; to David—the Psalter; to Jesus—the Gospels; to Muhammad—the Quran. The prototypes of all Sacred Scriptures and Books are kept eternally in the celestial "Preserved Tablet.

"The "Scriptures" and "Books" present by themselves the "dictum" or the "dictation," which comes from God both in content and verbal format. The other part of revelation is the "inspired word;" here the prophet is involved in its verbal expression. In particular, Muhammad's own dictums (so-called Hadiths or Sunnah) compose the kernel of the Islamic Sacred Tradition and refer to this second type. On the basis of the Hadiths and testimony by Muhammad's associates, various versions of his Sira (Biography) have been made. The last ones for Muslims are similar to the Gospel in Christian understanding, whereas the Quran, being an embodiment of God's primeval Logos, is comparable to the Jesus himself.

Social and Ethical Principles

In essence, the ethical and moral doctrine of Islam is closely related to Judaic and Christian ethics. In comparison to the social and moral outlook of the Arabs during the epoch of paganism, it represented a huge step forward. Instead of a sense of a tribal exclusiveness and isolation, the founder of Islam introduced the idea of the equality of all believers, irrespective of tribal and racial differences. Contrary to the well-known heathen custom of blood feud, the Prophet called for tolerance and mildness. Islam condemned the practice of burying newborn girls alive, a practice that was widespread among some tribes. By the sanction of having no more than four legal wives the Islamic law essentially constrained the practice of polygamy, which had been widespread hitherto. The opportunity to divorce, which was rather easy for the Arabic pagans, became difficult. The initiative in the cancellation of marriage, which hitherto had belonged exclusively to men, became accessible to women as well.

After entering Islam, the rights of widows and divorced women were rehabilitated: The heathen custom of levir was revoked. From this time, women could freely take care of themselves and, in particular, could get married again. In general, due to this new religion, the social-legal position of women was considerably improved. The current subordinate status of Islamic women occurred much later, partly on the ground of contacts with other peoples who joined Islam. Such institutions as seclusion of women, the harem, and the eunuch were also alien to the original Islam. The interdiction of wine and gambling, stipulated by Islam, promoted feelings of moderation and a serious attitude to life. At the same time, ascetism was rejected in Islamic ethics. The Prophet said: "The best of you are those not who, for the sake of the heavenly, neglect the terrestrial. The best of you take both."

Following this spirit, Islam does not accept celibacy, raising marriage to the level of a religious responsibility and calling for the pleasures of family life. According to the Prophet: "When spouses caress each other, God looks at them with a gaze full of kindness." A similar "grounding" in secularity is found in the attitude to work and wealth. The Prophet required each Muslim to earn his living. The Caliph

Umar, well-known as Muhammad's companion, said that God rewarded the efforts made by persons to earn their living much more than participation in the war for faith. Although the Prophet promised the poor that on Judgment day they would enter Paradise before the rich, this was not considered an attribute of the superiority of poverty over wealth. On the contrary, prosperity (gained, naturally, in a legal way and "cleared" by paying the religious tax—zakat) was a sign of heavenly favour. Muslims did not despise "The Beautiful Life," and even encouraged it. According to the Prophet, "If God made a great favour for one of His serfs, it is necessary for Him to see an attribute of that benefit in the serf."

The activist orientation characteristic for classical Islam agreed easily with the doctrine of divine predetermination (Qadar) of the destiny of each creature outlined on the heavenly Tablet. Understanding this doctrine called one to live and act in such a way as if predetermination did not exist. Each one should apply all their efforts to changing what is possible to change. But one should readily accept what seems to him unchangeable. Only after the 13th century, partly due to the Islamic mystic Sufis, did the divine determinism, in the religious consciousness of Muslims, turn into a passive fatalism and an inert quietism.

Problem of the Theocratic Ideal

The correlation of religion and state, spiritual and secular authority in the Islamic society was not so unequivocal and unconditionally theocratic as it appears. It is possible to characterize the authority of the founder of Islam as theocratic. He combined in himself the roles of teacher of dogma and leader of the secular community and the state (army commander). The theocratic idea is also peculiar to the doctrine of the Shi'ites, who trust in God's inspiration of their teachers—Imams from the line of Ali's descendants (son-in-law and Muhammad's cousin). By direct contact with Allah, they have not only legislative, but also God-given political authority. But the "majoritarian" Islam, known as Sunnism, did not share similar ideas and did not recognize the spiritual authority of the Caliph. The Caliph ("governor," "deputy") acts for Muhammad as a community head, but not as a religious lawmaker.

After the Prophet's death, the legislative, spiritual authority was embodied exclusively in the Quran and Sunnah. In contrast to the Pope, the Caliph was never considered as the carrier of sacral grace. That is why he could not introduce new doctrines and rites or establish such institutions as indulgences, interdicts, excommunications, etc. The Caliph possessed executive authority only. His main goal was to see that the life of the community proceeded according to religious prescriptions. Therefore, some researchers avoid applying the term "theocracy" to Islamic realities. When using this term they necessarily add such clarifications as "executive," "protective," and even "secular" theocracy.

State authority in the classical period was not surrounded by a religious aura, though it was considered a necessary institution. In the consciousness of Muslims of that epoch, only the first four companion-successors of the Prophet (Abu Bakr, Umar, Uthman, and Ali, who ruled from 632 to 661) were real "executive deputies" of the Prophet. Such understanding has remained until now, that is, the leaders of the state have never inherited his prophetic powers of prophecy. They were known only as the "rightly guided Caliphs." All subsequent governors were actually only ordinary kings (muluk), though they had the title of Caliph. There is a belief that such a transformation of power had been predicted by the Prophet: "After me the Caliphate will last for thirty years, and then a reign (mulk) comes." In reality, under the Umayyad (660—750), state authorities took an openly secular character. Under the Abbasids (750-1258), it remained the same in general, though the latter sometimes aspired to give to it a religious, theocratic coloring.

The "people of religion," the theologians (Ulama) and jurists (Faqihs) in their majority, obviously distanced themselves from state authorities, and at times were opposed to them. When some of the governors (in particular, in the 10th-11th centuries) declared themselves "deputies of God," such theocratic claims appeared only in idle declarations, because by that time the Baghdad Caliph had changed into a simple symbol of the empire, which entered into feudal dismemberment. Real power was concentrated in the hands of the Turk praetorian guards, and in the provinces the power had passed into the hands of secular governors, Emirs and Sultans. The emergence of the institution of the Sultanate meant the delimitation of religion and state. Islam (to be exact Sunnism) did not stipulate such an institution as church, that is, a hierarchically and territorially structured clergy, which would accumulate in itself the mystical presence of God in the world and act as an indispensable link between God and the individual.

Islamic faith does not recognize any intermediary who is to carry out the contact between earth and heaven, any organ that monopolizes the right of interpreting the Sacred Scripture, and any instance (like cathedrals and synods) that makes obligatory decisions for the whole community. In Sunnite Islam, only an Islamic community (Umma) is considered infallible or to be correct in its unanimous opinion—Ijma. But Ijma, usually reduced to the consensus of authoritative theologians, is actually represented as a legitimizing instance. As a rule, it legalized those beliefs and rites that long ago had taken deep root. An analogue of the indisputable authority of the church can be found only in theocratic and charismatic Shiism, in its doctrine on Imams as sinless and infallible. Among extreme Shi'ites, Ismailists, Druzes, and Alawits—this cult reached the level of their complete deification.

Sufism

Though paradoxical, in the Sunnite environment, the existence of some kind of an intermediary between God and believers was assumed by mystic Sufis. Arising as early as the Umayyad dynasty, Sufism (tasawwuf) initially had the form of asceticism, which expressed the lower class's protest against the sharp differentiation in the Islamic community, against the luxurious and idle life of the ruling strata. Later, in the 8th and 9th centuries, it was expressed in a movement oriented to a mystical knowledge of God. Rabya praised love between God and believers. Zun-Nun marked out different stages (maqami) on a mystical way (tariqa) to God. Al-Bistami considered the wanderer's goal on this way to his final annihilation (fana) in the Beloved (God). Al-Bistami is also known scandalously because of his ecstatic utterances (shatkh) in which theologians saw claims to joining with the deity and even self-deification.

His exclamation "Glory be on me!" was considered as most seditious, for in Islamic tradition the epithet "glorified" (subhan) is attributed only to God. The other famous daring saying is "I am the Truth (God)" by the greatest mystic of Islam al-Hallaj (d. 922), who developed the doctrine on an incarnation (hulul) of the deity in the human soul. Between the 8th and 9th centuries in Sufi groups, there was a charter of spiritual management: the neophyte Sufi (murid) could attain the mystical way of perfection only under supervision by the master (sheikh), the will of whom he should obey completely and implicitly. Further, Sufi groups began to unite into large and powerful brotherhoods or orders (tariqah). Each had a system of mystical practice, rites of initiation and investiture, and external insignia.

At the head of a hierarchically organized brotherhood was the "saint" (wali, "Friend of God "). As a rule, they considered that the "saint" had supernatural abilities, and at times even a divine nature. So the mystics of Sufism introduced into religious life institutions alien to Islam. In a certain sense, these institutions were a mediating link between a believer and God, some kind of a church to which some mystics in Christianity had objected. As a whole, Sufism acted as a many-sided phenomenon, in which there were the most various social, political, spiritual, and moral orientations: from praising poverty to blessing wealth, from an anarchic aversion of the state to its active support, from indifferent religious toleration to the zealous spreading of Islam by arms, from enthusiasm in speculative theorizing to the sharp aversion of discursive thinking as a dry way of thinking and a barrier between God and the mystic.

Rigoristic Islam, while rejecting the esoteric, libertarian, and pantheistic manifestations of Sufism, simultaneously legitimized the "nomistic" branches of Sufism, supporters of which insisted on strict observance of the instructions of the Islamic law, and obligatory coordination of their doctrines with the Quran and Sunnah. Also, they called the "union" of a Sufi adherent with the Deity a particularly psychological (instead of ontological) act. Thus, the cult of the Saints, not known in early Islam, became a notable element in the religious life of the majority of the people. In many regions, Sufism had become almost the main form of "popular" Islam.

Pluralism

The absence of church in Islam resulted in another feature of Islamic spiritual life: no uniform, institutional Orthodoxy of general importance. During the Middle Ages in the Islamic empire, there were three competitive Caliphates whose capitals were in Baghdad, Cairo, and Cordoba. Within each of them, there were numerous competing religious-political schools, the number of which in the 10th century could hardly squeeze into the framework predicted by Muhammad: "My community will be divided into 73 branches." Under such conditions, naturally, the appearance of conventional "orthodoxy" was impossible, though it did not prevent each Caliphate or each school from considering their own doctrine to be the only correct one. Gradually, the conflicting religious movements came to comprehend the need of peaceful coexistence, which was the dictum of the founder of Islam: "Differences in opinions within my community are a signal Divine favour."

An example was the peaceful coexistence of the four schools of Islamic (Sunnite) law (fiqh): Hanafism, Shafiism, Malikism, and Hanbalism. An adherent of any one could pass freely to another. In turn, it was possible to meet representatives of different schools of law in the same family. It is characteristic that since old times at the four corners of the main Islamic holy place—Kaaba (in Mecca)—there have been centers for each of the four schools. In the oldest Islamic university, al-Azhar (Cairo), teaching was distributed among the four corresponding chairs. The ideological variety of the Arab-Islamic society was supported also by the fact that alongside Islam, Christianity, Judaism, and Zoroastrianism were recognized as revealed religions. From one side, this coexistence of different confessional groups was an important factor for training in religious tolerance and universalism; from the other side, it determined the character of classical Islamic culture, as not only multinational, but also polyconfessional.

Urban Dominant

Another distinctive feature of classical medieval Arab-Islamic culture is its urban character. In the Islamic society, culture was not concentrated in closed, out-of-town centers of scholarship, as in the European monasteries. Culture was exclusively the product of townspeople. The high level of urbanization of that world is indicated by the fact that about 20 percent of the population lived in the three largest towns of Southern Mesopotamia: Baghdad, Basra, and Kufa. In the quantity of towns with a population of more than 100.000 people, Iraq and Egypt in the 8th to 10th centuries surpassed the most urbanized West-European countries in the 19th century, such as the Netherlands, England, and France.

The value orientations in the medieval Islamic burgher society is indicated by the reference group with which the society tried to comply. This group was the embodiment of those features supposed obligatory for an educated and well-brought-up person. Such groups were formed by adibi, the carriers of adab (in Greek, paideia and in Latin, humanitas), which combined the breadth of humanitarian interest and many-sided secular knowledge with high morals, refined breeding, elegant manners, and courteous behaviour. From the adabi environment, there were many outstanding representatives of liberal medieval thinking, which had a relatively wide circulation in the Islamic East.

This took diverse forms, from treatises about Moses, Jesus, and Muhammad as "three impostors,",to the "dandies" (zurafa), who sported their religious nonconformism and skepticism. Usually, the long list of such thinkers of the classical epoch opens with the names of the adibs Ibn al-Muqaffa and at-Tawhidi, the philosophers Ibn al-Rawanda and Abu-Bakr ar-Razi, and the poets Khayyam and al-Ma'arri. The action of these and other factors of the social-political and ideological kind has determined the character of the classical Arab-Islamic culture as a religious-secular one. Moreover, in many spheres of spiritual creativity, secular matters were not subject to religious matters, and sometimes came to the fore.

Intellectual Learning

Cult of Knowledge

It is noted by researchers in the Arab-Islamic culture that "knowledge" (ilm, also meaning "science") had a significance not found equally in other civilizations. The universal celebration of knowledge in Islamic civilization has been partly promoted by the Islamic religion. The Quran often emphasized ordering the world according to a system of, and compliance with, law, which is the main precondition for scientific knowledge. Many Quranic verses urge the human being to think of natural things because they bear in themselves the "signs" of the Creator and certify His skill, wisdom, and good intention. Moreover, the Quran declares the human being to be God's governor on the Earth. That is why one is called not only to study the world, but also to transform it. In many respects, the general moral-psychological atmosphere surrounding knowledge and science was determined by Quranic prescriptions that represent the world as something final rather than as relative and transient, that is, the emphasis is on the theistic rule of God as stabilizing rather than as capable of working all possible miracles, that would break the usual flow of cause-effect relations, which would subvert knowledge and science.

The Sacred Tradition is eloquent evidence to the worship of knowledge. The founder of Islam called the search for science a "responsibility of each Islamic man and woman." He talked about study as a continuous process which lasts "from cradle to tomb" and requires of a person a brave search for wisdom "even in far China." Such words, as the "ink of the scientist is as precious as the blood of the martyr who died for the faith," or "one hour of thinking is better than 70 years of divine service" belong to Muhammad as well. Orthodox adherents have vainly tried to attribute all these calls and similar ones to religious and theological knowledge. The rising civilization surrounded any knowledge with respect and honor. This is reflected in one saying, which is sometimes attributed to the Prophet: "Take wisdom even from a pagan's lips".

People of classical Islam not only cultivated knowledge and wisdom, but also enjoyed the magical charms radiated by the word of "knowledge". Knowledge was considered to be required for the soul ("heart") as food and drink is for the body. Sometimes knowledge was so tied to life that if the heart did not receive it within three days it definitely could die. Due to knowledge, one obtains immortality, because "knowledge and books are the eternal posterity of a wise man."The public prestige of knowledge is indicated by its position as a self-sufficient value, exceeding all religious and secular matters: Knowledge and education put a person on a level equal to the aristocracy and bestowed authority and power. With wide availability for education and the absence of any formal restrictions of caste, race, ethnicity, or even confession on obtaining knowledge, the real prospect of increasing personal social status was open for any ambitious young man.

A respectful attitude to the Book later spread to the Arabic alphabet, instruments and materials for writing, and the writer's profession and reflected the high position of knowledge. For Muslims, the purchasing of books turned into a matter of passionate enthusiasm, becoming a status position. In general, manufacturing paper (the secret of which was borrowed from the Chinese) in the Islamic East began in the 8th century and had vast significance for developing the book business and culture. Subsequently, paper manufacturing was taken over from the Arabs by the Europeans.

The whole Islamic world was covered with a network of numerous and diverse libraries. Libraries with up to 100,000 books (for comparison one notes that in 1340 the famous library of the Sorbonne had only 1720 books) became usual phenomenon. At the end of the 10th century, in the library of the Fatimids in Cairo, there were more than 600,000 volumes, and in Cordoba alone there were more books than in all the rest of Europe. In public libraries the readers, especially visitors who were not rich, not only used the books, but also received paper and writing materials free of charge. There they found both a quiet place and material support. Books from a library could be taken home without any subscriptions, and many libraries were also a kind of scientific club or literary salon.

Scientific Achievements

A tremendous role in the formation and development of classical Islamic culture was played by the so-called "translation movement." Begun in the 8th century, it became quite active in the next century, in particular after the Caliph, al-Mamun (813-833), established in Baghdad the "House of Wisdom." This served simultaneously as a library, academy, and translation office. Many works of the ancient, Iranian, and Indian wisdom were translated into the Arabic language, which became the language of science and culture for the whole Islamic empire. The greatest interest shown by the was in Greek/Hellenic scientific and philosophical culture. From the Greek language (at the beginning, via Syrian and Persian, there were translations of the philosophical works of Aristotle and Plato, medical works by Galen and Hippocratus, mathematical and astronomical works by Euclid and Ptolemy, and also works on chemistry, botany, pharmacology, zoology, mineralogy, agriculture, agronomy, mechanics, etc.

Works on astronomy were translated from Sanskrit, and works of the ethical instruction from Persian. Thanks to the "translation movement," a considerable number of ancient sources in their Arabic versions were saved for history. After the epoch of translations, which lasted about one century—until the mid 9th century—the period of actual creative development of the inherited cultural traditions followed. From the 9th to 12th centuries, Baghdad, the capital of the Abbasids, had became the center of world science, just as Athens -had once been a philosophical center, and Jerusalem a religious one. Intellectual life prospered also in other large towns of the Islamic empire. A great number of cultural centers were also formed as the result of feudal dissociation, which came after the 10th century, when each independent dynasty aspired to make of its capital a small Baghdad.

Scientists of medieval Islam (as well as the figures of the Arab-Islamic culture in general) were encyclopedically educated people. Often, one person combined a philosopher, mathematician, physician, physician, historian, geographer, poet, and philologist. Having mainly overcome the speculative character of ancient Greek science, they aspired to combine science and practice, theoretical knowledge and technical action. The interest in resolving practical problems resulted for such scientists as Ibn al-Hayssam and al-Biruni in the creation of experimental science long before its rise in Western Europe. In the Islamic world, points of the astronomical system by Ptolemy, Aristotelian physics, Pythagorean optics, and theory of music were experimentally checked and revised. At the same time, due to the high theoretical level of the development of mathematics, its influence on the sciences especially on physics, chemistry, astronomy, and geography was evident. Al-Biruni considered the language of mathematics as the most perfect language of science.

Based on their predecessors' achievements, Arab-Islamic scientists made their own contributions to the development of the exact and natural sciences. In mathematics they introduced a system with 10 numbers (ciphers), subsequently called Arabic numerals (but probably Indian in origin). This system replaced a cumbrous Greek-Roman system of figures/ letters and opened broad horizons for the development of mathematics. Both "zero" and "cipher," which with the Europeans originally meant "zero," originated from the Arabic name of zero—sifr ("empty", that is, "an empty place"). Along with the introduction of daily arithmetic, the merit of discovering decimal fractions, important for the extraction of square and cube roots, belongs to the Islamic scientists.

The mathematicians of medieval Islam transformed algebra into an exact science and considerably developed it. The term "algebra" (Arabian, al-Jabr) goes back to the name of a mathematical treatise by al-Khorezmi (11th century), and the term "algorithm" originates from the author's name, transformed into Latin. The algebraic symbol "X" was taken from the Spanish xay which is the phonetically transformed Arabic word shay—thing. Islamic scientists created plane and spherical trigonometry. By applying arithmetic and algebra in geometry, they laid the basis of analytical geometry. As a whole the astronomy of the medieval Islam adopted the Ptolemaic system. Though this system was erroneous in its essence, the Islamic scientists managed to reach important discoveries.

At the end of the 9th century, al-Battani was the first to calculate the deviation of the terrestrial axis (so-called ellipticity). In 920, the equinox or precession was predicted, which allowed an adjustment of the lunar and solar calendars. Having found a weakness in the Ptolemaic system, some scientists subjected it to criticism and reformation. Astronomers from Maraga, as well as Ibn al-Shatir (d. 1350)—from Damascus, created non-Ptolemaic planetary models, and al-Biruni conceived the benefit of heliocentrism. In the well-equipped observatories of Baghdad, Damascus, Cairo, Cordoba, Maraga, Samarkand, and other cities, the foundation of astrometry, the whole area of astronomical observation was began. More perfect than those of antiquity and India, the astronomical tables made in the Islamic East were popular in Europe until the middle of the 18th century.

Along with the well-known terms: "zenith", "nadir", "almanac," and "azimuth," more than 200 of the Arabic names of stars, among which Aldebaran, Altair, Betelgeyze, Vega, and Rigel, were adopted in Europe. In the Middle Ages, astrology was closely bound with astronomy. It became the subject of general enthusiasm, despite the negative attitude of rigorist theologians. Abu-Mashar (in Latin Albumasar, who died in 886) was the greatest Arabic astrologer. The Christians of medieval Europe honored him as a prophet. The geographical literature of Medieval Islam is characterized by an abundance of information and a variety of genres. Arabic geographers and travelers left the description of the whole Islamic world, and also some other countries of Europe, Northern and Central Africa, the East African coast, and Asia from Korea to the Malay Archipelago. They were interested not only in physical, geographical, or climatic conditions, but also equally in life, industry, culture, language, religious doctrines, miracles, and legends.

The geographer al-Idrisi (1165), native of Morocco, was the most known in the Christian West. He became famous after preparing for the king of Sicily, Roger II, descriptions of the world on the basis of direct observations obtained by an expedition under his supervision. As an illustration of his work, the scientist created a silver planisphere, on which all cities known at that time (1154) were marked. Beyond descriptive geography, scientists of the Islamic world successfully developed astronomical and mathematical geography. Under al-Mamun (9th century) in the Syrian desert, the meridian degree was measured with the purpose of subsequently measuring the Earth's circumference. The result of the measurement was incredibly accurate, within several hundred meters.

Arab-Islamic geographers had rules that make it possible to calculate the area coordinates, and also the table of latitudes and longitudes for all points worldwide. These tables, created from making corrections and additions by the Arabs to the data contained in the Geography of Ptolemy became known in the medieval West as well. For example, the length of the Mediterranean sea was considerably reduced in comparison with the calculations of Ptolemy: from 62 to 52 degrees (al-Khawarizmi), and then down to 42 degrees (az-Zarqali), which is close to correct. Arab-Islamic achievements in the field of navigation were taken up by the Christian West. In particular, the Europeans borrowed such technical innovations as the compass and the slanting (triangular) sail, which allowed one to move against the wind. Especially due to the latter it became possible to build larger ships which were able to cross the Atlantic and make longer voyages, resulting in great geographical discoveries.

Moreover, marine maps (the Portolans), important for seafarers, were made in Genoa on the basis of Islamic marine maps. The evidence of an Islamic contribution to the development of marine culture can be found in the acceptance by Europeans of many Arabic words as international terms: admiral, arsenal, barge, after mast, galley, cable, monsoon, still used today. The Islamic world promoted great geographical discoveries in other ways as well. Early Islamic geographers taught that there was a certain global center "Arin," looking like a dome and located in India, at the equator, midway between the extreme western and eastern borders of the inhabited part of the Earth. This theory, later perceived by Christian Europe, guided Columbus to the idea of a pear-shaped Earth. Additionally, in the western hemisphere, opposite to the Indian Arin, another center should exist, which was supposed to be higher than that located on the eastern side. So the Arabic geographical doctrine played a certain role in the greatest geographical discoveries of the modern epoch.

Columbus in his letter with the inscription "from Haiti" (October, 1498) said that the Arabic-Spanish thinker, Ibn Rushd (Averroes), was one of the authors who opened to him the existence of the New World. It is interesting, also, that Vasco da Gama, used the services of the Arabic pilot, Ahmad Ibn Majid, to first reach the coast of India on May 20, 1498. In the history of optics, Ibn al-Hayssam (d. 1039), known in Europe as Alhazen, discovered that the heavenly bodies emitted light, and that time is required for light's movement. He disproved the theory of Euclid and Ptolemy on visible rays, which go from the eyes to an object, and described the visual process as a pure act of perception. Studying light reflection in flat, spherical, cylindricalm, and conic mirrors, the Cairo optician investigated the question that to this day is called the Alhazen problem. Ibn al-Hayssam came close to discovering the principle of the magnifying lens that became an initial point for telescope design.

While studying light refraction, he managed to calculate the height of the terrestrial atmosphere with rare precision. The scientist's work, known in the Latin West under the name of the Treasure of Optics, formed the basis for optical research by Europeans, from Vitelo, Peckam and Roger Bacon to Leonardo da Vinci and Kepler. In the Middle Ages, chemistry and alchemy were indivisible disciplines, and in the Arabic East they were combined under the same term, al-kimiya, from which the European names of both sciences originated.

Having originated in Greek Egypt, alchemy reached the peak of its popularity in Islamic Iraq. Until the 14th century, the code of works ascribed to Jabir Ibn Hayyan (Lat. Geber, 8th century), served as the most authoritative manual on alchemy-chemistry both in Asia and in Europe.

Though the attempts to find such miracle substances as the "Philosopher's Stone" (which helps to transform the base metals into gold and silver) and the "Elixir of Life" (preserving youth and longevity) were doomed to failure, Arabic alchemists during their quests developed a new technology of smelting metals and made a number of valuable scientific discoveries. They essentially improved such main chemical operations as calcination and restoration, and also the methods of evaporation, sublimation, melting and crystallization. Due to these methods, the Arabs discovered the following new chemical substances: nitric acid, borax, arsenic, ammonium chloride, potash, saltpeter, antimony, aquaregia, etc.

The physician and philosopher ar-Razi (9th century), as well as the above-mentioned encyclopedist, al-Biruni (widely known due to his historical ethnographic work on India), who succeeded in measuring with a high degree of accuracy the specific weight of metals and minerals, are considered to be leaders in alchemy. The medicine of the Islamic East was the leader in the world till the European Renaissance. A powerful stimulus to the development of hygiene and public health services was given by Islam which required its adherents to take care of preserving not only the soul, but the body as well. Muhammad, being extremely scrupulous in matters of physical cleanliness, had given the status of a religious cult to the observance of hygiene (including daily ablutions). The mosques, where there was necessarily a room for ablution, served simultaneously as the centers of hygiene.

In addition to such rooms there were numerous public baths—hammams—which were a characteristic element of an Islamic town. The founder of Islam encouraged medical treatment, because, as he said: "God does not send diseases for which He does not send an appropriate medicine". Under his name some hundreds of sayings were given, mainly advising on prophylactic, diet and hygiene. Later they were collected under the name "The medicine of the Prophet". In Islamic cities medical services were performed not only by privately practicing doctors, but also by hospitals, usually established by donations from governors and rich people. Also there were mobile hospitals for the countryside.

More often medical aid was free, including the hospital care, medicine and food. Hospitals were subdivided into female and male branches, and also into various categories depending on an illness: fever, eye disease, gastrointestinal, or surgery. Attached to hospitals there were reading rooms, laboratories, a chapel and also a school of pharmacy. For the first time pharmacology became an independent science, and pharmaceutics a recognized profession. In hospitals students had their clinical practice; this tradition was not adopted by Europeans until approximately 1550. The Islamic world was familiar also with dispensaries, hospitals for lepers and mental hospitals, where experts on nervous diseases cared for patients.

The physicians of the Islamic middle ages carried out diagnostics based on anatomical and physiological data. They also resorted to psychotherapeutic methods, paying attention to the individuality of patients. During medical treatment much attention was paid to correct and balanced diet. The kitchen was considered an auxiliary means for medicine and had many special tasks. Also they used such anesthesiological means as opium, hashish and steam from wine. Physicians did not utilize a human corpse for disection which had been forbidden by both Islam and Christianity, but they did autopsies on monkeys and thereby gained knowledge of anatomy. In this way one physician discovered the pulmonary principle of blood circulation. In the 12th century an Islamic physician from Seville provided the first description of stomach cancer.

The surgical tools were made by highly skilled craftsmen. Ophthalmology was developed; and for the first time an operation to remove cataracts was performed. Admission to medical practice required approval by a state commission. The medical knowledge of medieval Islam was known in Europe in particular due to the translations of the encyclopedic works by such scientists, as ar-Razi (Lat. Razes, d. 926) and Ibn Sina (Lat. Avicenna, d. 1037). "The Canon of Medicine" by the latter was published in Latin in the 12th century and dominated the medical teaching in Europe at least to the end of the 16th century. In the 15th century, it was published in 16 editions, and in the 16th century in 20. Such terms as alcohol, soda, and syrup were borrowed by the European languages from Arabic medical language.

Theology of Kalam

The religious-philosophical thought in classical Islamic culture was represented by three main trends: Kalam-Islamic philosophical theology; falsafa, which evolved on the ancient Greek model of philosophizing, and speculative Sufism. Kalam first appeared in Islam and developed as various religious and political groupings appeared on the social and political scene, and in the disputes of the Muslims with the adherents of such other faiths as Mazdaism, Christianity, and Judaism. In these disputes, there took shape a characteristic theological problematic, which included the following main questions: God's attributes and their correlation with his essence; the eternity of the Quran as God's speech or its creation in time (while writing it on the Heavenly Tablet or sending it down to Muhammad); divine predetermination; and freedom of the will.

Mutazilites, the representatives of the first large school in Kalam, which prospered in the first half of the 9th century, opposed anthropomorphism and fatalism. Mushabbikhits, the adherents of such anthropomorphism, conceived God in human form. The most extreme of them—literalists or Hashawits—insisted on a literal understanding of the words of Sacred Scripture and Tradition referring to the creation of man in "God's image," to "eye," "hand," and "leg," and to His Throne. On the contrary, Mutazlites considered Islamic monotheism to be incompatible not only with polytheism and anthropomorphism, but also with the recognition of the reality and eternity of the divine attributes as certain entities or hypostases distinct from the divine essence. The traditional list of the main "positive" attributes of God usually included the following: knowledge, power, life, will, sight, hearing, and speech.

Among these as substantive or internally inherent to the divine essence, Mutazlites recognized only the first three considering them to be identical to the divine essence and in this sense eternal. The rest of the characteristics they considered "operative attributes" that arise within time, are changeable, and, hence, different from the divine essence. From this follows the Mutazilite doctrine about the creation of the Quran as God's Word, which does not comply with the prevalent Islamic theological conception of the eternity of the Sacred Scripture. Refuting the determinism of the fatalists, Jabrits, the Mutazlites considered divine justice to assume freedom of choice without which the moral responsibility of a human being for his actions and deeds is inconceivable.

Having become the main school of Kalam after the 10th century, Asharism developed its own way of resolving theological matters as the "golden mean" between the Mutazlites' position and the traditionalist theologians, between libertarians and fatalists in the perception of human action, and between nominalism and realism in their approaches to the divine attributes. In particular they believed, that the Quran was eternal in its meaning, but not in verbal expression. Moreover, according to the opinion of some Asharites, Sacred Scripture in its verbal expression had been generated within time, and was not necessarily divine: God handed over to the archangel Gabriel only the sense of revelation, which he passed to Muhammad. From this it follows that the verbal content of the Quran belongs to the Prophet.

In the above-mentioned religious discussions, there developed not only a special circle of theological problems characteristic of Kalam, but also a specific method for their resolution, which excluded references to any authorities (including Sacred Scripture and Tradition), except reason. Mutakallims (teachers of Kalam) proclaimed the unconditional priority of reason over faith, and proclaimed doubt as a methodological principle of cognition. They considered it necessary for each Muslim to pass through a stage in which he had to call into question all religious ideas, in order mentally to convince himself of their validity or falsity. The ability to think critically was trained and polished in numerous circles (or assemblies, Majalis) organized by the Mutakallims.

There, representatives of very different schools and orientations, represented by Muslims, Christians, Jews, and atheists demonstrated their skill in carrying on theological-philosophical dispute. Mutakallims also disputed before the general public; quite often even street shops and markets were places for theological disputes. However, the problems of Kalam was not reduced to theological questions. It is indicative, that in the classical works on Kalam (13th-14th centuries), theology takes less than one quarter of their volume. The rest of the research was devoted to epistemology, natural philosophy, and ontology. In Kalam were developed the original atomistic concepts, in which the finitist approach to the structure of physical bodies was applied to movement, space, and time. The teachers of Kalam thus continued the ancient atomistic tradition, which had been forgotten in medieval Christian Europe.

The aforesaid main features of Kalam—rationalism, antifideism, and primary attention to actual philosophical problems—explain the fact that the activity of the

Mutakallims was perceived suspiciously and sometimes with hostility by the majority of Islamic theologians. On the whole, in Islam, there was no aspiration to rationalize and conceptualize dogmatism and develop speculative theology. It was more focused on developing not orthodoxy as the "correct faith," but orthopraxy as the "correct deed." Therefore, Islamic civilization institutionalized and canonized the law or fiqh but not theology. In addition to law, such disciplines as the science of the Quran (exegetical) and the science of hadith—the sayings and deeds of Muhammad—were included in the traditional number of "religious sciences," but not dogmatic theology. Hence subjects similar to Kalam were not taught at religious schools (Madrasahs).

Eastern Aristotelism

If Kalam was born in the bosom of religious disputes, falsafa was a child of the "translation movement." The translation activity, where the Nestorian Syrian scientists played a large role, had resulted in the Islamic world engaging an extensive circle of philosophical ideas of the Greek-Hellenic tradition, the most important of which were the ideas of Plato, Aristotle, Neo-Platonists, Stoics, and Neo-Pythagoreans. Aristotelism and, in particular, its encyclopedic scope attracted the attention of Islamic scribers for the most part. Therefore, falsafa (Arabian, Calque) was represented mainly by the Peripatetics (Aristotelians), who were guided by Aristotle's logic, physics, metaphysics, and ethics. For politics (as the doctrine of the "ideal state" or the "virtuous city"), they used Plato's Republic.

The most outstanding Peripatetics of Islam were: Al-Farabi (d. 950), who combined Aristotelian cosmology with the emanationist doctrine of Neo-Platonians, Ibn Sina (in Latin, Avicenna, d. 1037) who systematized Aristotelism, and Ibn Rushd (in Latin, Averroes, d. 1198) known in Europe also under the honorary name of the Commentator par excellence. Where the attitude to religion on the part of some represen-tatives of falsafa was characterized by either formal recognition of the superiority of prophetic over philosophical knowledge (al-Kindi, 9th century), or open criticism of the prophets as deceivers (Abu-Bakr ar-Razi, d. 925 or 934), the Eastern Peripatetics considered religion an important "political art" aimed to control moral and legal relations among people. Such a position was determined by the belief that philosophy could be the property of the intellectual elite, the "select" (hassa), while society consisted of the "popular masses" (amma, jumhur), unable to think conceptually.

That is why it is necessary to express the norms of behaviour required for society's well being in the form of laws sent down from above. Religion and philosophy are united by the fact that their subject is the highest basis of existence. But their methods of interpretation vary in principle. According to al-Farabi, religion is a stepdaughter of philosophy, or in the words of Ibn Rushd, its sister. The Eastern Peripatetics gained new life in medieval Europe. As remarked by R. Bacon, it was due to the Islamic commentators that the Aristotelian philosophy, which had been in oblivion, became popular in the Latin-speaking world.

Also, the original works of falasifa left a deep imprint on the philosophy of medieval Europe and the epoch of the Renaissance. Medieval European scribers were familiar with the works of al-Kindi and al-Farabi. The philosophical Robinsonade of Ibn Tufayl was very popular among European readers, especially after its translation into Latin in 1671. But the deepest imprint on the philosophical thought of Christian Europe was left by Ibn Sina and Ibn Rushd. Their names were bound up with such trends, as Avicennian Augustinianism and the Latin Averroism. As a whole, classical Arab-Islamic philosophy promoted the seculari-zation of European philosophical thought and its consolidation with the natural sciences. Thus it prepared the development of early modern philosophy.

Theosophy of Sufism

The aspiration to self-reflection, the rational understanding of mystical experience, can be found in the al-Hallaj's works and in particular, in the works of al-Ghazali (d. 1111). It gained its most advanced form in the theosophical systems of al-Suhrawardi and Ibn Arabi. The doctrine of al-Suhrawardi (d. 1191), known as Ishraqism (from ishrak, "inspiration") or illuminism, represents a version of the "Metaphysics of Light," proceeding from the concept that light is the primary origin, which ontologically is represented as a substantiation of all existence, and gnoseologically as a principle of cognition. From the point of view of illuminism, the world consists of a hierarchy of "lights," at the top of which is the Higher Light of lights (God). On this basis, al-Suhrawardi revised the peripatetic system combining it with a Platonic "theosophy of inspiration," above any Aristotelian "Philosophy of Discourse."

The school of Ibn Arabi (d. 1240), the "Great Sheikh" of Islamic mystics, was more widespread in the Sufi environment. The characteristic feature for this school was the doctrine of the "unity of being" (Wahdad al-Wujut), for which it received the name of Wujudism, "ontic monism." According to Ibn Arabi, being is the one and single principle, equally present in all things; it allegedly forms their substance of primary matter, but they are its forms or modes. This Unique Being is identical to God. On this thesis, Wujudits formed the most significant system of philosophical pantheism in the Arab-Islamic culture. The other important theme of the Wujudism is the concept of "perfect man," reflecting in itself the richness of both the Deity and the universe. This concept was developed for the first time in the philosophy of classical Islam by Ibn Arabi; his follower, al-Jili (d. 1428), devoted to it his main book al-Insan al-Kamil (The Perfect Man).

The maghribian Ibn Khaldun (1406) was among the pleiad of celebrated members of the philosophical culture of medieval Islam. He was not a member of any of its schools, but founded the Human Civilization (umran) doctrine. This doctrine aimed to transform history from a chronicle of kings and prophets into a strict scientific discipline, which should form one of the important branches of philosophy. The creativity of the thinker was ahead of his time, and only in the 19th century was his true worth appreciated as the founder of historical criticism and of sociology.

Art

The Triumph of Poetry

The artistic genius of the Arabs found its brightest expression in poetry. In heathen Arabia, poetic creativity was especially cultivated by the nomad Bedouins, almost all were men. In special cases, women could compose verses. Each tribe had its own recognized poet, called to protect its honor by word, and to strike its enemies by poisonous abuse. It was believed that the poet was inspired by the Jinn, which resulted in the poet's magic charm toward the phenomena of nature. The poet's authority was important in decision-making related to private life. For example, it was enough for the poet, al-Asha, to recite a small poem eulogizing the generosity and the hospitality of one of his friends, for members of the most famous families of Arabia to come to the aid of the poor Bedouin, who still had eight daughters to establish in marriage.

At the annual fair in Ukaz (near Mecca), to which people from all ends of the Arabic peninsula came, there were competitions of poets. The verses judged the best were embroidered on silk with gold letters and hung on the walls of Kaaba, to be admired by all the pilgrims visiting Mecca. According to one of the legends, the Mu'allaks (literally, "hung up"), that is, the seven (or nine or ten) poems by the poets of the 6th century, originated from that. The Mu'allaks, in later medieval Arabic culture, were considered ideals for imitation. The composite form of Mu'allak, which is the main form of the ancient Arab poetry, is the Qasida or ode, consisting of 50-120 lines, or, more exactly, of couplets. The verses (beits) have not only a uniform size, but also a uniform rhyme.

Therefore, poems are often named with reference to their rhyme: lamiya, that is, ended with the lam ("L"), nuniya with the nun ("N"), etc. Each verse of the classical Qasyds is drawn toward the semantic completeness and, sometimes, toward the topic-figurative independence. Its connections with other verses are determined not so much by the development of a plot, as by the associations prompted by a trick of the imagination. Actually, the ode (Qasida) represents a mono-drama, usually about love, the hero of which is invariably a poet. It begins with a poet traveling by desert who stops at a site that had been left by a tribe. The poet's beloved usually is a member of that tribe, and the poet falls into his memories of her, describing her beauty and mourning his living apart from her.

Then the poet, starting again on his journey, turns to the description of his fellow travelers, horse or camel, views of the Arabic nature, animals and birds. In the final part of the Qasida, the poet eulogizes himself, re-reasoning about his arms and feats or the persons to whom he devoted this ode, glorifies his tribe, and derides his personal or tribal enemies. The ancient Arabic poetry, which was associated with paganism, originally was met with hostility by Muhammad. In the 26th chapter of the Quran, entitled "Poets," they were blamed for its invention. Probably, the founder of Islam was confused by the fact that he was accepted as an ordinary prophet or poet. Apparently, he had also personal collisions with poets and narrators, who sarcastically and disrespectfully criticized the doctrine he propagated.

Nevertheless, at the last stage of his activity, Muhammad drew upon the services of poets. Two of the most outstanding poets of the time, Kab ibn Zuhayr and Hassan ibn Sabit, delivered panegyrics in his honor. Kab, who previously composed a poem deriding the Prophet and even was wounded in a collision with the Muslims, had been an outlaw. Out of fear for his life, he came to the Prophet in repentance and began to read him a laudatory poem. It touched Muhammad so much that he threw his cloak over the poet's shoulders. As a result, the poem received the name of Burda (Cloak). As to Hassan, the Prophet presented him with a captive, the sister of his own Coptic concubine Maria. From there on, the poet recited many poems with much phraseology from the Quran and became known as the father of Islamic religious poetry.

However, the poetry of classical Islam did not become a religious poetry; on the contrary, with some exceptions it had a secular character. The Christian, al-Akhtal, who was the main poet of the Umayyad's court, sang proudly about his unwillingness to accept Islam and openly derided the Islamic cult. The love lyrics and the "wine" poetry of Abu Nuwas, the predecessor of Omar Khayyam, was widely popular. As in pagan times, poetry was recognized as the sole "high" form of literature and held a special place in Arab-Islamic society. In each court, there were poets called to glorify their patron. The study of poetry was one of the elements of general education, and erudition in this area was considered an attribute of good manners. The poetic art of classical Islam strengthened a feature characteristic of ancient Arabic poetry, namely, close connection with recitation, music, and singing. Shows starring poets, musicians, singers, and dancers were the main means of secular entertainment for the nobility and the educated people. In many respects, poetry defined the Baghdad style, and then, in general, the Arabic style of a magnificent and beautiful life.

Medieval Arabic poetry reached its zenith in the 9th to 10th centuries. In this epoch there appeared the drinking and hedonistic lyrics of Abu Nuwas and the freethinking, philosophical, and, sometimes, pessimistic verses of al-Maari, as well as the solemn lyrical odes by al-Mutanabbi who up to now is considered by many the greatest Arabic poet. During the following centuries, in particular in the 12th to 13th, the philosophical lyrics of Sufism flourished in Arabic (Ibn al-Arabi, Ibn al-Farid) and Persian ("Mesnevi" al-Rumi). The mystical poems, which were rich with bacchanalian and erotic images, were widely popular even far from the actual Sufi environment. Classical Islamic poetry remained faithful to lyricism. The epos genre presented in the Persian language by the famous Shah-nameh (Book on the Kings) by Ferdowsi (10th to 11th centuries), was not appreciably developed. At times, the genre of the "knight novel," Syra (literally "Biography") was attributed to the epos genre.

This is the product of collective folk creativity, where prose alternates with verses. From more than 20 such novels have come, up to now, the Syras of the pre-Islamic poet-warrior Antare, the Mamluk sultan Beybarse and, most famous, the migration of the Hilalits tribe to Egypt and Northern Africa. The tradition of the performance of these works in the streets, squares, and coffee shops by professional speakers, accompanying themselves on the rabab (viola), has continued until now. A significant place in Arabic prose writing is taken by adab. This is the original semi-didactic, semi-fictional genre, intended for the education and entertainment of the above-mentioned humans or adibs. In the middle of the 8th century, Ibn al-Muqaffa, who was one of the founders of this genre, translated into Arabic and carried out the literary processing of the collected fairy tales and fables, approaching the Indian Panchatantra, and played by animals. This book, known by the Arabs as the Kalila and Dimna, made Ibn al-Muqaffa famous and provided the basis for the framed story genre, at the peak of which is the famous folk fairy tales of The Thousand and One Night.

Life in the large cities gave birth to an original kind of short story called Maqama. This was a cycle of picturesque stories about the adventures and transformations of a clever tramp. Maqamas were written with refined and rhymed prose mixed with poetic inserts. The best example flowed from the pens of al-Hamadhani (d. 1008) and al-Haryri (d. 1122). Drama was not cultivated in the culture of Islam. Shadow theater plays were in folk language (oral language only). The Egyptian Ibn Daniyal (13th century) became an outstanding figure in such theater and wrote for it three librettos, which were recognized as belonging to high literature, and in this sense were unique. Later on, there was a doll theater known as the Aragooz, named after the main character. A serious kind of folk drama was represented in the Shiite mysteries (Tazia, literally Consolation), which were shows about the tragic death of Imam al-Huseyn and performed during anniversaries of this event.

As far as the Quran is concerned, it is considered a unique work, which did not belong in the frameworks of traditional poetry or prose. Written in the form of a rhythmic and sometimes rhymed prose, this book is a divine, not human, word and is inimitable and inaccessible in its artistry. The perfection of the Quranic form is also the justification of its heavenly origin, proclaiming the authenticity of Muhammad's prophetic mission.

Calligraphy

In Arab-Islamic artistic culture an extremely high position is held by calligraphy, which represents an alternative to Christian iconography. A respectful attitude to handwriting was incorporated in the Islamic religion, based on the Quran, not without similarity in Christianity to respect for the person of Jesus. According to Islamic conceptions, the first of God's creations, which appeared even before the sky and earth were created, were writing tools, that is, the pen and the tablet. The Prophet Muhammad guaranteed a dwelling place in paradise to one who beautifully reproduces God's words, particularly from the Quran, by means of the pen. Arabic handwriting became the sacred symbol of Islam. Some people considered that each letter from the alphabet represented one of the "most perfect names" of God. During the whole Islamic history, there was a wide circulation of "the science of the letters," which attributed magical and physical properties to the letters, the perception of which was the key to the mysteries of nature.

In the medieval Arab-Islamic culture, the aesthetic, emotional, and artistic perception of handwriting has been brilliantly expressed, not only in the endless efforts of artists to create new, more perfect forms of writing, but also in numerous sayings in which the writing is compared to such objects of beauty and emotional appeal as jewelry, flowers, fabrics, and gardens. Beautiful handwriting has been described as bringing pleasure to the heart and eye. "Where saffron is a maid's spirit, ink is the spirit of men," the poet exclaimed. In literature, the comparison of corporal features with letters became a standard component of poetic figures: A ringlet on the temple of the beloved can remind the poet of the "nun" letter, and a birthmark on the cheek a point above the "nun," the ligature of the "lam" and "alif" letters, written as interlacing each other, symbolizes love and union.

Being rectilinear, angular and monumental in form, Kufi calligraphy (named from a town in Iraq) was a favorite for the Quran for more than five centuries. Subsequently, it was replaced by new, uncanonized styles, mainly by naskhi ("italics"). Both calligraphies were ornamental, often with symbolic content. Calligraphy was not only a matter of patterns; sometimes it represented the completed whole in the form of some kind of a frieze or panel. Sometimes its capricious flourishes, merging together, created images of animals and even people in stories and poems.

Arabesques

Islamic art, especially in its Arabic version, developed mainly as a decorative art. This characteristic ornamentation was given in the West the name "arabesque", which reflects the aspiration to create abstract patterns in infinite variations of the same motifs filling all the graphic space. Arabesque is a complex interlacing of vegetative, geometrical and calligraphic (epigraphic) elements. The vegetative elements (acanthus, palms, grape leaves, trefoil, pine cones, tulips, roses and almond tree flowers) are stylized and have some elements in common with Hellenic tradition. But geometrical figures are characterized by rich abstractness. A circle or a star are not so much the objects of contemplation, as self-sufficient and perfect figures characteristic of the perception by Greek geometricians as the initial point for creating new figures. The third element of arabesque and the most original is calligraphy. The Arabic letters are the most suited for such a purpose and may have no analogues in this respect except possibly the Chinese hieroglyphs.

Arabesque has left a rich heritage in Islamic Spain, and hence in Europe, where it was known as the "Moresque" ("Mauritanian style"). It is remarkable that Europeans did not always realize the Islamic character of the innovations adopted by them, perceiving Arabic inscriptions on fabrics imported from the East only as geometrical patterns. Arabic calligraphy is clearly visible on the coronation attires of German emperors; it can be distinguished even on the band decorating the shoulder of Jesus in Giotto's "Resurrection of Lazarus".

Miniatures

The flourishing of the ornamental arts in the Arab-Islamic culture arose partially from the characteristic Islamic tendency to struggle against icons, according to which depicting not only God, but also creatures (in particular people) is forbidden. Such anti-iconism reflected unitarism, the denial of any anthropomorphic features of God, the fear of idolatry, and the conception of God as the creator (Mussawir, literally "Form-maker") who gave forms to creatures, but whom it is impossible to imitate. According to this point of view, the artist who depicts a person or an animal encroaches on the prerogative of the Creator and will be strictly punished on Judgment Day when he will be required to breath life into the pictures he created.

However, the interdictions by the theologians on painting and sculpture in aristocratic environments was sometimes no more effective than those on wine. Figured images can be seen on the surviving frescos in the Umayyad Caliphs country castles in Syria and on the Abbasid palaces of Samarra (in Iraq). The Baghdad Caliph al-Mansur (754-775) is mounted on a horse statue on the green dome of the palace in the capital. The Arabic-Spanish Caliph Abd-ar-Rahman III (912-961) crowned with a statue of his favorite wife, az-Zahra, the palace named in her honor. The governor of Egypt, Humarawayah (834-895), decorated the residence with his own image and the images of his wives wearing golden crowns. But nowhere in an Islamic mosque do we find an image of a person or animal. Thus Islam did not resort to the fine arts as a means of propagating religious ideas, as did Christianity and Buddhism. Sculpture, and especially painting, became secular arts patronized by the governors and the aristocracy.

The creative talent of Islamic painters is shown most brilliantly in the miniature, multicolor images by which they decorated and illustrated manuscripts. In the epoch of classical Islam the two main schools of miniatures: the Arabic (or Arabic-Mesopotamia, Baghdad) and the Iranian were developed. The epoch of the glory of the Arabic school was at the end of the 12th century and the first half of the next century. The artists of this school illustrated the scientific works: "Automatics" by al-Jazari, "Pharmacology" by Dioscarides, and the medical treatises ascribed to Galen; as well as the literary works: "Kalila and Dimna" by Ibn al-Muqaffa and "Maqama" by al-Hariri. Whereas the Arabic school was under Byzantine influence, the Iranian miniature was more oriented to the Chinese tradition. Often there were illustrations for the chronicles "Shah-name" by Ferdowsi, those of at-Tabari and Rashid-ad-Din, and the "Quinary" ("Hamse") by Nezami. The Eastern miniature reached its zenith in the creativity of Behzad (15th to 16th), the Raphael of the East.

The miniaturists, who easily overcame the interdiction against the figured images, did not overcome the temptation to reproduce sacred persons, which the rigoristic Islam prohibited. In the illustrations for the story about a mystical Muhammad's ascendancy to the Sky (Mi'raj) and in the books of sacred history, the Prophet is sometimes presented with a veil on his face, sometimes with his face bare and a flame of nimbus. There were also pictures of the pre-Islamic prophets, Muhammad's companions, Islamic saints and angels. The "Antifigure" rule was also circumvented in applied works of art. The utilitarian purpose of such subjects as though excluding God's respectful attitude to them, partly explains a relative tolerance of figured images in this sphere. Alongside calligraphic and ornamental motives, bronzes and glass, fabrics and carpets, ceramics and other products were decorated with figures of people and animals (including some that were three-dimensional).

Architectural Style

As has been said already, Arab-Islamic civilization is mainly urban. In the conquered countries the Arabs kept all the existing towns, and when founding new towns they did not feel a need to establish a special "Arabic" architectural type of town. In this respect the medieval Arab-Islamic towns are remarkable for their variety. The general features determining a classical "Islamic town" are mainly connected with some types of cult buildings, first of all a mosque, and also a madrasah (religious school, college) and mausoleums. The additional universal modes are set by such public structures as baths (Hammam), hospitals, fountains (sabyl), caravansaries and covered markets. Private residences are oriented on the inside court with only high solid fences turned toward the streets, thus preserving the inhabitants of a house from immodest stares.

The mosque (from Arab. Masjid, "the place of worship") represents the main center and the main symbol of Islamic religious life. With all the historical and geographical variety in mosque architecture a number of general unifying elements were maintained. The main one is the orientation of the prayer hall toward Mecca, to which the Mida (a covered room or a door with a fountain or a pool) is adjoined, where a short ablution (Wudu) is made prior to praying. In the back wall of a prayer hall there is a Mihrab or niche indicating for the believer the direction (Qibla) to address while praying. The Mihrab is considered the symbol of Islamic unity because it forces all to look toward the Kaaba, the spiritual center of the Universe, or to the symbol of Muhammad's mystical presence during the prayer of an Imam. The vicinity of the Mihrab is the most sacred and the most decorated part of a mosque.

In the principal mosques, to the right of a Mihrab there is a rostrum—Minbar—from which is read the sermon prior to the Friday prayer. Under Muhammad the Minbar was a high seat, and within the first centuries of Islam it was a symbol of power, similar to the throne. In the middle Ages announcements and addresses of the governors to people were made from Minbars. Here they performed the solemn ceremonies of crowning the governors. Rising above a mosque is a Minaret (Arab. manara), a tower with a balcony, from which the call to prayer is announced. According to one interpretation, the Minaret symbolizes Islamic monotheism, because it resembles the forefinger, which a Muslim raises upwards when pronouncing the formula "There is no God, except Allah".

Islamic civilization developed different types of mosques, the following three of which are the main types: "Arabic", "Iranian" and "Turkish". The Arabic (or hypostyle, columnar with courtyard) type mosque was developed within the first centuries of Islam. Such a mosque (the mosque of the Umayyads in Damascus, Ibn Toulon in Cairo, Sidi-Ukba in Kairouan, the Great mosque in Cordoba) had a rectangular plan, this included a multicolumnar prayer hall, more often latitudinal with a flat roof (later with a dome) and also a spacious courtyard with a fountain for ablution.

This was surrounded by covered galleries where it was possible to rest and be protected from the heat. Beginning from the 12th century, and especially in the Eastern regions of the Islamic world, the Iranian type (Aiwan) of mosque was more prevalent. It had a relatively small prayer hall under a dome (but without columns), four aiwans (high positioned niches under an arch) on the axes of a courtyard and monumental portals (with two decorative minarets) on the main facade. The Dark Blue mosque in Tabriz, the Great mosque and the Shah mosque in Isfahan are famous buildings of this type. The Turkish type of mosques, with a dome in the center, spread under the Ottomans and is represented by such masterpieces as the Suleymaniya and the Ahmadiya in Istanbul, and the Selim in Edirne.

Palaces were also remarkable samples of Arabic secular architecture, the fabulous luxury and the fantastic magnificence of which made a magic impression on foreigners, especially from Western Europe. Their characteristic feature is open courtyards surrounded by colonnades, around which there were groups of halls and rooms. An abundance of mirror pools, fountains and babbling streams also were typical. Around the palaces there were shady rustling gardens. Unfortunately, not many of these numerous palaces remain, but one is the magnificent Alhambra palace-fortress in Spanish Granada.

Music in Islam

Research on the religious and cultural originality (in particular emphasizing its difference from Christianity) reveals that Islam did not allow instrumental music in cult. Nevertheless, the prophet Muhammad was tolerant of such musical genres as military, pilgrim and holiday (public and family) songs. Moreover, from the beginning of his stay in

Medina the Prophet founded Azan, a call to prayer, performed by a harmonious human voice. Later he permitted the believer "to decorate reading the Quran with a good sounding voice", which is the basis for the art of Tajwid, the melodic recitative of the Sacred Scripture. Other kinds of spiritual music were also developed in the Islamic religious tradition. During the nights of Ramadan (month of fast), special melodies, fazzariyat, were performed. On the Prophet's birthday (Mawlid) hymns and songs telling about his birth and life were performed. Music accompanied celebrations devoted to the famous Saints, in particular during the above-mentioned Shiite mourning ceremonies (Tazia).

Music has been especially popular in the Sufi orders. Dhikr, a ritual mentioning the name of Allah, became the main element of religious practice of Sufism. The ritual of Dhikr was combined with certain body movements, which in some brotherhoods was performed with a drumbeat. At similar "meetings" it was the practice to sing love and drinking verses, quite often accompanied by musical instruments, in particular keys. Thus Dhikr developed into the practice of sama' (literally "listening"), sometimes with ecstatic dancing (raqs). The "Swirling Dervishes", who were the members of the Mawlawi order founded by the famous Sufi poet, ar-Rumi (1273), performed these dances most brilliantly.

Strict adherents of theology, as a rule, condemned these practices and similar forms of joining music with religious cult. They allowed only vocal music, calling musical tools the instruments of temptation. Therefore, the music of classical Islam was primarily secular in character and focused mainly on the tastes of the palace aristocracy and other higher levels of the urban population. The hostile attitude to secular music from the side of pious theologians and society was stimulated in particular by its association with erotic dances and wine parties, and also by the socially reprehensible moral character and behaviour of many woman-like (mukhannasun) actors and musicians.

Developing as a synthesis of ancient Arabic, Persian, Byzantine and other traditions, Islamic music was always closely connected with poetry. Primarily it was vocal in character. The most common genre was a small vocal and instrumental group, consisting of a group of soloists of whom usually the singer was dominant. The other feature of the music of medieval Islam is its micro-key, tonal richness, in which can be found not only semi, but quarter tones as well. The four or five-string lute (al-'Ud) became the favorite instrument for Arabic classical music. This instrument was glorified by poets and played an important role in theoretical and cosmological constructions. National storytellers accompanied their recitation by playing rabab (the base of the European "Rebeck", an original viol). The trapezoid eve (European "kanoon" originated from it) and kaman (a kind of viol) were the other popular string instruments.

There were a variety of flutes and pipes, often double. Among percussion instruments a drum tambourine was the main instrument, while a regular tambourine was popular at all levels of the society. The drum (tambl, transformed by Europeans into timbal), the kettledrum (nackara, transformed into European naker) and the dulcimer (kasat) were parts of a military orchestra, which also included the wind instruments, horn (buk) and pipes (nafir, plural anfar, origin of fanfares). Besides the purely military function military orchestras played an important role in public processions and ceremonies. In Europe minstrels spread the music of the Arabs, with their manner of singing and playing instruments.

"The Morris dancers" (came from "moorish"), who made shows with toy horses and bells, were reminiscent of that. European names of the notes: do, re, mi, fa, sol, la, ti, came from the names of those Arabic letters which represented the notes in Islamic countries in the middle ages. After the fall of Baghdad under Mongol pressure in 1258 and the destruction of the Abbasid Caliphate, the Golden Age of Islam and its culture ended. After the 13th century there was a deep fragmentation of the culture which previously had been uniform. Such relatively independent regional cultures as Arabic, Iranian, Turkish and Islamic culture in India as well as óthers became prominent.

Within the next two centuries, 14th and 15th, the heart of Arabic culture continued to beat, though not strongly under the Mamluks in Egypt and Syria, and also in Andalusia. That was its Silver Age marked mainly by the epoch of compilations and commentaries. The Arabic world began to overcome the economic decline and cultural semi-stagnation only since the middle of the 19th century. Modern culture in the Arabic countries developed in the process of a complex interaction of the three major factors: reforming religion, revival of the classical cultural heritage, and the adoption of the values of European (Western) civilization.

Theology of Power

"Supremacist puritanism in contemporary Islam is dismissive of all moral norms or ethical values." Since the early 1980s, commentators have argued that Islam is suffering a crisis of identity, as the crumbling of Islamic civilization in the modern age has left Muslims with a profound sense of alienation and injury. Challenges confronting Muslim nations — failures of development projects, entrenched authoritarian regimes and the inability to respond effectively to Israeli belligerence — have induced deep-seated frustration and anger that, in turn, contributed to the rise of fundamentalist movements, or as most commentators have preferred to say, political Islam. But most commentators have been caught off guard by the ferocity of the acts of mass murder recently committed in New York and Washington. The basic cruelty and moral depravity of these attacks came as a shock not only to non-Muslims, but to Muslims as well.

The extreme political violence we call terrorism is not a simple aberration unrelated to the political dynamics of a society. Generally, terrorism is the quintessential crime of those who feel powerless seeking to undermine the perceived power of a targeted group. Like many crimes of power, terrorism is also a hate crime, for it relies on a polarized rhetoric of belligerence toward a particular group that is demonized to the point of being denied any moral worth. To recruit and communicate effectively, this rhetoric of belligerence needs to tap into and exploit an already radicalized discourse with the expectation of resonating with the social and political frustrations of a people. If acts of terrorism find little resonance within a society, such acts and their ideological defenders are marginalized. But if these acts do find a degree of resonance, terrorism becomes incrementally more acute and severe, and its ideological justifications become progressively more radical.

To what extent are the September 11 attacks in the US symptomatic of more pervasive ideological undercurrents in the Muslim world today? Obviously, not all social or political frustrations lead to the use of violence. While national liberation movements often resort to violence, the recent attacks are set apart from such movements. The perpetrators did not seem to be acting on behalf of an ethnic group or nation. They presented no specific territorial claims or political agenda, and were not keen to claim responsibility for their acts. One can speculate that the perpetrators' list of grievances included persistent Israeli abuses of Palestinians, near-daily bombings of Iraq and the presence of American troops in the Gulf, but the fact remains that the attacks were not followed by a list of demands or even a set of articulated goals. The attacks exhibit a profound sense of frustration and extreme despair, rather than a struggle to achieve clear-cut objectives.

Some commentators have viewed the underpinnings of the recent attacks as part of a "clash of civilizations" between Western values and Islamic culture. According to these commentators, the issue is not religious fundamentalism or political Islam, but an essential conflict between competing visions of morality and ethics. From this perspective, it is hardly surprising that the terrorists do not present concrete demands, do not have specific territorial objectives and do not rush to take responsibility. The September 11 attacks aimed to strike at the symbols of Western civilization, and to challenge its perceived hegemony, in the hope of empowering and reinvigorating Islamic civilization.

The "clash of civilizations" approach assumes, in deeply prejudiced fashion, that puritanism and terrorism are somehow authentic expressions of the predominant values of the Islamic tradition, and hence is a dangerous interpretation of the present moment. But the common responses to this interpretation, focusing on either the crisis of identity or acute social frustration in the Muslim world, do not adequately explain the theological positions adopted by radical Islamist groups, or how extreme violence can be legitimated in the modern age. Further, none of these perspectives engage the classical tradition in Islamic thought regarding the employment of political violence, and how contemporary Muslims reconstruct the classical tradition. How might the classical or contemporary doctrines of Islamic theology contribute to the use of terrorism by modern Islamic movements?

2

Classical Islamic Law

By the eleventh century, Muslim jurists had developed a sophisticated discourse on the proper limits on the conduct of warfare, political violence and terrorism. The Quran exhorted Muslims in general terms to perform jihad by waging war against their enemies. The Quranic prescriptions simply call upon Muslims to fight in the way of God, establish justice and refrain from exceeding the limits of justice in fighting their enemies. Muslim jurists, reflecting their historical circumstances and context, tended to divide the world into three conceptual categories: the abode of Islam, the abode of war and the abode of peace or non-belligerence. These were not clear or precise categories, but generally they connoted territories belonging to Muslims, territories belonging to enemies and territories considered neutral or non-hostile for one reason or another.

But Muslim jurists could not agree on exactly how to define the abode of Muslims versus the abode of others, especially when sectarian divisions within Islam were involved, and when dealing with conquered Muslim territories or territories where sizable Muslim minorities resided. Furthermore, Muslim jurists disagreed on the legal cause for fighting non-Muslims. Some contended that non-Muslims are to be fought because they are infidels, while the majority argued that non-Muslims should be fought only if they pose a danger to Muslims. The majority of early jurists argued that a treaty of non-aggression between Muslims and non-Muslims ought to be limited to a ten-year term. Nonetheless, after the tenth century an increasing number of jurists argued that such treaties could be renewed indefinitely, or be of permanent or indefinite duration.

Importantly, Muslim jurists did not focus on the idea of just cause for war. Other than emphasizing that if Muslim territory is attacked, Muslims must fight back, the jurists seemed to relegate the decision to make war or peace to political authorities. There is a considerable body of legal writing prohibiting Muslim rulers from violating treaties, indulging in treachery or attacking an enemy without first giving notice, but the literature on the conditions that warrant a jihad is sparse. It is not that the classical jurists believed that war is always justified or appropriate; rather, they seemed to assume that the decision to wage war is fundamentally political. However, the methods of war were the subject of a substantial jurisprudential discourse. Building upon the proscriptions of the Prophet Muhammad, Muslim jurists insisted that there are legal restrictions upon the conduct of war. In general, Muslim armies may not kill women, children, seniors, hermits, pacifists, peasants or slaves unless they are combatants.

Vegetation and property may not be destroyed, water holes may not be poisoned, and flame-throwers may not be used unless out of necessity, and even then only to a limited extent. Torture, mutilation and murder of hostages were forbidden under all circumstances. Importantly, the classical jurists reached these determinations not simply as a matter of textual interpretation, but as moral or ethical assertions. The classical jurists spoke from the vantage point of a moral civilization, in other words, from a perspective that betrayed a strong sense of confidence in the normative message of Islam. In contrast to their pragmatism regarding whether a war should be waged, the classical jurists accepted the necessity of moral constraints upon the way war is conducted.

An Offense against God and Society

Muslim jurists exhibited a remarkable tolerance toward the idea of political rebellion. Because of historical circumstances in the first three centuries of Islam, Muslim jurists, in principle, prohibited rebellions even against unjust rulers. At the same time, they refused to give the government unfettered discretion against rebels. The classical jurists argued that the law of God prohibited the execution of rebels or needless destruction or confiscation of their property. Rebels should not be tortured or even imprisoned if they take an oath promising to abandon their rebellion. Most importantly, according to the majority point of view, rebellion, for a plausible cause, is not a sin or moral infraction, but merely a political wrong because of the chaos and civil strife that result. This approach effectively made political rebellion a civil, and not a religious, infraction.

The classical juristic approach to terrorism was quite different. Since the very first century of Islam, Muslims suffered from extremist theologies that not only rejected the political institutions of the Islamic empire, but also refused to concede legitimacy to the juristic class. Although not organized in a church or a single institutional structure, the juristic class in Islam had clear and distinctive insignia of investiture. They attended particular colleges, received training in a particular methodology of juristic inquiry, and developed a specialized technical language, the mastery of which became the gateway to inclusion. Significantly, the juristic class engaged as a rule in discussion and debate. On each point of law, there are ten different opinions and a considerable amount of debate among the various legal schools of thought. Various puritan theological movements in Islamic history resolutely rejected this juristic tradition, which reveled in indeterminacy.

The hallmark of these puritan movements was an intolerant theology displaying extreme hostility not only to non-Muslims but also to Muslims who belonged to different schools of thought or even remained neutral. These movements considered opponents and indifferent Muslims to have exited the fold of Islam, and therefore legitimate targets of violence. These groups' preferred methods of violence were stealth attacks and the dissemination of terror in the general population. Muslim jurists reacted sharply to these groups, considering them enemies of humankind. They were designated as muharibs (literally, those who fight society). A muharib was defined as someone who attacks defenseless victims by stealth, and spreads terror in society. They were not to be given quarter or refuge by anyone or at any place. In fact, Muslim jurists argued that any Muslim or non-Muslim territory sheltering such a group is hostile territory that may be attacked by the mainstream Islamic forces. Although the classical jurists agreed on the definition of a muharib, they disagreed about which types of criminal acts should be considered crimes of terror.

Many jurists classified rape, armed robbery, assassinations, arson and murder by poisoning as crimes of terror and argued that such crimes must be punished vigorously regardless of the motivations of the criminal. Most importantly, these doctrines were asserted as religious imperatives. Regardless of the desired goals or ideological justifications, the terrorizing of the defenseless was recognized as a moral wrong and an offense against society and God.

Demise of the Classical Tradition

It is often stated that terrorism is the weapon of the weak. Notably, classical juristic discourse was developed when Islamic civilization was supreme, and this supremacy was reflected in the benevolent attitude of the juristic class. Pre-modern Muslim juristic discourses navigated a course between principled thinking and real-life pragmatic concerns and demands. Ultimately, these jurists spoke with a sense of urgency, but not desperation. Power and political supremacy were not their sole pursuits. Much has changed in the modern age. Islamic civilization has crumbled, and the traditional institutions that once sustained the juristic discourse have all but vanished. The moral foundations that once mapped out Islamic law and theology have disintegrated, leaving an unsettling vacuum. More to the point, the juristic discourses on tolerance towards rebellion and hostility to the use of terror are no longer part of the normative categories of contemporary Muslims. Contemporary Muslim discourses either give lip service to the classical doctrines without a sense of commitment or ignore and neglect them all together.

There are many factors that contributed to this modern reality. Among the pertinent factors is the undeniably traumatic experience of colonialism, which dismantled the traditional institutions of civil society. The emergence of highly centralized, despotic and often corrupt governments, and the nationalization of the institutions of religious learning undermined the mediating role of jurists in Muslim societies. Nearly all charitable religious endowments became state-controlled entities, and Muslim jurists in most Muslim nations became salaried state employees, effectively transforming them into what may be called "court priests." The establishment of the state of Israel, the expulsion of the Palestinians and the persistent military conflicts in which Arab states suffered heavy losses all contributed to a widespread siege mentality and a highly polarized and belligerent political discourse. Perhaps most importantly, Western cultural symbols, modes of production and social values aggressively penetrated the Muslim world, seriously challenging inherited values and practices, and adding to a profound sense of alienation.

Two developments became particularly relevant to the withering away of Islamic jurisprudence. Most Muslim nations experienced the wholesale borrowing of civil law concepts. Instead of the dialectical and indeterminate methodology of traditional Islamic jurisprudence, Muslim nations opted for more centralized and often code-based systems of law. Even Muslim modernists who attempted to reform Islamic jurisprudence were heavily influenced by the civil law system, and sought to resist the fluidity of Islamic law and increase its unitary and centralized character. Not only were the concepts of law heavily influenced by the European legal tradition, the ideologies of resistance employed by Muslims were laden with Third World notions of national liberation and self-determination. For instance, modern nationalistic thought exercised a greater influence on the resistance ideologies of Muslim and Arab national liberation movements than anything in the Islamic tradition. The Islamic tradition was reconstructed to fit Third World nationalistic ideologies of anti-colonialism and anti-imperialism rather than the other way around.

While national liberation movements — such as the Palestinian or Algerian resistance — resorted to guerrilla or nonconventional warfare, modern day terrorism of the variety promoted by Osama bin Laden is rooted in a different ideological paradigm. There is little doubt that organizations such as the Jihad, al-Qaeda, Hizb al-Tahrir and Jama'at al-Muslimin were influenced by national liberation and anti-colonialist ideologies, but they have anchored themselves in a theology that can be described as puritan, supremacist and thoroughly opportunistic. This theology is the byproduct of the emergence and eventual dominance of Wahhabism, Salafism and apologetic discourses in modern Islam.

Contemporary Puritan Islam

The foundations of Wahhabi theology were put in place by the eighteenth-century evangelist Muhammad ibn 'Abd al-Wahhab in the Arabian Peninsula. With a puritanical zeal, 'Abd al-Wahhab sought to rid Islam of corruptions that he believed had crept into the religion. Wahhabism resisted the indeterminacy of the modern age by escaping to a strict literalism in which the text became the sole source of legitimacy. In this context, Wahhabism exhibited extreme hostility to intellectualism, mysticism and any sectarian divisions within Islam. The Wahhabi creed also considered any form of moral thought that was not entirely dependent on the text as a form of self-idolatry, and treated humanistic fields of knowledge, especially philosophy, as "the sciences of the devil."

According to the Wahhabi creed, it was imperative to return to a presumed pristine, simple and straightforward Islam, which could be entirely reclaimed by literal implementation of the commands of the Prophet, and by strict adherence to correct ritual practice. Importantly, Wahhabism rejected any attempt to interpret the divine law from a historical, contextual perspective, and treated the vast majority of Islamic history as a corruption of the true and authentic Islam. The classical jurisprudential tradition was considered at best to be mere sophistry. Wahhabism became very intolerant of the long-established Islamic practice of considering a variety of schools of thought to be equally orthodox. Orthodoxy was narrowly defined, and 'Abd al-Wahhab himself was fond of creating long lists of beliefs and acts which he considered hypocritical, the adoption or commission of which immediately rendered a Muslim an unbeliever.

In the late eighteenth century, the Al Sa'ud family united with the Wahhabi movement and rebelled against Ottoman rule in Arabia. Egyptian forces quashed this rebellion in 1818. Nevertheless, Wahhabi ideology was resuscitated in the early twentieth century under the leadership of 'Abd al-'Aziz ibn Sa'ud who allied himself with the tribes of Najd, in the beginnings of what would become Saudi Arabia. The Wahhabi rebellions of the nineteenth and twentieth centuries were very bloody because the Wahhabis indiscriminately slaughtered and terrorized Muslims and non-Muslims alike. Mainstream jurists writing at the time, such as the Hanafi Ibn 'Abidin and the Maliki al-Sawi, described the Wahhabis as a fanatic fringe group.

Wahhabism Ascendant

Nevertheless, Wahhabism survived and, in fact, thrived in contemporary Islam for several reasons. By treating Muslim Ottoman rule as a foreign occupying power, Wahhabism set a powerful precedent for notions of Arab self-determination and autonomy. In advocating a return to the pristine and pure origins of Islam, Wahhabism rejected the cumulative weight of historical baggage. This idea was intuitively liberating for Muslim reformers since it meant the rebirth of ijtihad, or the return to de novo examination and determination of legal issues unencumbered by the accretions of precedents and inherited doctrines. Most importantly, the discovery and exploitation of oil provided Saudi Arabia with high liquidity. Especially after 1975, with the sharp rise in oil prices, Saudi Arabia aggressively promoted Wahhabi thought around the Muslim world. Even a cursory examination of predominant ideas and practices reveals the widespread influence of Wahhabi thought on the Muslim world today.

But Wahhabism did not spread in the modern Muslim world under its own banner. Even the term "Wahhabism" is considered derogatory by its adherents, since Wahhabis prefer to see themselves as the representatives of Islamic orthodoxy. To them, Wahhabism is not a school of thought within Islam, but is Islam. The fact that Wahhabism rejected a label gave it a diffuse quality, making many of its doctrines and methodologies eminently transferable. Wahhabi thought exercised its greatest influence not under its own label, but under the rubric of Salafism. In their literature, Wahhabi clerics have consistently described themselves as Salafis, and not Wahhabis.

Beset with Contradictions

Salafism is a creed founded in the late nineteenth century by Muslim reformers such as Muhammad 'Abduh, al-Afghani and Rashid Rida. Salafism appealed to a very basic concept in Islam: Muslims ought to follow the precedent of the Prophet and his companions (al-salaf al-salih). Methodologically, Salafism was nearly identical to Wahhabism except that Wahhabism is far less tolerant of diversity and differences of opinion. The founders of Salafism maintained that on all issues Muslims ought to return to the Quran and the sunna (precedent) of the Prophet. In doing so, Muslims ought to reinterpret the original sources in light of modern needs and demands, without being slavishly bound to the interpretations of earlier Muslim generations. As originally conceived, Salafism was not necessarily anti-intellectual, but like Wahhabism, it did tend to be uninterested in history.

By emphasizing a presumed golden age in Islam, the adherents of Salafism idealized the time of the Prophet and his companions, and ignored or demonized the balance of Islamic history. By rejecting juristic precedents and undervaluing tradition, Salafism adopted a form of egalitarianism that deconstructed any notions of established authority within Islam. Effectively, anyone was considered qualified to return to the original sources and speak for the divine will. By liberating Muslims from the tradition of the jurists, Salafism contributed to a real vacuum of authority in contemporary Islam. Importantly, Salafism was founded by Muslim nationalists who were eager to read the values of modernism into the original sources of Islam. Hence, Salafism was not necessarily anti-Western. In fact, its founders strove to project contemporary institutions such as democracy, constitutions or socialism into the foundational texts, and to justify the modern nation-state within Islam.

The liberal age of Salafism came to an end in the 1960s. After 1975, Wahhabism was able to rid itself of its extreme intolerance, and proceeded to coopt Salafism until the two became practically indistinguishable. Both theologies imagined a golden age within Islam, entailing a belief in a historical utopia that can be reproduced in contemporary Islam. Both remained uninterested in critical historical inquiry and responded to the challenge of modernity by escaping to the secure haven of the text. Both advocated a form of egalitarianism and anti-elitism to the point that they came to consider intellectualism and rational moral insight to be inaccessible and, thus, corruptions of the purity of the Islamic message. Wahhabism and Salafism were beset with contradictions that made them simultaneously idealistic and pragmatic and infested both creeds (especially in the 1980s and 1990s) with a kind of supremacist thinking that prevails until today.

Between Apologetics and Supremacy

The predominant intellectual response to the challenge of modernity in Islam has been apologetics. Apologetics consisted of an effort by a large number of commentators to defend the Islamic system of beliefs from the onslaught of Orientalism, Westernization and modernity by simultaneously emphasizing the compatibility and supremacy of Islam. Apologists responded to the intellectual challenges coming from the West by adopting pietistic fictions about the Islamic traditions. Such fictions eschewed any critical evaluation of Islamic doctrines, and celebrated the presumed perfection of Islam. A common apologist argument was that any meritorious or worthwhile modern institution was first invented by Muslims. According to the apologists, Islam liberated women, created a democracy, endorsed pluralism, protected human rights and guaranteed social security long before these institutions ever existed in the West.

These concepts were not asserted out of critical understanding or ideological commitment, but primarily as a means of resisting Western hegemony and affirming selfworth. The main effect of apologetics, however, was to contribute to a sense of intellectual self-sufficiency that often descended into moral arrogance. To the extent that apologetics were habit-forming, it produced a culture that eschewed self-critical and introspective insight, and embraced the projection of blame and a fantasy-like level of confidence. In many ways, the apologetic response was fundamentally centered on power. Its main purpose was not to integrate particular values within Islamic culture, but to empower Islam against its civilizational rival.

Muslim apologetics tended to be opportunistic and rather unprincipled, and, in fact, they lent support to the tendency among many intellectuals and activists to give precedence to the logic of pragmatism over any other competing demands. Invoking the logic of necessity or public interest to justify courses of action, at the expense of moral imperatives, became common practice. Effectively, apologists got into the habit of paying homage to the presumed superiority of the Islamic tradition, but marginalized this idealistic image in everyday life. Post-1970s Salafism adopted many of the premises of the apologetic discourse, but it also took these premises to their logical extreme. Instead of simple apologetics, Salafism responded to feelings of powerlessness and defeat with uncompromising and arrogant symbolic displays of power, not only against non-Muslims, but also against Muslim women.

Fundamentally, Salafism, which by the 1970s had become a virulent puritan theology, further anchored itself in the confident security of texts. Nonetheless, contrary to the assertions of its proponents, Salafism did not necessarily pursue objective or balanced interpretations of Islamic texts, but primarily projected its own frustrations and aspirations upon the text. Its proponents no longer concerned themselves with coopting or claiming Western institutions as their own, but defined Islam as the exact antithesis of the West, under the guise of reclaiming the true and real Islam. Whatever the West was perceived to be, Islam was understood to be the exact opposite.

Alienation from Tradition

Of course, neither Wahhabism nor Salafism is represented by some formal institution. They are theological orientations and not structured schools of thought. Nevertheless, the lapsing and bonding of the theologies of

Wahhabism and Salafism produced a contemporary orientation that is anchored in profound feelings of defeat, frustration and alienation, not only from modern institutions of power, but also from the Islamic heritage and tradition. The outcome of the apologist, Wahhabi and Salafi legacies is a supremacist puritanism that compensates for feelings of defeat, disempowerment and alienation with a distinct sense of self-righteous arrogance vis-à-vis the nondescript "other" – whether the other is the West, non-believers in general or even Muslims of a different sect and Muslim women. In this sense, it is accurate to describe this widespread modern trend as supremacist, for it sees the world from the perspective of stations of merit and extreme polarization.

In the wake of the September 11 attacks, several commentators posed the question of whether Islam somehow encourages violence and terrorism. Some commentators argued that the Islamic concept of jihad or the notion of the dar al-harb (the abode of war) is to blame for the contemporary violence. These arguments are anachronistic and Orientalist. They project Western categories and historical experiences upon a situation that is very particular and fairly complex. One can easily locate an ethical discourse within the Islamic tradition that is uncompromisingly hostile to acts of terrorism. One can also locate a discourse that is tolerant toward the other, and mindful of the dignity and worth of all human beings. But one must also come to terms with the fact that supremacist puritanism in contemporary Islam is dismissive of all moral norms or ethical values, regardless of the identity of their origins or foundations. The prime and nearly singular concern is power and its symbols. Somehow, all other values are made subservient.

The Notion of Orientalism

Orientalism is the branch of scholarship that uses traditional Western methods as a means of understanding and gathering knowledge pertaining to the Orient. The term was also used by Edward Said (1978) to elucidate his own challenge to the validity of such methods. On the one hand, Orientalism has given us much of what we know about the Oriental world at large. Late nineteenth-century authors are especially worthy of consideration for their contributions to an understanding of foreign cultures and peoples. On the other hand, however, several problems arise from the attitudes and methods used in traditional Orientalist discourse, which in turn has had an impact - often negative - upon Western consciousness. This influences and distorts the framework through which the West approaches the Orient in general and Islam in particular.

The Orient encompasses a far greater area than simply that of the Arabs and the Muslim community; exotic images from India, China, Japan and Korea are conjured up in the minds of Western people when they think of the Orient. However, Orientalism has had a particular impact on the study and understanding of Islamic philosophy. Many scholars' understanding of Islamic philosophy is, 'that Islamic civilization as we know it would simply not have existed without the Greek heritage'.

Orientalism as a Political Doctrine

Orientalism has several different but interrelated meanings. In its general sense, it describes the way in which the West looks at the Orient in order to understand it within the context of Western experience. More specifically, Orientalism is a categorical approach by Western scholars as an attempt to form a collective body of knowledge about the Orient. Included in this enterprise is the study of Eastern philosophies, history, religion, culture, language and social structures. To understand the effect of Orientalism on Islamic philosophy, however, we need first to understand it as a political doctrine; from its inception, Orientalism was primarily political and secondarily cultural and philosophical. Orientalism as a system of the knowledge began in the late seventeenth century, reaching its zenith in the late nineteenth and early twentieth centuries. During this period Britain and France, and later the USA, were involved in the struggle for Western domination.

This Anglo-French-American experience was essentially imperialistic. Implicit in the Orientalist attitude, therefore, is the belief that the Orient had passed its golden age as the West was being 'born', and was thus in decline. This view of the Orient as backward and barbaric led to interpretations which resembled more closely what scholars wished to believe, rather than what actually was the case. In philosophy, this attitude led to the belief that the entire system of Islamic philosophy was based upon the Greek inheritance; this in turn led to the belief that Islamic philosophers were not good Muslims, as philosophy and religion apparently could not be reconciled. Along with this attitude, Orientalism also played an active role in advancing Western interests in the East. The pursuit of knowledge of the Orient was often not an end in itself. The study of Islamic philosophy merely confirmed many Western scholars in their belief of the superiority of their own culture.

Orientalist Approach to Islam

From the beginning, Orientalists have viewed Islam in two ways. First, as it had borrowed liberally from Abrahamic (Judaeo-Christian) traditions, Islam was considered to be a crude parody of Christianity. Second, Islam was looked upon as an alien menace which historically had enormous military and political success throughout the world, and consequently was a threat to Western civilization. In Orientalism, Islam first had to be placed within the realm of Western understanding with respect to Christian concepts rather than regarded on its own terms. One way of accomplishing this was to make analogies between Christian religions and Islam. The obvious parallel is the one which some Orientalists draw between Muhammad and Christ. Since Christ is central to the Christian faith, Westerners assumed that Muhammad holds the same place in Islam. This misconception helped to popularize the use of the name

'Mohammedanism', a term highly offensive to Muslims.

The Christ analogy also served to reinforce the notion that Muhammad was nothing more than an 'impostor' and a pale version of the Christian Messiah. Islam also provided a provocation to the West in another respect. From the time of the Arab conquests in the seventh century to the ascendancy of the Ottoman Empire, Islam itself posed a formidable challenge to the Christian world. Islamic empires - Arab, Ottoman or those in Spain and North Africa - had quite effectively challenged and, at least for short periods of time, dominated Christian Europe.

Orientalism and Islamic Philosophy

The first wave of Muslim conquest in ad 632- 4 secured for the Arab Muslims the strongly Hellenized territories of Syria and Egypt along with the western part of the Sassanian Persian empire. At first the new conquerors may have been suspicious about the culture of classical antiquity, as both religion and language separated the Arab Muslims from the vanquished peoples. However, the former overcame their anxiety remarkably quickly and began instead a cultural conquest and assimilation of ancient knowledge.

Philosophers such as Ibn Sina, al-Kindi, al-Farabi and Ibn Rushd all interpreted the Islamic inheritance of classical philosophy and attempted an assimilation of it into mainstream Islam in their writings. The classification of the sciences, in encyclopedic proportions, was carried out by the likes of al-Khwarizmi in his Mafatih al-'ulum, and by a group of scholars in the ninth and tenth centuries who called themselves the 'Brethren of Purity' (Ikhwan al-Safa'). The attitude of these and other philosophers was one of acceptance and the transferring of intellectual history, rather than an adoption of so-called 'foreign' ideas. Many of these ideas were foreign indeed, as we do not see any mention of them in the Quran and earlier traditional works, but the underlying theme was the gaining and spread of knowledge, 'ilm. Gaining of knowledge is obligatory according to the tradition of Muhammad, the prophet of Islam, who said: 'Seeking knowledge ('ilm) is obligatory upon all Muslims, men and women.'

This approach is clearly brought out in the epistles of the Ikhwan al-Safa'. During a lengthy debate in these epistles, between humans and animals in the court of the king of the jinn, examples from history are given in which the conquering nations took over, translated into their language and made their own the knowledge of vanquished peoples. Solomon is cited as a classic example:

> Our sciences and the sciences of all the nations are [acquired] one from the other. If this was not the case, from where did the Persians get astrology, astronomy and observatories? Did not they take it from the Indians? If it was not for Solomon, where did the Israelites get the sciences.... He took it from the kings of all nations when he conquered their territories and transformed them to Hebrew...(Rasa'il Ikhwan al-Safa' 2: 288)

This transcendental open-mindedness has been misrepresented many times by Western scholars, who are more interested in finding something new in the Islamic sciences than in attempting to understand the transmission of the corpus of human knowledge from one people to another. The Orientalist outlook mentioned above appears clearly when scholars such as Walzer and Rosenthal expend much effort in finding faults within the Islamic philosophical system, rather than using their impressive abilities to develop a better understanding of the amalgamation and legacy that has been left by the Islamic philosophers. In Walzer's important work, Greek into Arabic, the attitude is that everything the Arab philosophers had to say was 'borrowed' from the Greeks. Even when we are not able to find the source, according to Walzer, it can be assumed safely that the original Greek source is no longer extant.

This imaginary dichotomy between philosophy and theology, as assumed by the Orientalists, has led to a severe crippling of the understanding of the achievements of the Islamic philosophers. This attitude itself has its roots in the initial reaction to the impact of Greek philosophy upon Christianity. Orientalist scholars assume that the Muslims felt exactly the same as the early Christians did about the conflict between philosophy and theology. Of course there were debates between Islamic philosophers and theologians, but in the Arab and Islamic milieu the attitude was rather different from that in the Christian world; in the former, the philosophers were simply taking what they assumed was their legitimate inheritance from the corpus of human knowledge.

In conclusion, these notions about the Orient eventually 'created' the Orient. The 'Orient' (East) is, in fact, only East from an European perspective: it is a relative, not absolute, term. More precisely, the 'Orient' is whatever the Orientalists say it is: it is a series of abstractions based upon Western-generated ideas rather than upon Oriental realities. Islamic philosophy needs to be studied as more than just a reflection of Greek ideas; it needs to be considered as an area of thought which came into contact with a variety of different cultures, and which developed out of these and out of a meditation on the Islamic sciences themselves into an independent and original form of philosophical thought.

3

Translation Technique and Textual Criticism

The intention to move towards a plain English redaction of the Quran (or Qur'ân), the recital of Islam, came with the discovery of different original Arab redactions of the Quran, as well as various translations of the canonical Arab text. Sound translations in Dutch, English and French evidenced various possible "approaches", whereas in Sufism, the great mystics of Islam made use of the "roots" of the Arab words of the Quran to justify their theologies and mystical philosophies (their champion in this being Ibn'Arabî). Moreover, for a number of "key problems" there is as usual no other way left than to decide on the basis of the original language of the text.

Everytime a problem was encountered which demanded the command of Arab (both linguistically and intuitively), native speakers were called upon. A plain redaction on the basis of different translations in English, French and Dutch could thus continue and be completed. The outcome of this is therefore a redaction rather than a new translation of the Quran. For is the Book translatable? Clear semantics, a fluent style, the identity of the author and a critical reading were important general hermeneutical guidelines.

- *Clear semantics*: A lot of translations prefer complex sentences and a complicated choice of words, while maintaining the "Thee" and "Thy"forms of the biblical tradition. This obstacle had to be removed if a plain text had to be the outcome;

- *A fluent style*: When it was discovered that a plain English text could be arrived at, no trouble was avoided to make sure that the overall style remained simple and straightforward;
- *Identity of the author*: Besides focusing on the meaning of the text we must try, by means of the text, to catch a glimps of the identity of the Author of the Book. It is inevitable that every book contains traces of the psychology and philosophy of its author. This is also the case with the Quran, a book in which ALLAH is speaking in 113 of the 114 chapters. To remember the Author of the Quran is the most challenging, interesting and rewarding feature of this work;
- *Critical reading*: Let us distinguish between three kinds of signs:
    a. In green: The essence of the Recital, considered transhistorical, like all spiritual themes, stories and verses touching upon the unity of the Divine as well as these elements which constitute the particular form of Islam worship (like the direction of the Ka'ba, the food laws, the fast, the pilgrimage, etc.)
    b. In orange: Containing elements which need to be reinterpreted in the light of historical circumstances, like the laws for slaves and by extension all legal matters;
    c. In red: Conflicting with the universal declaration on human rights and possibly interpolated and/or purely historical and circumstancial, like severing the limbs of thieves, whipping adultors, beating women, placing woman a degree below men.

Study of Middle Egyptian enabled to understand the functional role of an unvoweled consonantal system, as well as appreciate certain grammatical features which Egyptian has in common with Arabic: the absence of the verb "is", some of its verb and noun roots, its pronouns, two genders with the feminine marked by the ending -t, the system of number and the endings used to denote plural and dual, the presence of the stative as well as the important aspectual distinction between "perfective" (state) and "imperfective" (action) forms. Egyptian verbforms recorded two aspects: the perfective singleness (momentariness) of state or the imperfective continuity of action, once considered to be fundamental (cf. the outdated verbal system of Sethe and Gardiner).

Particular forms to indicate past and future time existed. However, as in Arabic, Dutch, German and French, Middle Egyptian had a "static" verb form, expressing a state of being and the result of a completed action. In English, the past participle of most intransitive verbs can be used instead, but this always expresses an action, never a state. Hence, English has no stative. The French sentence: "Le soleil est paru." can easily be translated into Dutch ("De zon is verschenen.") or German ("Die Sonne ist erschienen."). In English, it has to be rendered as "The sun has appeared.", for "The sun is appeared." makes no sense.

Egyptian belongs to the Afro-Semitic languages such as Arabic, Ethiopic, Hebrew and Hamitic -North African- languages such as Berber and Cushitic. With the discovery of the bones of the free Egyptians who had built the Great Pyramids (to erect, ca.2500 BCE, the pyramid of Khufu, ca.20.000 workers had been placed in rotation for 20 years) and the comparison of its ancient DNA with that of contemporary Egyptians, geneticians could prove a direct ancestral relationship between the Ancient Egyptian builders and their Arab speaking offspring (although ca.4500 years stands between them).

In previous studies of Ancient Egyptian spirituality (cf. the theology of Memphis, the Aten of Akhenaten, the constitution of man and To Become a Magician) a distinction was made between the mythical, pre-rational and proto-rational stages of cognition (Piaget) and their co-relative presence in the genesis of Ancient Egyptian language and its "magical" (power). In her recent publication, Sagesse Sémitique: de l'Égypte ancienne à l'Islam (1998), the French egyptologist Claire Lalouette tried to define the broad "Semitical" horizon on which the images of the ancient Middle-East dawned to enlighten the heart of both Ancient Egyptian, Judaic, Christian and Islamic spirituality. The reassimilation of Ancient Egyptian civilization also allows African civilization to be part of the total picture of a possible multi and metacultural model on human spirituality.

This allows for a more refined understanding of the two major historical events of Mediterranean Antiquity: Greek rationality and the birth of Jesus, "the Christ":

- With Greek rationality, proto-rationality was superceded, i.e. the concrete particularism and/or geo-sentimentalities and their patronizing influence on cognition were eliminated by abstraction and stable concepts used in a formal scheme. The Greek temples were finished constructions, whereas the Egyptian ones were always open to allow context and concrete eventualities to demolish, add or reconstruct structures. The Greeks liberated the mind by linearizing it.
- The teachings of Jesus "Christ" introduced the principle of one's personal conscience in the face of God. Everybody could be forgiven and saved. Everybody could be damned. To each human his choice.

In Ancient Egypt, the theological realization of the Great One with many forms came with the New Kingdom, although the mythical and pre-rational forms of the "Great One" were attested in the Old Kingdom and continue to play a role throughout Egypt's long history. Ramesside theologians invented the idea of a "divine trinity", which returned in its rational form in neo-Platonism (or substance by itself, in relation and as returning). The various forms of this "hidden" "King of the gods" called "Amun") were his outer manifestations or epiphanies and first among these was the creator-god Re, visible to us as the sun (hence, "Amun-Re").

They are the gods and goddesses of creation. Only in Amarna theology (under the reign of the heretical king Akhenaten), was Egypt briefly forced to accept that the "Aten" (the physical light of the sun) was the sole god and that Akhenaten was his only prophet. The experience was repressed but is, thanks to the climate of Egypt, a fact of history (whereas Moses is completely of memory). In Genesis, the theology of Akhenaten was perfected with great success by excluding all imagery of the Divine (cf. next to the inevitable pictorial features of Ancient Egyptian culture, Akhenaten's theology had made ample use of "light", "disk of the sun", "rays as live-giving arms" etc to explain his concept of the One).

The Hebrew "name" of the "Great One Alone" was "YHVH ALHYM" (or: "Yahweh Elohîm"). "YHVH" referred to the "hidden" Essence (or Face) of God, whereas "Elohîm" was a plural to indicate the Divine Names or Existences of God. In the Greek translation (the Alexandrian Septuagint), "Elohîm" was replaced by "Theos" or "God" (i.e. a plural by a singular), eclipsing the modi operandi of Divine Presence! In Greek rationality, the Supreme Being was the object of philosophical discourses. The ultimate idea in Platonism, the unmoved mover for Aristotle... This Ultimate Being or "first cause" was understood to be identical with the material world (as in Stoicism, allowing for a "logos" of a subtle material nature) or transcending the order of being (as in Platonism and neo-Platonism). These philosophical conceptions did not offer redemption and salvation.

For Plotinus, liberation was understood as the outcome of a purification of the soul, a return to its original state. The soul was able to do this unaided. Although helped and guided, nobody could and should take away that which prevented the soul from reuniting with the One. Contrary to the Semitical theologies, Greek mysticism needed no salvic archetype (as was Pharaoh in Ancient Egypt and the Messias in Israel). This intellectual approach (cf. Plotinus), was clearly for an elite and did not attempt to understand the devotional difficulties and barriers encountered by ordinary people who trusted in the national deities of Greece or Rome. In Ancient Egypt, Greece or Rome, the deities were the occupation of only 10% of the population. Popular devotion existed, but could not compete with state religion, on the contrary, it was at work at its periphery.

And so the rich and powerful could more easily win the favour of the deities. In Q1 however, the historical Jesus only speaks of the merciful "Father" and teaches utter simplicity, renunciation of the world, charity and unconditional trust in His love. He reduced the complex Hebrew law to a few precepts: the love of God and the love of the other as your own self. In Paulinian Christianity, everybody was called to be baptized and reborn "in Christ" (also uncircumcized males and criminals). Jesus "Christ" liberated the soul irrespective of anything the bodily passions and the ruses of the mind might have done or do. After the "Deus ex machina" of baptism, the old world was eliminated, for the kingdom of Elohîm had come to light in one's most inner chambers of intimate consciousness (that's why later Constantine was baptized just before he died !)

Around the time Jesus was born, the ancient gods and goddesses seemed to have become powerless and philosophical discourses were unable to put the soul at ease (quite on the contrary). The spiritual vacuum of the time being an indication that an epoch had ended. With the rapid rise of an organized Christianity (late 3th century), the institutional phase of Christianity (initiated by First Clement) was consolidated by Constantine as Roman Catholicism (making the actual Catholic and Pontifical Church the last imperial order on earth). As Early Christianity indicates, Jesus was a Jew who founded a Jewish sect (and there were many around). Among the Jews, Messianic expectations ran high, for Hellenized Judaism under Roman occupation failed to satisfy the Semitical vision of the "golden age".

The first followers of Jesus (the embryonic social formation of original folk witnessing Jesus at work) were Jews interested in his teachings. They must have been much impressed by his spiritual force and charisma, often forgotten by those intellectuals who, two millenia later, never experience spiritual states and/or never witness the charisma of mystics and those humans adept to be truly themselves, called "saints", "guru's", or "masters" etc. To them, Jesus was the Messiah. They composed Q and the various stories told about Jesus. Paul, who never witnessed Jesus while he was alive, universalized Jesus and transformed the adjectival use of the word "Christ" (by the original Jewish Christians, as in "Jesus, the Christ") into a nominal one: Christians are told that they are "in" Christ, or belong to the mystical body "of" Christ. If Jesus "Christ" was the Messiah of Israel, then Judaism ended were Christianity began.

Christianity had answered the call of late Hellenistic astral millenarianism (and Jewish Messianism) and it had successfully superceded the boundaries of race, gender and nationality. It was a "universal" religion of the One Supreme Being and would subsequently try to use rational thought to justify its claims (early Christian philosophy till Thomas of Aquinas). However, ironically, early Christian churches were fundamentally divided regarding the nature of Christ, both ontotheologically (Where does Christ stand in the salvic model?) as well as anthropologically (What is the nature of Christ?). Also Christ's miraculous presence in the holy host remained a crucial matter of debate, for East (Constantinopel) and West (Rome) differed regarding the precise moment this miracle actually happened during Mass (and thus had conflicting liturgical practices concerning an essential spiritual enactment, namely the true and continuous Presence of Christ during Holy Mass !).

These scandalous division of Christianity fixated the dogmatic attitudes and many "consensual" Christ-models saw the light (of which, in both churches, a lot were condemned as heresies). How can the religion of the "One Being" remain justified, if inner conflicts divide it? It can not. Hence, around the time of Constantine, Christianity became divided (in accord with its neo-Platonic schemes) in clergic (active) and monastic (contemplative). Is it surprising that the Christian monastic tradition was initiated in the South of Egypt? Or that those who started it, had enough of the administrative centrism of Rome and Constantinople? Of course, monasticism had to follow the rules of the bishops, patriarchs and popes. Hence, the early monastics (and later the mystical monastics) were not trusted (for heresy and non-centrist "gnostic" -read: prophetic- uprisings had to be avoided - cf. the 5the century Nag Hammadi hiding).

The "monastic rules" and the "walls of Pachomius" were indeed invented to keep the monks within certain centrist parameters. But these were apparently broad enough to allow genuine Christian spirituality to blossom and so let us affirm that the purest expression of Christianity is found in monasticism. For it is close to the true life of its founder, the laconical wisdom-teacher who taught Q1. The Christians who, in the 6th century, spoke with prophet Muhammad, peace be with him, were probably not Roman Catholics. But it is likely that they spoke about them. Scholars found spurious data of so-called heretical sects, like the Christian Gnostics of Basilides and the Marcionites. We also know that Muhammad had a Coptic handmaiden called Mary (Coptic was the last phase of Ancient Egyptian). So it is also likely that the prophet of Islam was aware of the schisms and conflicting views within the Jewish faith and had knowledge of Zoroastrism.

Marcion, who founded his own church, was excommunicated by the church of Rome in 144 CE. He had reinterpreted the gospels, did not accept the writings of the apostles and claimed that they had misunderstood Jesus (apparently Marcion was right). In his teachings, he eliminating the physical body of Jesus (early docetism). Monophysite theories must also have circulated. In these teachings, Jesus had another kind of physical body than ordinary people, i.e. he was primarily Divine and not human as other humans. The Christian gnostic elaborated all kinds of fantastic notions about Jesus and maintained that an evil deity had created the universe, not the merciful Heavenly Father of Jesus "Christ".

These various schisms within early Christianity were answered by Muhammad's fundamental teaching (in accordance with the Quran) that ALLAH has no second. The Philonic "logos as second God"-model (rooted in Ancient Egyptian filiation between Pharaoh and the creator-god Re and Jewish reverence for the Messiah) was radically rejected. The monophysite model (Jesus is only Divine) as well as the Nicene "son of God"-model were discarded as the most serious basphemies ever ! If a monophysite model was used, then in it, Jesus was a human like us all. For how could ALLAH have a second and be the One Being? Either ALLAH is ALL or He is not ALLAH. If there would be a place for the "son of God" to be really this son, then the absolute would somehow be limited by this filial reality. As ALLAH is absolute and unlimited there can really be no "son of God". Ergo, to claim that there is a "son of God" is to deny the absolute His Absoluteness. What can be worse?

When Islam started to conquer foreign nations, it usually considered those who adhered to any of the "false" ideas about Jesus "Christ" as its enemies. For the Quran contains many signs dedicated to Jesus, a prophet gifted with the spirit of holiness, and who is called "the word" (i.e. "logos"). This adjectival use of "logos" being in harmony with how first century Jewish Christians had seen Jesus, namely as "the Messiah". For them, the name "Jesus" was powerful (in Hebrew, this name "splits" the secret Name of God:

YHshinVH = Yeheshua, with the spiritual letter "shin" as copula). "Christ" was the Greek version of "Messiah", or: "the anointed one". So in Islam, the expression: "Jesus, the logos", is orthodox, if under "logos" is understood one of the many revelations (albeit exceptional) of ALLAH through the spirit of holiness (and not the "second God" of Philo of Alexandrian, one of the teachers of Paul). The Paulinian contribution, a nominal use of "Christ", is rejected by the Author of the Quran, who insists upon a radical definition of the absolute.

What follows is divided into three parts:

1. A general outline of the use of criticism in religion and mysticism;
2. A critical study of the authenticity of the Quran;
3. A few major themes: hermeneutical levels, vertical approach, etc.

At the end of this webpage, there is a link to Towards a Plain Recital. This publication contains an English edition of the first two chapters of the Quran, based on several Dutch, French and English sources and assisted, whenever necessary, by capable native speakers. The publication of the complete text (although finished) was avoided in view of the overall balance of this website.

Critical Approach in Religion

Importance of Critical Philosophy

The advent in Western Europe of critical philosophy has dramatically influenced all subsequent scientific endeavours. The core of Kant's "Copernican Revolution" and its impact on epistemology has been studied in Kennis (1995). This fundamental reorientation has placed its stamp on nearly all scientific disciplines, and altered our views on the possibility and the expansion of knowledge fundamentally. Especially in the last century, has the critical (anti-dogmatic and anti-sceptic) perspective been assimilated by all major disciplines like physics (Kopenhagen interpretation), psychology (depth-psychology), sociology (Wertheimer) and biology (psychosomatism). In philosophy (Wittgenstein), Kant triggered the "linguistic turn", rooted in the transcendental method initiated with the Critique of Pure Reason.

Before Kant, empiricism held the conviction that the conditions determining the processes of thought (sense-data) are themselves part of the real world "out there", and hence constitutive for our knowledge (realism). In Hume's scepticism, only mathematical truths and direct observation are doors to knowledge. For him there are no universal empirical statements. The so-called "law" of causality is nothing more than a psychological habit. Kant's revolution attacks and refutes exactly that, for he showed that what we usually call "reality" is not the result of a perception of the real as if it were an open book, but is undoubtedly co-determined by the normative, conditional structure of cognition rooted in the subject of experience itself. So nature does not condition us, but it is we who impose our categories upon nature.

Kant still hoped to radically escape scepticism by trying to universalize these conditions themselves (reality would then be "our reality"), but this was of no avail. For in the 20th century epistemology and the psychology of observation clearly demonstrated that observation itself is never before or after subjective theoretical connotations, but rather happens within the context of expectation itself. Insofar as the latter are standardized in a particular historical method of investigation (set of rules for observation and dialogue conventionally accepted by the majority of relevant sign-interpreters), a relative, conventional "reality-for-us" may be arrived at when both observation (testing) and dialogue (discussion) yield a common experience of reality (for-us and its a posteriori criteria of knowledge-production). But this is not the same as our personal, intimate "reality-for-me" (the realities of my personal "Lebenswelt"), neither necessarily identical with "reality-as-such", i.e. reality as it is for and by itself without any subjective influence (also called "absolute reality").

In Rules for the Game of True Knowing (1999), the rules involved with this critical, normative theory on the possibilities knowledge (theoretical epistemology) and the methodology of producing facts (practical epistemology) are summarized. The latter are further elaborated and encompass both a hermeneutical technique (to understand various "religious" texts) and participant observation of actual communities in which particular ideas, beliefs and myths circulate (to understand the major "religious" communities).

Major Difference

Religions experiences (re)connect the individual or a group with a fascinating larger, totalized whole which is experienced as awesome and mysteriously transcending the ordinary (cf. Otto's "mysterium tremendum et fascinans"). This whole may be certain particularly intense natural phenomena, nature as a whole, the state, the god-man, the deities or one Supreme Being. All these components may have different relationships and operational contexts. Let us call this larger whole "radical otherness". Religious experience reveals this as a "Gegenstand", which opposes one's everday conscious identity (the realm of the "others").

In the case of mystical experience, "otherness" can in no way be compared with our (socio) nominal experience of the otherness of nature, our fellow human beings, the forces of nature or the world, for here, the other is experienced as outstandingly exclusive and this has a dramatical impact on its subject of experience. Hence, in mysticism the "other" is "radical" and "rhetorical". Religion is always socially organized. A good reason for this is the fact that the approach of radical otherness may affect the religious singleton so intensely, that he or she may become physically ill, psychotic or in other ways unfunctional (cf. the experience of the desert fathers). Hence, social formations become necessary to embank this possibly dangerous flow towards transcendence and soften the ill effects of too much loneliness on a social animal expressing its humanity.

Special places to gather and express this religiosity as a spiritual community emerge (communal caves or gathering places, loose spiritual groups, monasteries, temples, churches, synagogues, mosks, lodges, etc.). Specific rules are found which allow the individual to save him or herself (soteriology) within the context of the religion at hand. This salvation is generally preceded by adhering to a variety of rules touching upon the physical, psychological and moral characteristics of the person (virtues). This also implied purification, leading to or inviting salvation. In most religious systems the latter can only be realized as long as the individual accepts the rules of the game (each religion having its own set of rules and rationally conflicting themes).

In the 20th century, comparative religion has shown that the source of most (if not all) religions is the direct experience of radical otherness by a single or a few individuals. Their experience is not limited by the need to reconnect the individual in group with a larger, numinous whole (as does religion). Exclusive theologies (only one religion saves) were replaced by inclusive, pluralist models (each religion saves in its own way). The speculative quest for the "nuggets of gold" radiating a meta and multicultural theology is just beginning. The founders of the religions either belong to myth (like Osiris in Ancient Egypt or Krishna in India), to history (Akhenaten and Amarna, Jesus in Christianity, Muhammad in Islam) or to memory (like Gautama in Buddhism, Lao Tzu in Taoism and Moses in Judaism). Insofar as this special individual has a more or less permanent experience of radical otherness (= the mystical state), he or she is called a mystic.

Mystical experiences are far more independent of the imaginations and conceptualizations of a religious group than are religious experiences. The act of adhering to a religion is impossible without assimilating a particular religious doctrine or code. This indicates that religious experience calls for a group standard (a totem, flag, way-marks). Mystical experiences move beyond a particular religious doctrine, which does not mean that (a) the mystical individual has no theoretical superstructures (cf. Staal) or (b) that he or she does not adhere to a religion (the latter condition is however not necessary for the experience to happen).

Inner ideas and (to say the least) adherence to the philosophical longing satisfied by the unconditional (absolute reality), often serve to prepare and to (afterwards) understand the direct experience of radical otherness. But also: these superstructures may (in the case of a social mystic who reveals Divine signs in the different phases of a prophetic life) become the dogmatic articulations characteristic of a particular religion, fideistically considered holy and eternal... wereas only the absolute can be named such. So religious experiences are always mediated by a doctrine. The latter is "invented" (in the constructive sense) by those who really witnessed the radical experiences of the founding mystic(s) and collected the necessary information to save their insights for posterity and to formulate a common picture for the group to imitate.

Nevertheless, the limitations of their religious experiences are such that they are not really (only allegorically or metaphorically) entitled to say anything about the contents of the mystical experience of any mystic (which is an exclusive, vertical matter between this mystic and the absolute). Hence, religious experiences are not radical because they are always more indirect than direct (i.e. more determined by explicit or implicit religious dogma). They are a door and an opening. At their best, they do offer a safe straight road when one's house is left. But if the soul's love of absolute unity is answered, can anything else than that absolute exist? And what if the straight path is left? Peaceful religions indeed represent the aspiration of human groups, their inner quest for the experience of the Divine. Only if they are in "permanent revolution" are they able to cope with the "spiritual lag" between the intentions of the mystical founder and the subsequent generations of theologians... This points to a religion which fosters mysticism.

Let us distinguish between, on the one hand, the extraordinary experiences associated with orgasm, strong and intense emotions, awe, falling in love, serendipity, aha-experience, inventivity, synchronicity, intuition, etc. and, on the other hand, the experience of radical otherness. The former are clearly stations, i.e. intermediate, dynamical states of consciousness, prone to change and determined by continuous (linear, cyclic, chaotic) processes (or changes of events in their phase-space). These extraordinary "everyday" experiences contain clear traces of the element of transcendence and the co-relative tendency to break through barriers, which seems inherent in the autostructuration which is operative (as the unconditional) in intelligent beings. In the direct and radical experience of the mystics, has the radical and completed form of this urge to move beyond limitations become observable.

The waking consciousness of the individual who at least had one mystical experience (a mystic) differs from that of a non-mystic insofar as the past mystical state is always remembered. The radical experience was so profound that it left a trace or deposit in consciousness (cf. the deposit in classical yoga or the "reshimu" in qabalah). This deposit influences the morality of the "one time" mystic, more focused now to serve his fellow living beings (the criteria to decide between genuine and bogus mysticism are to be found in ethics). Mystical states alone are powerful enough to immediately and permanently influence the morality of the subject of experience, raising his or her level of ethical engagement and charity (cf. Burcke).

Recurrent mystical experiences not only allow consciousness to encompass the "process" of the transcendent experience, but they also make it possible to observe the relationships between the color of the glass and the water poured into it. At some point the mystical stations (always ending in waking consciousness) rotate around one central mystical state, constantly enlightening the waking state (like an open door through which light enters into the rather dark room of nominal consciousness). The pendulum-movement characteristic of the stations is replaced by the integrated state.

This analysis raises the following points:

1. Agifted mystic has more or less an immediate access to the direct experience of radical otherness, triggering superstructures which may or may not be made explicit;
2. The companions are guided by the mystic and collect (after his or her death) the stable components of what they think (or have been told) the superstructure of the founder looked like, making it into a religious dogma or a particular canonical discourse on radical otherness;
3. Those who adhere to the dogma which usually calls for an imitation of some of the practices of the founding mystic may indirectly experience radical otherness through the eye-glasses of the particular dogma, veiling and limiting the real thing. This is then their religious experience;
4. A religion is born if the soteriological (salvic) power of the dogma triggers the formation of a solid spirito-social structure (i.e. the companions have followers). This can only mean that the eye-glass was strong enough to allow for a succesfull albeit derived and indirect imitation of the founder's mystical experience, transforming it into the religious experience of the disciples who claim to walk the path of the master...;

The more time has elapsed between the mystical experiences of the founder and the religious experiences of the followers of the companions, the more likely it is that the original superstructures (of the founder) become intermixed with elements which are foreign to the original direct experiences of radical otherness, moving the religion away from the message of its founder (as has been the case in all world religions).

Religion and Criticism

It took more than a century to fully understand how critical thought might play a constructive role in the study of comparative religion and mysticism. In fact, in the 19th century this was deemed impossible, for around 1850, religious experiences were seen as an outdated mode of relating with the world (Compte), a projection of humanity (Feuerbach), an epiphenomenon of the brain, an instrument used by the upper classes to keep the masses sedated (Marx, Engels), a psychopathology (Freud) etc. In the same way, mystical experiences were considered psychotic, i.e. involving delusionary thinking, hallucinations and the construction of an illusionary world (a theory unfortunately still popular in some conservative psychiatric circles in Belgium today).

At the end of the 19th century, psychic research (later called parapsychology) was born, and materialistic science was confronted with the inadequacies of its own model of the world. Also from the inside did the Newtonian monolith show its first cracks, namely as (a) the ultraviolet-catastroph, suggesting that nature jumped (cf. Planck's quantum), and (b) the experiment of Michelson and Morley, proving the constancy of the speed of light. In the last quater of the 20th century, chaostheory added the insight that very small changes in the initial conditions could produce massive effects.

It took till the end of the previous century, to realize that no advancement of science is possible if both object and subject of observation are not taken into consideration, meaning the end of reductionistic approaches, i.e. exclusive materialism (objectivism, positivism, realism, scientism) and spiritualism (subjectivism, idealism). Pushed too far, this relativism became absolute itself, giving way to "anything goes" (Feyerabend), radical scepticism regarding "all-emcompassing stories" (Lyotard) and the denial of absolute standards for reason (Rorty).

The postmodern approach allowed for "double coding" (Jameson and Derrida's deconstruction) and a new king of spectrology (the study of the invisible, the unseen, the absent). Furthermore, contemporary parapsychological studies proved the existence of extraodinary individuals able to read minds and objects at a distance (remove viewing, psychometry), project themselves out of their physical body (astral projection), cause small and large changes in objects inexplicable by the current laws of physics (telekinesis), etc.

Axiom:

- Concept C is a mental construct based on perceptions in time and space of a subject x;

  Given are:

  1. A singular perception p of a particular fact f by x or p(x)f;
  2. A string of perceptions P of facts f, f', f''... f^n in time (.dt) by x or P(x)f.dt = p(x)f, p(x)f', p(x)f''... $p(x)f^n$;
  3. An ungoing process of perceptions in time (.dt), shaping a perception-bank B concerning P(x)f.dt or $BP(x)f^{(1\dots n)}$.dt.

- Each p(x)f is an elemental building block of C:

  1. The rules of the game of "true" knowing teach that all possible facts (or aggregated events) -so do we fancy-possess the credentials of absolute being itself, i.e. facts correspond with reality-as-such. In p(x)f, f is not written as f(x), for no fact can be totally subjectified.

     These same rules teach that knowledge is unthinkable without active, constructive, creative subjects of knowledge, involved in many forms of communication. The more symmetrical and free their multiple and varied discourses are, the better a consensual interpretation of the facts ensues. No communication can be totally deobjectified.

2. Hence, p(x)f depends on fact f and the mindgrid mg of x or p(x)f = mg(x) + f which also applies to string of perceptions with co-relative mindgrids: $P(x)f.dt = mg(x) + f, mg'(x) + f', \ldots mg^n(x) + f^n$.
3. The generalization C arrived at by a particular subject x on the basis of the given perception-bank $BP(x)f^{(1\ldots n)}.dt$ is a general notion which has been combined over time. As it is not logically possible to justify when the jump from the particular to the universal is to be made lawfully, the logical genesis of the concept remains a priori incomplete. Comparison (i.e. convention) alone explains why singular perceptions become strings. In fact the only thing we really know are singular instances, nothing more (cf. the Buddhist logic of Dharmakîrti and the scepticism of David Hume).
4. The original concept C is communicated to other subjects and confronted with other people's perceptions of facts. Through dialogue and argumentation a consensual, intersubjective concept $C^{(1\ldots n)}$ regarding $f^{(1\ldots n)}$ arises. The movement from C to C', C''... C^n is the evolution of a concept. If the process of perception stops, the evolution is halted and gradually the meaning of the original C withers.
5. Over a period of time the process of ungoing perceptions coupled with quasi permanent intersubjective confrontations define a constellation of consensual general notions $C^{(1\ldots n)}$ regarding $f^{(1\ldots n)}$ which form a tradition $T(f^{(1\ldots n)})$.

The moderate postmodern position of this system implies that objectivity is only guaranteed if, on the one hand, it is understood that observational statements are impossible without some extralinguistic, absolute reality, which so do we believe makes itself known to us through the letters of belief provided by the facts observed during experiments and which correspond with our ideas and discussions about reality. On the other hand, no knowledge can be gained without subjective linguistic activity (the articulation of theories, dialogue, discussion and consensus), for both the organization and the assessment of an experiment are impossible without (a) a particular theoretical background which, by mutual agreement, is considered constant (cf. the "ceteris paribus"-clause) and (b) opportunistic rules-of-thumb allowing one to measure (cf. the Kopenhagen interpretation of the experimental context and the work of Knorr-Cetina).

Hence, science does not produce eternalized knowledge (Kwant), but knowledge which we can consider as true for the time being (Polyani). Moreover, the discovery of the fallibility of knowledge (Popper), the dependence of science on the relative, historical context of knowledge-production (Knorr-Cetina) and the theory-ladenness of observation (Lakatos, Kuhn) have paved the way for the notion that the language of science and the language of religion are two separate language games (Wittgenstein) with their own set of realities.

The two may thus exist next to each other, but should never interact. In this view, science mainly deals with the objective, significant state of affairs of the world, whereas religion is concerned with the subjectively relevant conditions of life, like values, morals and personal salvation (seen as subjective well-being). Science, finally awakened out of its dogmatic slumber, no longer claimed to have access to absolute reality. But, the language game of science was and is considered to be superior, for inter-subjectively valid and dealing with a reality shared by all concerned sign-interpreters (i.e. a "reality-for-us").

Challenge of Comparative Mysticism

In the 20th century, comparative mysticism showed how this artificial dichotomy between science and religion was not satisfactory and possibly flawed. Firstly, because mystical experiences (independent of their different religious contexts) share common characteristics, proving that some objective elements are present in the subjective process of enlightenment (as classical rationalists and intuitionists had claimed cf. the role of intellectual perception and intuition). Especially the fact that (besides parapsychological and other internal constants) the mystics of the world articulate a more or less common cognitive model of reality (based on unity-in-differentiation or bipolarity, the coincidence of the opposites and unsaying) suggested that mystical experiences may be significant to understand the rather hidden and mysterious layers of the real (constantly veiled by our inalienable subjectivities which colour the water of life).

Secondly, mystics claim to experience absolute reality, i.e. the experience is so radical that most if not all subjective and objective conditions of the mystic are temporarily cancelled and a paradoxical "station of no station" (Ibn'Arabî) beyond subjectivity and objectivity is ex hypothesi attained. If this is truly the case, then it would mean that mystical experience probe deeper into reality than do scientific theories. Do mystics catch glimpses of the real as it is for and by itself? Science always remains dependent of the subjective conditions of observation and dialogue (which always change) and hence a forteriori deals with aspects of reality conditioned by subjectivity.

Ironically, this is exactely what was said about religion in the 19th century, when science was still thought to be founded on the rock-bottom of the "absolutely objective" sense-data and the various conflicts between the religions were seen as sufficient proof of their fundamental subjective conditionings, deemed incommensurable and ideosyncratic.

We had to wait for Bergson to understand that the world religions all share the same core, namely the mystical experiences of their respective founder.

1. Indian classical yoga was systematized by Patañjali;
2. Buddhism goes back to prince Gautama;
3. Judaism is unthinkable without Moses;
4. Christianity would not be without the historical Jesus;
5. Islam came with Muhammad.

Ideally, the authentic elocutions and actions of a founding mystic become the sacred symbols of the tradition initiated by the first direct witnesses or companions of the founder. These symbols encompass a model of the world, a theory on man, ethics and the afterlife and a salvic road, defined as the "right path". This superstructuring is also and always political, i.e. meant to organize the mass of believers. Mostly within a couple of centuries after the founder's death, a large number of texts see the light, and a so-called "sacred" tradition ensues. A lot of this may be purely legendary and mythical.

History shows that this traditional testimony is always questionable because quickly after a founder's physical death corruption occurs, redundancy and conflicts rise, schisms are proclaimed and battles are unleached. This is the sad history of the glorification of human inventions. In Hinduism, Buddhism, Judaism, Christianity and Islam differences operate and continue to do so and hence the fundamental message of unity was and is -historically- lost (each in its own way and with its own particular stories and intensities.)

Ontological Illusions of the Religions

The difficulties involving the confrontation of religion with critical thought circumambulate the fact that most if not all religious authorities and their traditions were and are deeply rooted in what Kant called the "ontological illusion", namely the confusion of the conditions of knowledge which are rooted in the subject of experience with objective states exclusively belonging to the world (and hence independent of any subjective condition). This illusion is not surprising. Firstly, because the superstructures developed by the religions are all precritical. This means more precisely that they make use of a conceptual realism which claimed a direct, one-to-one relationship between our thoughts (assumptions, theories) and reality. Hence, what we think is a reflection of what is.

Plato and Aristotle were both conceptual realists, although not in the same way (for Plato, ideas existed outside our minds in a world of ideas and for Aristotle, ideas were abstractions produced by the active intellect). Plato had a major influence on Hellenistic Judaism (Philo of Alexandria) and Christian neo-Platonism, whereas Aristotle influenced the Arabs (Ibn Sina, Ibn Roesjd) and Thomism. Proto-critical sounds, like Dionysian negative theology in Christianity or Nagarjuna's views on vacuity in Buddhism never became mainstream. Secondly, religions are meant to organize the masses... they end up serving political ends. So simple answers to complex problems are necessary. Apologies based on critical thought are bad marketing tools and so the religions prefer to accept the escape-route of the "mysteries" than to attack the core: a continuous adaptation of the dogma in the light of other mystical experiences (i.e. continuous reformation).

Thirdly, religions tend to sanctify the founder in such a way that s/he becomes too far removed from the disciples to stimulate them to imitate the mystical experience of the founder. For this is considered as an exclusive matter between radical otherness and the founder, and hence the dogmatic superstructures developed by the religions themselves, become a system which barrs one from the core of the matter: the experience of otherness, either directly (mystical experience) or indirectly (through an everchanging and adaptive, flexible religious model). What happens is that dogma becomes fixed for ever. Without criticism it is thought that religious concepts represent the absolute reality to which they refer (in fact they are just one inter-subjective historical interpretation of this reality, not the reality itself).

Two Examples: Buddhism and Christianity

Let us take Buddhism and Christianity as two histoical examples of the principle. Although a more extensive list of criteria has been published elsewhere, we focus on (1) the conceptual structure of the salvic theory (not the method) and (2) the authenticity of the historical sources.

Buddhism

For most Buddhists, so-called "objective reality" is a sheer construction. They conceive that a "real object" is actually a rapid succession of vacuous, singular and momentary aggregates which rise and vanish with no substantial, continuous or self-subsisting features. No two points or states are identical. The continuities witnessed are psychological habits constructed by our own minds and have no foundation in the "outer" world. The only reality mentioned is called "Buddha-nature" and it dwells deep down inside ourselves. To bring it to the surface and to let it permeate our whole personality being the sole goal of Buddhism. With the individual having awakened to Buddhahood, absolute reality (cf. "nirvana") is attained and all has been said.

No objective criterion exists to isolate the original teachings of Siddhârtha Gautama, called "the Buddha" (the awakened one), probably born in 566/563 BCE in Kapilavastu in present-day Nepal (and who probably died at 80 after eating spoiled food). His birth, life and work is shrouded in legends (like the stories in the Buddhavamsa of the Khuddaka-nikâya of many Buddha's before Gautama, the historical Buddha or "Shâkyamuni Buddha"). The history of the first four Buddhist councils ("samgîti") remains partially obscure. Tradition holds that the first council (480 BCE) was that of Râjagriha which was held shortly after the Buddha entered "parinirvâna" (coinciding with his physical death around 486/483 BCE). It is said that the first collection of writings took place on that occasion (the Vinaya-patika - Upâli's responses- and the Sûtra-pitaka -Ânanda's responses- of the Tripitaka).

Some of the oldest part of the Tripitaka, the "canon" of Buddhist scriptures -the Vinaya-patika which mentions the first council- probably did originate relatively early, i.e. in the first decades after the death of Gautama. He himself did not write a single word and the problems discussed during the first council were related to the fact that his pupil Ânanda had neglected to ask the Buddha for precise instructions concerning certain less important rules and the latter's contention to found an order of nuns ! At this council, Ânanda was the object of forceful reproaches.

The "Basket of Discipline" (Vinaya-patika) only contains accounts of the origin of Buddhism and the rules and regulations needed for the communal life of monks and nuns. Although some collections did see the light relatively early, it remains unknown whether the discourses said to have come from the mouth of Gautama the Buddha (the Sûtra-patika or part two of the Tripitaka, the "Basket of Writings") are part of this, as tradition claims without no real textual evidence. It is interesting to mention that tradition also claims that Ânanda at the time of the council had not yet realized arhathood, which happened during the council. What does this mean for the "Basket of Writings" composed on the basis of his responses? All historically authentic texts of Buddhism were written in the context of a spirito-communal entity. This is something different than the original teachings of the first historical Buddha, apparently lost or unknown.

This salvic theory has an idealistic structure. Objectivity is the result of subjectivity, for all of reality is constructed, except for absolute reality, which is identical with the Buddha-nature, part of each subject of experience. Because of its idealism and the fundamental ineffable features of Buddha-nature, Buddhism is a priori unable to articulate a consistent ideology. It is forced to absolute silence, for every word or thought is only a reflection of a particular construction and thus irrelevant in the awakening of Buddha-nature. Hence, Buddhism is not a religion, neither a theology, philosophy or a morality. It is only a state of mind.

Christianity

We are told by the Christian churches and other groups of Christian denomination that Christianity was founded by Jesus Christ, the unique son of God, born in Bethlehem. He came to this world to redeem all those who believe that He is God become flesh (God-with-us) who died on the cross for the sins of those who believe in Him, who resurrected and ascended to heaven. Without Him and His church there is no salvation. The teachings of the historical Jesus can be found in Q (especially Q1). When he died (ca.30 CE), his teachings were written down as well as the many stories told about him. Although in Q1, Jesus does not want to be associated with Solomon or the Messianic "Teacher of Righteousness" invoked by the Qumrân-people, he nevertheless defines himself as belonging to another spiritual level. His message was at least proto-Christic (Q1 27).

Jesus, as son of man, announced the Kingdom and sent his chosen disciples out to do their work of peace and healing (Q1 32 - 41). The salvic factor was their missionary work, showing that the Kingdom of Elohîm had come over the world (with Jesus). Saving the world from the oblivion of unawareness (Q1 23-25, 54, 61) which represses the memory of the fact that the Father does not forget us (Q1 49, 53, 63-71) is all what was needed to experience the Divine Presence (realized without people being open enough to notice it).

Jesus' Jewish adherents recognized the expected Messiah of Israel in Jesus, but these original Christians continued go to the temple to sacrifice and to accept the Jewish law, and also the verses related to circumcision, as Genesis 17:14: "And the uncircumcided man child whose flesh of his foreskin is not circumcized, that soul shall be cut off from his people; he hath broken My convenant." It was this double morality at work in the church of Jeruzalem headed by James (i.e. the mixture of "old" and "new" convenant) and the fact of painful circumcision as "natural" deterrent, which Paul intended to eliminate to allow gentile Christianity to prosper.

The difference between the Jesus of history and the Christ of Paul is not small. It is very likely that a lot of the teachings of the historical Jesus were lost or did not fit into the centrist plot. The differences between the orthodox and the gnostic churches became clearly visible after the apostolic period (the death of John), but shortly after the "son of man" was gone, a lot of different opinions circulated about Jesus.

The massive output of fantastic and mythological texts, makes it probable that it was very difficult for anybody to really understand what had happened or what had been said. Does their later destruction suggest that the texts of those who burned the originals (the orthodox male bishops) can not be trusted either? Is this not the original sin against truth? The Jesus of history was clearly too quickly recuperated by these "new" Christians (orthodox centrists, gnostics, self-proclaimed apostles, pneumatics and wandering prophets alike).

Historically, the earliest movements around Jesus (first century CE) were (cf. Mack, 1995):

1. An oral, "lore" tradition (20 - 50 CE), especially interested in the teachings of Jesus and less in his biography;
2. Several major textualizations pre-dating the synoptic gospels of Mark, Matthew and Luke, such as:
    a. Q1 (ca. 50 CE, in Galilee): this is the earliest layer of the sayings or source Q and
    b. Miracle-stories (ca. 50 CE in the North of Palestine);
3. The "kerygma" or "announcement" of Paul in his

authentic letters, introducing a "gospel of Christ" (ca. 50 CE in Greece and Asia Minor - cf. Romans, Corinthians I and II, Galatians, Philippians, Thessalonians I and Philemon);

4. The teachings of the Jewish Christians of the Didache (ca. 50 - 100 CE, in Galilee), containing traces of Q1;
5. The synoptic gospels of Mark and Matthew (between 75 and 90 CE), of which Mark is the first to introduce the Jeruzalem drama and the suggestion (voiced by the demon) that Jesus is the "son of God";
6. Textualizations which reflected the intimate realizations of some of his apostles which were not fully integrated in the narrative gospels of Mark and Matthew, neither in the letters of Paul, namely the Gospel of Thomas (75 - 100 CE), the Gospel of John and the Apocalypse of John (ca.90 - 100 CE).

However, the escatological mythology found in Paul, John, Thomas and the Didache was not part of Q1. Especially the authentic writings of Paul (strongly influenced by Philo of Alexandria) suggest this "pneumatic" interpretation of the historical founder (cf. "being in Christ"). Paul never met Jesus as a man. The first Christians were Jews. The so-called "church of Jeruzalem" was a Jewish sect. Paul was therefore the true founder of Christianity as a universal church. Jesus came to fulfill the Jewish laws. Only after Paul, did the Christian myth gain social and ideological body and focused (in the early years) on the "Holy Spirit". The contradictions which emerged when the teachings of these new prophets "in Christ" confronted each other led to more orthodoxy and also to the notion of "false prophecy."

It is very likely that this orthodoxy was largely a political invention which became necessary to divulgate the new myth in more civilized subcultures and societies (rich intellectuals and administrative people became Christians too). More than one scholar showed that the Christian myth mostly contains (often recuperated) superstructures that clash with what is really known about the historical founder "malgré lui". For the impression is, that Christianity was not founded by Jesus born in Bethlehem but by his Jewish apostles and by the apostle of the gentiles.

In the second century "heresy" and "apology" were invented. The "power" of the bishop of Rome was not built on some spiritual fact but only on the (sacramental or sympathetic?) magic of the dead bones of Peter and Paul (cf. the early cult of celebration on graves, the cult of the relics of the bloody martyrs which rapidly became part of the liturgy of the altar). The "canon" of the "sacred" texts of the New Testament emerged rather late (and this after a lot of other texts had been probably burned, perhaps hidden away or fled with their rejected authors).

Moreover, the narrative gospels themselves contain contradictions concerning the genealogy of Jesus and (not unlike contemporary political agreements) develop the "Christ of compromize". How to trust a constructed account like this? Only blind authoritarian dogma maintains the authenticity of the evangelical, biblical figure of Christ. The Christian churches failed history, Jesus and of course... the truth ! Only their radical transformation may alter things.

This implies the reformulation of Christian theology on the basis of Q1, the Gospel of Thomas and the Christ of the Didache. Of the traditional canon, only the authentic letters of Paul, the Gospel of Mark and the Gospel of John are important, but already reveal a wide gap between the historical Jesus and the "Christ" of salvation. Hence, to reveal Jesus "Christ" is a delicate exercise in balance for, on the one hand, the more "gnostic" and "soteriological" we allow this "Christ" to become, the less historical the total picture becomes. On the other hand, the more the Jesus of Q is put into perspective, the less universal Christianity is. To unite the best of both worlds is the task and the reward.

How to erect a coherent ideology with self-defeating texts? Does "Credo quia absurdum est" summarize

"Christian philosophy"? Can philosophy be "Christian" and still be philosophy? In Western theology, the problem of the nature of Jesus Chris (being a complete but sinless human and also completely God) and the neo-Platonic "mystery" of the "Holy Trinity" (three Divine Persons but One God) have caused the dialogue between genuine intuition ("gnosis", intellectual perception, unveiling, universal prehension etc.) and modern empirical-formal operations to be nearly impossible. Although with Vaticanum II, Roman Catholicism tried to incorporate modernism, recent developments prove its inner orthodoxy, dogmatism and fixation on largely Medieval concepts like primordial sin, the ordained patriarchy, unworldly sexuality, papal authority, a celebate male priesthood and many other more sectarian concoctions.

This slip into the wood of the Cross and not into its resurrection has caused massive disbelief in Europe. Moroever, the conjunction of this ideological poverty with Roman pump and circumstance remains shocking, unacceptable and a permanent object of criticism by all honest intellectuals. Recently, in full Constantinian regalia, with golden cross and ring, the pope, his cardinals and bishops confessed that their church is holy but that its "sons and daughters" have been very sinful.

The pontifex asked God to forgive these "sons and daughters" and to "purify our memory". In the so-called "orthodox" East, emphasis on apophatism and change through pneumatic experiences are present but fossilized orthodoxy is even more omnipotent! The Protestant movement at large remained biblical and hence largely mythical and fantastic (Paulinian). What is necessary is a theology of Jesus based on what is known. In this historical picture, the ascetical, laconical and hermetical teacher of wisdom is far more prominant that the mythical savior. The Jesus of history was hence more the "son of man" rather than the unique "son of God".

Main areas of critical study of the religions:

a. The investigation of the historical, psychological, sociological and political influences on the formation of the religions; and

b. A hermeneutical study of their major texts and traditions and the participant observation of the practices of the living religions.

It must be said that in the previous century, Judaism, Christianity, Islam, Hinduism and Buddhism have been scrutinized using sound critical standards, thus allowing for a clearer perspective on the original and even suggesting ways to perfect the tradition. For example. The qabalah of Judaism refers to a universal model of existence (the Tree of Life) which can be used outside the dogmatic formulations or rabbinical Judaism. It is largely mathematical and hence open to adaptions and critical expansions.

The mass of critical studies show that Christianity, being today an unsound amalgam and unworkable hybrid, can not be recuperated without assimilating gnosticism and the results of the seminars on Jesus. This however would make Christianity move away from the particularities of the institutionalized aspects. But as so little is known, how to avoid that the nugget of gold (Jesus) is again immersed in irrelevant myths and metaphysics? Moreover, the valid elements of the creed were mostly forms of worship recuperated from Jewish debris and pagan cults and subsequently "christified" ("in the name of Christ" or "through Christ" added). In that respect, Christianity offers the best example of the drama of the difference between the founding experience and its superstructure (namely life and teachings of Jesus son of Mary) and the resulting religion.

Hinduism (if such a term may be used) is a complex phenomenon. Nevertheless, of the six schools of philosophy, classical yoga proves to be a fairly independent, ortho-practical and workable approach of the absolute. It focuses on practice, not on theory, and although its classical form calls for a theistic component, Ishvara's role is reduced to that of being the archetypal yogi. This shows that the realization of the direct experience of the absolute is the only goal of yoga.

This makes yoga to be the oldest conceptualization of the methods leading the individual to his or her own direct experience. i.e. instead of promoting an ideology (orthodoxy) based on past direct experiences (of some extraordinary individual), classical yoga promotes the direct experience of the absolute by every individual during his or her lifetime (orthopraxis). Hence yoga is mystical and the most honest and practical traditional path leading to enlightenment. Insofar as Buddhism is limited to the realization of Buddha-nature, it has a lot in common with yoga, except for the latter's theist component and the acceptance of the material world as real and substantial.

4

Criticism of Islam

Let us now turn to the matter at hand: Islam or the complete and irreversible submission to ALLAH, the Merciful, Compassionate Most High. The first thing to be remarked is that a critical understanding of Islam by Muslim scholars is still on its way. Studies by Western scholars on the other hand are available since the 19th century. They focus on the reception of the Quran and the trustworthiness of the historical information about Muhammad, the prophet of ALLAH. Indeed, these are the two main sources necessary to approach Islam: the revelation sent down to Muhammad (the Quran) and the traditions ("hadîth) ascribed to the latter, believed to clarify the Quran... One of the reasons why a critical study by Muslim scientists of the Quran poses difficulties (and this despite the fact that to increase knowledge is explicitly mentioned in the Quran) is their devotional approach of the book, described by Western critics a superstitious (like putting it on the highest shelve in a library).

For Muslims, the Quran, also called "the book" is the most important text ever, while critical literary atheists have described it as boring, nonsensical and of a very poor literary quality... and its author as a fraudulent man who devised revelations for convenience sake... It goes without saying that a critical mind must remain open enough to understand why believers understand the Quran as the highest form of literature, for in its 114 sûra's or "series" there is only one in which ALLAH is not speaking (namely the first one, called "al-Fatihah", the Opening). Hence, because of this direct textual contact between the Divine and humanity offered through the book, it must a forteriori be the excellence of excellences. This claim has to be weighed against the historical authenticity of the text as we have it, which brings us to the criticism of the reception of the Quran. Along with this study is the question of originality.

Furthermore, it is not because one adheres in the field of rational research to the methods of criticism, that one has to reject theism or the existence of the Supreme Being for that matter. So although critical minds may be atheists (making their position easier), it is certainly not a necessary condition or a requirement. It is not because one accepts the existence of the absolute (the Supreme Being exists) that every revelation is a priori accepted as genuine. In fact, how can an atheist develop enough sensitivity to understand the deeper layers put into revealed texts? Hence, critical "friends of God" are the best guarantee for an honest and open study of the relevance of any revelation. These friends may even adhere to none of the religions at all, and propose a rational concept of the Absolute (cf. the "God of the philosopher") based on what the mystics of all traditions claim and on the best of the religions.

Their honesty can only be doubted if it has been proved that their critical study is a mask or apology for a particular creed. So two things have to be avoided here:

1. The critical atheist has to remain open and flexible enough to be able to change his or her position. If the study of revelation is undertaken with a prejudice (or hate) against the absolute, then clearly some points will be missed and although the worse blunders (if any) will be put forward, it remains extremely unlikely that a total picture will be attained. The critical atheist often forgets that the existence of the absolute has not been disproved by science, which deems itself unfit to answer that question

(in the same way as scientific language is inadequate to describe what happened before the Big Bang). This begs the question whether atheists, and sceptics in general are valid investigators of the religions, mysticism and the peripheral disciplines in particular. For unlike critical minds, sceptics already have a proposition to prove (albeit a negative one) and hence come nearer to dogmatism (as Kant so admirably demonstrated);

2. The critical theist, deist, pantheist or pan-en-theist has to be rational enough to be able to see the contextual and personal elements which may creep in during the reception of the revelation. This can be guaranteed if the investigator is not set in advance to "prove" this or that creed. In fact, all historical creeds, being manmade, contain falsehoods...

It is clear that this type of scientist has to focus on the direct experience of radical otherness itself, and hence will not throw the child away with the bathwater, meaning that errors in superstructures not necessarily dismiss the experience of the mystic or (in the case of Islam), the prophet Muhammad. As Staal suggested, the true critical investigator of the religions in general and of mystical experience in particular has him(her)self to experience (directly or indirectly) radical otherness in order to erect a firm inner foundation, which then may be contrasted with the historical creeds (rooted in the mystical experiences of their founder). The author of the present text tries to belong to the second category and his experiences and studies have turned him into a critical pan-en-theist disciplined enough to daily perform a series of spiritual exercises (the one remembrance of the absolute).

Redactions of the Quran

Several redactions have to be distinguished:

1. The texts of the "al-Qurra", a class of men in Medina, who lived near the prophet, and had a fairly complete

knowledge of the revelations and of the rules of life. It is possible that they memorized most of their knowledge but also recorded parts of it. It is not unlikely that independent collections of "al-Quarra" texts existed before the first redaction under Abu Bakr.

2. Tthe independent texts on "pieces of papyrus, flat stones, palm leaves, shoulder blades and ribs of animals, pieces of leather and wooden boards, as well as from the hearts of men" mentioned by Zaid ibn Thabit.
3. The private, first redaction of Zaid ibn Thabit: a codex of what he had collected on sheets or leaves made under Abu Bakr, caliph between 632 and 634, and given to the second caliph 'Umar when Abu Bakr died in 634 and upon 'Umar's death to his daughter Hafsa.
4. The second, "official" redaction of Zaid ibn Thabit under 'Uthman (650 - 656 CE).

In 1 - 3, all textual elements were in "scripta defectiva" meaning that the consonantal text was unpointed, so that the distinction between letters was blurred and several others indistinguishable. The 'Uthman collection was meant to standardize the text, changing it into a "scripta plena" (a fully voweled and pointed text).

"It must be emphasized that far from there being a single text passed down inviolate from the time of 'Uthman's commission, literally thousands of variant readings of particular verses were known in the first three (Muslim) centuries. These variants affected even the 'Uthmanic codex, making it difficult to know what is true form may have been."

The last redaction, official collection or second reaction of Zaid ibn Thabit was completed between 650 and 'Uthman's death in 656. This collection was sent to Kufa, Basra and Damascus, and all other versions were ordered to be destroyed ! The collection of Ibn Mas'ud of Kufa survived (he was indignant that the text was established by someone like Zaid), as did many others. In fact, scholars like Jeffery (1937) listed fifteen primary codices, and a large number of secondary ones. The "official" text of modern Islam is based on Asim of Kufa through Hafs (cf. Egyptian edition of 1924). The presence of an authentic Quranic tradition before the official redaction, the probability of different collections in Arab before the one made by Zaid under Abu Bakr, as well as testemonies of trustworthy sources, make it clear that we do not possess the complete text of the Quran.

Absence of a Redaction Ordered by Muhammad

If Muhammad had wished for a collection of his independent revelations he would have ordered its redaction himself. This does not mean that the text we have is totally untrustworthy, but to consider it as complete and of inviolate origin (as fundamentalists do) runs against its historical criticism and, as we shall see, against what is written about it in the Quran itself (cf. infra).

"... the Prophet, who was more probably an unlettered man, had never thought of writing a book, or of gathering together, in a complete code, the scattered verses which he had recited to his friends, in some circumstances of his life..."

Originality of the Contents of the Quran

Critical studies of the Quran prove that many of its themes, as well as the stories about the Hebrew prophets largely came from the Jews of Arabia (cf. the Bani Quraiza, Qainunqa'a, Nadhir near Medina), whereas parts of the sections on Jesus and Mary were influenced by certain Christian opinions circulating at the time of Muhammad (spurious data of so-called heretical sects like Gnostics of Basilides and Marcionites or of plain domestical origin - cf. his Coptic handmaiden Mary). Muhammad himself confused Miriam, the sister of Moses, with Mary, the mother of Jesus and he makes the fertility of Egypt depend on rain instead of the inundations of the Nile (12:49).

Furthermore, the content of certain passages is at times purely for the sake of rhyme. Instead of the usual seven angels around the Throne, sometimes eight are introduced in order to assure that "thamaniyah" happens to fall in with the rhyme (69:17). This shows its underlying poetical (recitatoric) intention. The Book claims that Christ announced to his followers to expect a prophet named Ahmed ("the praised one"), because they fancied that the word "Paraklete" meant "Periclete" (praised, celebrated) etc. Apparently, the Christians around Muhammad did not know the book of Revelations, nor the role of the Holy Spirit in Christian theology. The tales of Christ's childhood were taken from the non-canonical (i.e. heretical and fabulous) literature of early Christianity (with its variety of non-centrist, gnostical sects depending heavily on the gift of prophesy).

Moreover, some Quranic verses have without doubt been taken from poems anterior to Muhammad. Passages from the Sabaa Mu'allaqat of Imra'ul Qays appear in the Recital. The story goes that it was the custom of the time for poets to hang up their compositions upon the Ka'aba and it is known that the seven Mu'allaqat were exposed. Fatima (the daughter of the prophet) was repeating a verse and was overheard by the daughter of Imra'ul Qays, who said: "O that's what your father has taken from one of my father's poems, and calls it something that has come down to him out of heaven.", a story told amongst Arabs until today. Moreover, before the time of Muhammad, at Mecca, Medina and Tayif, the Hanefites had stressed the unity of The God and abandoned their idols. Their influence upon the prophet is beyond doubt (especially Zaid ibn Amr).

Arabian and Greek historians tell us that previous and during his life, many parts of the peninsula were ruled by Persian kings. Undoubtedly, many of the Eastern descriptions of the garden of paradise were overheard and known by the prophet, as well as the "balance" of judgment (of Ancient Egyptian origin via the so-called The Testament of Abraham, originally written in Egypt). Traditions tells us how often Muhammad conversed with people of every nation in their own tongue.

The principle of theology of the Book is a radical dogmatic articulation of monotheism hand in hand with the idea that The God sent many messengers with His messages (or clear communications) before Muhammad. The first part of the "declaration of unity" can also be found in the Torah and even in the Amarna religion. Was the idea of the multiplicity of communications (sealed by Muhammad) developed properly? Indeed, nothing is said about the scriptures of the Hindus (Vedas), Buddhists (Tripitaka), Ancient Egyptians (Pyramid Texts) or Assyrians (to name but a few of the great and pre-Arabic religions).

If one concludes that these religions were unknown to Muhammad, then he too had his limitations and reflected what he knew through the forms of his own mind and senses (cf. the Sûfî dictum: "water takes the color of the glass"). He never got in touch with the Ancient Egyptian quest for the Great One Alone, nor with the monotheistic monuments of enlightened Brahmanism or the teachings of the historical Buddha. Some scholars conclude that the Quran was filtered by the mind of its prophet (cf. the Quranic distinction between the prophet as a human being and Gabriel as "rasul karim ALLAH")... These and other examples (like the verse on beating women) have been thoroughly criticized by contemporary scholarship. Changes very probably occured as soon as the text was canonized.

As soon as Muhammad died in 632 A.D., important organizational problems rose. It was unclear who the rightful successor ("khalîfa") of the prophet was ("khalifah rasul Allâh" or "successor of the Messenger of God"). Would the emergent Arab culture relapse into its former ancestral tribal consciousness? A central focal point seemed necessary. "Canonization and stabilization of the text of the Quran go hand in hand with the formation of the community, according to Wansbrough. A final fixed text of the scripture was not required, nor was it totally feasible, before political power was firmly controlled; thus the end of the second/

eighth century becomes a likely historical moment for the gathering together of oral tradition and liturgical elements leading to the emergence of the fixed canon of scripture and the emergence of the actual concept 'Islam'."

Those who's interests had been purely political, argued that the death of Muhammad meant the end of their allegiance with the community of ALLAH. This shows that the historical community was not the unity of ALLAH Muhammad had projected it to be (the rejection of hypocrisy is often repeated in the Quran). But most of the Muslims gathered around Abu Bakr, the first calyph, or successor of Muhammad as spiritual leader of the Islam. He was very clear about his authority, claiming no Divine status, nor human excellence (cf. Ibn Ishaak's account in 1017). But only two years later he died and was succeeded by 'Umar and 'Uthman. In 656 (only 24 years later) 'Ali became the last of the founding calyphs of Islam after Muhammad.

'Ali, Muhammad's son-in-law who married Fatima, Muhammad's only daughter, had stressed that the leader should in all cases care for his people. But 'Ali never quite received the allegiance of all the Muslims. He had to wage increasingly unsuccessful wars to maintain himself in power. He was murdered in 661, and Mu'awiyah, his chief opponent, became caliph. After Ali's murder, Mu'awiyah the governor of Syria during the early Arab conquests, a kinsman of 'Uthman, and a member of the Quraysh lineage of the prophet proclaimed himself caliph and established his capital in Damascus.

From there he conquered Muslim enemies to the east, south, and west and fought the Byzantines to the north ! He is considered by some as the architect of the Islamic empire and a political genius (the Constantine of Islam). Under his governorship, Syria became the most prosperous province of the caliphate. Mu'awiyah created a professional army and won the undying loyalty of his troops (like Alexander the Great, he paid them their generous salaries on time). Heir to Syrian shipyards built by the Byzantines, he established the caliphate's first navy. He also conceived and established an efficient government.

'Ali's second son, Al-Husain, refused to recognize the legitimacy of Mu'awiyah's son and successor as caliph, Yazid. This led to the schism between Sunnites and Shiites (the later party of 'Ali). The community of the direct followers of the prophet had considered themselves to be the guardians of the orthodox core or spiritual "sunna" (the habitual practices) of the prophet. These Sunnites were in the majority. This unity was breached when the dynasty of the Omayyads (initiated by Mu'awiyah) ruling the Empire of the Caliphate (CE 661 - 750) was rejected by the Shiites. The followers of 'Ali claimed that only the direct relatives of 'Ali could inherit the caliphate. The Shiites stressed (not unlike the Zoroastrians) inspired leadership ("imam") and actually venerated Husain, the second son of 'Ali.

As a result a fundamental division rose between the orthodox majority (following the "sunna" of the prophet) and the growing opposition, condemned for heresy. At present 60 to 80 million people (or 10% of Islam) are Shiites. The first four calyphs, so-called rightly guided, had more or less assured the unity of the community which had also been very important to the prophet. With the rise of the Shiites this unity was broken and would never be restored again...

The prophet's direct successors, the "perfect caliphate" and later Mu'awiyah effected the expansion of the Islamic state beyond Arabia into Iraq, Syria, Palestine, Egypt, Iran, and Armenia and, with it, the development of an elite class of Arab soldiers. They were also responsible for the adoption of an authoritative reading of the official Quran, which strengthened the Sunnite Muslim community and encouraged religious scholarship. By 732, the dynasty founded by Mu'awiyah had conquered Spain and Tours in France and stretched in the east to Samarkand and Kabul. It exceeded the greatest boundaries of the Roman Empire.

The Omayyads followed the traditions set by the Hellenistic monarchs and the Romans. The conqueror's (Muslim) law applied only to those of the same faith or nationality as the conquerors. During the 89 years of Umayyad rule, most Syrians became Muslims, and the Arabic language replaced Aramaic. The Omayyads minted coins, built hospitals, and constructed underground canals to bring water to the towns. Foreign trade expanded, and educated Jews and Christians, many of them Greek, found employment in the caliphal courts, where they studied and practiced medicine, alchemy, and philosophy. However, during their expansion the Muslims encountered Zoroastrism in Persia, monophysite Christianity in Syria and Asia Minor (especially in Anatolia), Nestorian Christianity in the Euphrate region, Buddhism and Hinduism in Nordwest India, fertility cults in North Africa and Roman Catholicism in Spain. All these religions influenced Islam, especially its mystical current (Sufism).

Rise of Orthodoxy

A century after Muhammad's death, Islam was not considered to be a religion for all of humanity. Only Arabs could convert. But, the other religions "of the book" ("ahl al-kitâb") received freedom to practice and were protected minorities ("dzimmî"). Moreover, especially after the period of the "ar-râsjidun" (the first four so-called rightly guided successors), when all of Muhammad's companions had died, one argued that the text of the official Quran could not be understood properly without the oral tradition or "hadîth's" (the stories about the "sunna" of the prophet).

So the "Sharî'ah", or sacred codex of Islamic practices was written down (9th - 10th century). It was based on:

1. The Quran;
2. The "Sunna" (the way) of the prophet as recorded in the Tradition (the "hadîth");
3. The "Ijma'", or universal agreement, which probably has been the most important factor in defining what the Quran and the straight path imply but which itself has remained the least clearly formulated religious institution of Islam. Its full nature and implications have never been really analyzed neither in Medieval Islam nor by modern scholarship. Far from working as unique standard, "Ijma'" came to operate as a principle of toleration of different traditions within Islam;
4. "Qiyas", or analogical reasoning, is the genuine basis of interpretation and thought ("ijtihad") in Islam. It is this which makes progressive "Ijma'" possible. Its earlier form was personal thought and opinion, criticized by traditional authorities as "arbitrary."

Four new sciences, known as the "sciences of the Sharî'ah", saw the light: the prophetic tradition ("hadîth'), Quranic exegesis ("tafsir"), theology ("kalam"), and law ("fiqh"). As a result of increased exposure to other religious systems, a cleavage occurred between the law and the doctrine, and the former, which ideally presupposed the latter as its base, came not only to be an independent discipline but to claim for itself the title of the science of the Shari'ah par excellence and was even identified with the Shari'ah itself. Thus "fiqh", which originally meant an understanding of the entire range of the faith, came to be applied to law alone.

Later, several new disciplines focused one the more philosophical aspects of these scriptures and these fractions often disagreed. Heresy became in effect in Islam. Although Islam stresses the importance of a political organization in accord with the laws of ALLAH, i.e. unity, it lacks the necessary tools to realize this: no canon, no centralized authority and many fractions and sects fighting each other for supremacy.

Even today in our secularized societies this remains a problem. In France, Muslims were till recently not represented in the national council for religions because it remained unclear who represented the community as a whole. The same happened in Belgium, were till 1999 the Muslims could not benefit from the official support offered to Judaism, Catholicism, Protestantism and Orthdox faith. Moreover, often after these councils have been established, they do not receive the support of everybody, diminishing their executive power. "According to general belief, ahâdîth were orally transmitted at least for one hundred years. (...) On the authenticity of this statement, there are differences of opinion among orientalists. Muir accepts it with the remark that there are no authentic remains of any such compilation of an earlier date than the middle of the 2nd century of the Hijrah. While Guillaume in referring to this statement says, 'The hâdîth must be regarded as an invention', Ruth also refers to Guillaume and some other scholars who doubt the trustworthiness of the report."

Moreover, the famous imam Malik Ibn Anas (born in Medina in the 8th century A.D.) never stopped saying that he did not record any of the Hadith they recounted, because he saw that they were dealing in matters for which they were not qualified. "After having tried to set straight the historical record the line of transmitters and witnesses who gave their account of a troubled historical epoch I can only advise redoubled vigilance when, taking the sacred as an argument, someone hurls at the believer as basic truth a political axiom so terrible and which such grave historical consequences as the one we have been investigating. Nevertheless, we will see that this 'misogynistic' Hadith, although it is exemplary, is not a unique case."

Is it strange that political matters like succession, power and territory played such an important role after the prophet of ALLAH died? Anyway, these considerations make Western scholars prudent enough not to blundly accept as genuine all (oral) stories in circulation after 632. Furthermore, it discredits any attempt to sanctify them. The Recitation ended when Muhammad died and the Muslims did not regress by reconstituting the tribal mosaic and its worship of the 360 gods, although polytheist practices prevail (cf. the kissing of the Ka'aba). During his lifetime they believed that Muhammad was a very evolved human, perhaps the archetype of the emerging Arab spiritual state of mind able to confront and transcend all former revelations. Apparently the language Muhammad used guaranteed the survival of a pan-Arabic cultural form. In the light of this achievement, all conflicts between the political fractions seem irrelevant. But they continue to exist till today. \

The Quran's Authenticity

To most traditionalists, asking questions about the authenticity of the Quran is considered as blasphemy. The same incredible attitude is found in Christian fundamentalists. It is part of the complex of fossilizing effects which install themselves after the process of canonization of the superstructure erected by the followers of a founding mystic is over. In the case of the Quran, this is surprising, for the Quran itself contains a lot of information concerning its own authenticity. Is it not strange then that the learned doctors of Islam did not develop their theories on the basis of these data? Why? Instead of answering this question, let us focus on what the Quran teaches.

In it is made the fundamental distinction between the revealed text (a recitation or "qur'ân") and its original guarded by ALLAH:

"Yes ! This glorious Quran is written on a tablet guarded with great care." (85:21-22)

This is confirmed:

"Recite what has been revealed to you of the book of ALLAH. Nobody can change His words. Apart from Him, you will find no refuge." (18:26)

The "book" of ALLAH or "kitâb" is a written piece, not the historical text to be recited (or a "qur'ân"). Nobody can change these words or decrees ("kalimât"). Hence, there are two entities: an original, celestial writing which never changes and which is guarded by ALLAH and its copy revealed to Muhammad through Gabriel. This original is given a special name:

"Ha Mim By the clear book. We have made it an Arabic Quran so that you would understand it. The mother of the book is with Us. It is indeed sublime and wise." (43:1-3)

The word "mother" implies center, source, origin. The mother of the book is hence the matrix from which the copy is made. This distinction is suggestive of the genetical relationship between an unchanging original and a copy exposed to all kinds of risks... Although the copy may be in peril, its mother remains the same all the time. The relationship between both is expressed by the verb "saddaqa", i.e. to be loyal to the celestial original. But this conformity is not a literal reproduction, for the same verb is used to indicate that the scripture of the Jews and those of the Christians are conform ("musaddiq"). Hence, the copy revealed to Muhammad is far from being a literal reproduction of the book written on the guarded tablet, although the copy conserves the general sense of the guarded tablet.

When Pharaoh asks Moses about the past generations and their teachings:

"Moses answered: 'The knowledge of them is with my Lord, in the book. My Lord goes not astray, nor forgets." (20:54)

That ALLAH possesses and guards the scriptures of the ancient peoples of 'Âd, Thamûd, etc. is thereby confirmed. The "book" mentioned is nothing less than a complete celestial library containing all the spiritual knowledge of humanity. The guarded tablet is the most revered book in it, but it does not stand alone. Nevertheless, the original tablet is the object of special care:

"No ! I swear by the falling stars, (And this is indeed a mighty oath, did you but know !) that the noble Quran, the prototype of which is in a hidden book, should be touched by none except the purified. Its a revelation from the Lord of all being." (56:74-79)

Nowhere is it said that the purified angels occupy themselves to guard the revealed copy of the hidden tablet. Hence, alterations during its transmission are not excluded.

Transmission of the Sense Only

The notion of conformity is used in the Quran to indicate the relationship between the revelations of the ancients, namely those that became before the revelation to Muhammad. Also: the Gospel is said to be conform ("musaddiq") with the Quran. This potential non-conformity between the original and the copy (the written book and the revealed recital) has been confirmed by Muslim theologians.

Suyûtî (who died in 1505 CE) put forward three possibilities: (1) there is a literal conformity; (2) Gabriel received the sense which Muhammad put down in Arab and (3) Gabriel received the sense and expressed it in Arab (the inhabitants of heaven read the book in Arab)... The latter two options imply that the sense of the book is unlike the words of Muhammad... Al-Juwaynî proposed to settle the argument, by conjecturing that part of the Quran is literal and another was transmitted in accordance with the sense of the revelation only.

Abrogation of Verses and the Satanic Revelations

Two other important intra-textual problems prevail: (1) the Quran itself mentions the fact that ALLAH abrogates and confirms certain verses and (2) some revelations were caused by Satan with the accord of ALLAH.

"Before you, We sent messengers, and We assigned to them wives and a lineage. None of them brought signs, except by ALLAH's leave. Every period has had its sacred book. ALLAH blots out or maintains whatever He will. In His hands rests the essence of the book." (13:38-39)

If every period has its sacred book, then clearly the distinction between the guarded, unaltered tablet and a revelation which adapts to historical circumstances (the law of periods "ajal") becomes acute. Without solving his dilemma, the Quran merely points out that those who are of bad faith see in this the proof of prophetic imposture.

"And when We exchange in this Quran a verse for another verse (ALLAH knows very well what He is sending down), they say: 'You are a mere forger !' No ! Most of them have no knowledge. Tell them that the spirit of holiness sent it down from your Lord in truth to confirm those who believe, to guide them and to bring good tidings to those who surrender.'" (16:104-105)

To propose that it is necessary to adapt the revelation to a changing situation and to new problems may lead to another, more fundamental question, namely how to maintain the validity of the revelation in the light of the authenticity of the unchanged Divine text? Apparently, according to the Quran, only the spirit of holiness is able to bridge this gap by inspiring the friends of ALLAH. Hence, the whole matter is made dependent of the depth of the faith of the believers and their ability of submit to ALLAH, to affirm Him even if reason is confronted with superficial inconsistencies which can only be resolved in and by ALLAH Himself.

Moreover, it seems that with His revelation, ALLAH did more than just bring the final law for humanity. The recital itself is testing those who are confronted with it...

"So We have appointed to every prophet an enemy; among Satans of men and jinn, they reveal tawdry speech to each other, all as a delusion. Yet, had your Lord willed, they would never have done it." (6:112)

The Quran explains how ALLAH's messengers are tested and also test. The Old Testament introduced prophets who were called by the Lord to utter falsehood (1 Kings 22:21-22). They have to be distinguished from false prophets, i.e. crooks who "reveal" something without the backing of the Lord. In the Quran, a distinction is made between confirmed signs and allegorical ones.

The latter were revealed to test the believers and to distinguish between them:

"It is He who sent down to you the book. Among its verses, some are firmly established and contain the essence of the book, and others are allegorical. Those whose hearts swerve follow the ambiguous part, desiring dissension, and desiring its interpretation. But none save ALLAH knows its interpretation. Those firmly rooted in knowledge will say: 'We believe in the book, all it contains is from our Lord.' Nobody remembers, but men possessed of minds." (3:5)

Those who fall in the trap see their sins increased. The others witness how the demonical words are eliminated. Hence, the firmly establised verses are the essence of the recital, whereas the allegorical ones are secundary and marginal, intended to test the believers. The Satanical revelations are a temptation too but eventually they are eliminated.

"Not once did We sent a messenger or prophet before you or Satan suggested errors to him in the recitation of a divine book. But ALLAH annuls what Satan casts and then He confirms His signs. Surely ALLAH is All-knowing, All-wise. But ALLAH permits this so that what Satan casts may be a trial for those whose hearts are sick and hard. The evildoers are plunged into a wide schism. This so that they who have been given the science may know that it is the truth from your Lord and believe in it, so that their hearts be humble unto Him. ALLAH ever guides those who believe towards the straight path." (22:51-53)

Muhammad's Limitations, the Lost Texts and Interpolation

The Quran tells the story of the pressures felt by Muhammad. His enemies tried to change his mind or claim to have had revelations too. Muhammad hesitated to reveal certain verses, was taught by ALLAH how to speak, forgot verses and/or was made to forget them (by ALLAH) and, according to tradition, was asked by Zaid ibn Thâbit (one of his secretaries) to add verses. Some of them just changed his words around... The Quran also makes clear that Muhammad is a mortal human who therefore is bound to make mistakes. Hence, ALLAH admonitions his prophet when the latter does a mistake (like talking to a rich man while leaving a blind one outside). The distinction between all the words of ALLAH and the words revealed in the Quran is maintained:

"Say: 'If the sea were ink to write the words of ALLAH, the sea would be spent before they are spent, even though We brought another sea the like of it.'" (18:109)

"If all the trees on earth were pens, and the seven seas ink, yet the words ALLAH would not be spent. ALLAH is All-Mighty, All-Wise." (31:26)

The Quran is just a divine drop of water facing the oceans of Divine Words. So who is able to maintain that the Quran contains the science of the universe? Moreover, tradition itself teaches that a lot of texts were lost. Muhammad's wife Aisha said that sûra 33 had 200 verses instead of the 71 today. The same is true for sûra's 2, 9, 15 and 24... In the corpus of Ubayy, two sûra's more are present than in the canon of Uthmân. Both resemble the first sûra and could have been omitted for that reason. In the recension of Ibn Mas'ûd, both are rejected, together with sûra's 1, 113 and 114! Finally, there is the question of interpolation.

Tradition has never hid the fact that interpolations happened. These were seen as authentic passages of the Quran by virtue of the fact that Gabriel is said to have dictated to Muhammad the places were they had to be inserted. This scenario clearly points to corrections a posteriori. Hence, the majority of sûra's of the Quranic canon were formed by aggregates of revelations, making them into heterogeneous compositions.

The Variations

Ergo, the unity of Quranic revelation is broken up by the fundamental distinction between a literal revelation and one of sense only. Moreover, purely literal differentiations prevail in the copy because of a variety of literal expressions, causing the literal meaning to be multiple. This is the theory advanced by traditionalists as "the seven letters" or "the seven readings", based on a hadîth told by Utmân and attributed to Muhammad: "The Quran came down according to seven letters."

Suyûtî explains that this has been interpreted in fourty ways ! Among these, Ibn Qutayba explains the seven letters as seven "modes of variation" in:

1. The declination without changing the sense;
2. The tenses of the verbs;
3. The diacritical signs on identical graphisms;
4. The letters which are near in graphism;
5. The place of groups of words in a sentence;
6. The text itself because of addition or suppression of words;
7. The words according to their synonyms.

Other traditionalists advanced other differentiations, like the one between gender, number and pronunciation (Al-Râzî). Ibn Hanbal conjectured that every word in the Quran may be replaced by seven synonyms... Ubayy, one of the most important scribes of Muhammad, established the legitimacy of an infinite freedom of variations, except if this led to contradictions and countersense (like changing chastisement for pardon - cf. Umar).

The story goes that one evening, after diner had been offered to him by Abû Bakr, Muhammad was walking with Umar. He heard a man, called Ibn Umm Abd, reciting the Quran in a very particular, personal manner. "Who has said," Muhammad asked Umar, "to read the Quran in its original form ('ratb'), as it descended? That they read it as Ibn Umm Abd reads it !" This anecdote clearly shows that Muhammad himself distinguished between an original state of the text and a worked state. The original form is associated with "ratb", or fresh dates, called to be modified and corrected.

Recitation in Arab

The Quran confirms that the copy of the guarded tablet was meant to be in Arab because the Arabs had not yet received a revelation in their own language. Moreover, nobody would have believed Muhammad if his revelation would have come down in another language altogether.

"We have sent it down from heaven as an Arabic Quran so that you may understand it." (12:2)

"If We had made this Quran a book written in a foreign language, they would have said: 'If, at least, its signs had been distinguished ! But what? It is a book in a foreign language and the one who teaches it speaks Arabic?' Answer them: 'It is a guidance and a healing to those who believe. But in the ears of those who do not believe is a heaviness, and they do not see it. They are like those called from far away.'" (41:44)

Extra-textual evidence: the verses, sûra's, preamble, mysterious letters, the bismala. Without going into the scholarly details of the matter, it should be mentioned that the Quran as we know it today is the result of the work of redactors. The division of the text in verses had liturgical purposes and does not correspond with the original situation. The same goes for the chapters... Let us try to summarize this process.

The Verse:A Set of Revealed Signs

The word "âya" (used 382 times in the Quran), meaning "Divine sign", may indicate a miraculous event, a decree or any other manifestation of the Divine will. It points to the essence of the revealed text, for the Quran itself is a Divine sign, commanding respect, obedience and bringing faith. In that sense, every word of the revealed text is a sign.

If these words are put together to form a textual division or set, the notion of verse emerges. Indeed, before the Quran came into existence as one text of more than 6000 verses long, it existed as individual carriers which showed no organic relationships and contained no perspective on their unity as one Quran. Hence, the revelation was multiple... The idea of bringing these elements together met with resistance. "How would I dare to do a thing the prophet himself did not do?" asked Abû Bakr when Umar proposed him the project. Even Zayd ibn Thâbit was at first scandalized, but he eventually accepted the task. The order of the verses has been fixed only late, namely during the Omayyad dynasty.

The Sûra: A Chapter of Revealed Themes

In the Quran itself, the word "sûra" (mentioned 9 times) is used not to indicate a textual division or chapter, but a revealed text. This implies that the real standard of Quranic revelation is a particular theme or subject (i.e. a set of verses). Most chapters however contain a multitude of revelations covering different subjects. Each of these, in its original Quranic sense, is a unity of revelation, or a "sûra".

Only after Muhammad died did the word "âya" designate a subdivision of the sûra's. The varying length of the latter can be explained by the change in style between the beginning of the revelation (with its verses of one word only) and its end (with verses of a page). It is likely that in the first phase of the redaction, sections of revealed text (i.e. "sûra" in the Quranic sense) were not provided with isolated letters and preambles. These "floating" chapters were inserted in the collections of the second phase, which were fractionated (in 29 fractions headed by the isolated letters?).

In the third phase, that of the constitution of the actual "vulgate", they remained part of existing chapters (and were grouped together) or constituted new individual chapters. The redactors can be felt at work in the choice of the titles and in the order of the chapters. The scribes of the first century AH (the Hegira of 622 CE) used the formula "end of sûra x". Then it became: "end of sûra X and beginning of sûra y". Eventually, only the last part was retained, stabilizing as: "sûra x". The titles of the chapters were added later than the isolated letters. Their order, from the longest to the shortest, was introduced by the canonical "vulgate" of Uthmân.

Isolated Letters: Original Divisions

Only 29 of the 114 chapters begin with groups of letters which are isolated. Different hypothesis have been put forward, giving them numerological, historical or geographical meaning. Some have associated them with the Divine Names, whereas others understand them as being part of the title of the chapter.

The study of these letters suggested to scholars like Welch, Loth, Nöldeke, Schwally, Bell and Jones that they are an integral part of the revealed text. Others doubt this. For Sfar they played an important role in the elaboration of the chapters, i.e. they are criteria to classify the chapters. Welch showed that the letters used were selected because of the graphism of the Arabic letters in the time of Muhamad. Hence, the isolated letters are the earliest witnesses of the organizational concerns which sprang into life as soon as the revelation had to be written down. Hence, the chapters are the result of dividing the first collections into smaller fractions, a process which was assisted by the letters. For the vulgate, the process can be summarized as follows:

The unity of revelation is a sign ("âya") or theme. Each sign or theme is a set of verses. Each "sûra" (chapters or series) is a set of signs or themes.

The Preamble: Introducting a Chapter

The preambles of the Quran belong to an ancient Oriental literary tradition of which we also find proof in the literature of Ancient Egypt. They are placed at the beginning of a chapter and introduce the theme which immediately follows it. However, the preamble is concerned with this theme alone, suggesting that new themes were added to the chapters a posteriori. It is unknown whether these additions happened during the lifetime of Muhammad or afterwards. Hence, the proof that the individual revelations were divided into chapters is given by the preamble, announcing the nature of the revelation or the theme at hand. It is probable that these introductory formulæ were put there after the collection of all the units of revelation (or signs) into chapters had been completed.

The abence of the bismala in chapter 9 in the redaction of Uthmân was for example caused by the resemblance between this chapter and chapter 8: "That is the reason why I did not separate these two chapters by the formula of the bismala." The fact that preambles sometimes also occur in the middle of a chapter evidences that the sign at hand once was an individual chapter which got integrated in another chapter when new collections ensued. All of this points to a loose compositional structure based on the individual signs.

The "Bismala"

All chapters, except one, are headed by: "In the Name of ALLAH, the Merciful, the Compassionate." This formula was probably also introduced after the collection of signs into chapters had been finalized. Tradition explains that Muhammad did not recite the "bismala" inbetween the chapters. Neither did Hamza (one of the seven canonical reciters) and this because (according to Qaysî) he did not consider it to be a verse. The isolated letters and the bismala show that they belong to a later phase, when the necessity was felt to incorporate into the canonical text elements which had not belonged to the revelation in the first place, but which were part of the tools used by the first redactors to organize the multiple units of revealed text into units needed in the liturgy.

The Quran as we know it today is a composition of signs or sets of verses revealed to Muhammad in the course of his prophetic life, work and teaching as separate units of revelation in time. Each sign containing verses which deal with the same theme and which vary in length (from one word to one page). It is probable that during Muhmmad's lifetime, small units with identical themes were put together. Proto-chapters of a book emerged which still had to be collected to form a physical unity. During his lifetime, some bits and pieces were probably written down on various media (not to fashion a book, but to help those with weak memories). No book or Quran as we know it today ensued. Why? The prophet himself was the best example the believers had and moreover he was their living point of reference, a person to whom all questions could be addressed to. He did not order such a collection.

However, to organize this growing Muslim community after his death, a new focus became necessary: the revealed texts themselves. Thus, the unity of this revelation became the most important concern. Several critical studies identified the compositional phases at work before the actual canon of Uthmân emerged. These stages explain the presence of compositional tools like the chapters, the isolated letters, the titles and the bismala. Moreover, collections which differed from each other ensued and these variations were also related to contents. Texts were omitted and others were interpolated. The result was the presence of several authoritative collections (used in the major cities of the emerging Islam).

It is clear that although no other book than the canonical collection had to survive (cf. Uthmân's order to burn all others except his), several alternative collections saw the light and continued to be used... So we may conclude that the Recital is not a literal copy of the celestial one. Neither is the canonical copy a literal transcription of the spoken words revealed to Muhammad as "fresh dates".

Hence, besides the differences between the Recital and the celestial book announced by the Quran itself (together with the other intra-textual evidence), extra-textual evidence makes it very likely that differences between the original collections and the canonical one continued to exist after the latter was sanctified by the Sunnite community.

These critical remarks however do not eliminate the fact that:

1. Those in charge with the original collections knew or had known the prophet personally;
2. They started collecting the revelations shortly after Muhammad had died;
3. They did not had to choose between texts which contained themes which radically contradicted themselves (like changing "pardon" for "retribution") and
4. They were motivated by no other reason than to establish a reliable text which could function as a guideline for a Muslim nation in state of chock and dismay (they could not believe that Muhammad had disappeared).

Compare this with what happened when the narrative gospels were formed (invented?). Only Matthew and John knew Jesus personally, but both of their gospels were probably written by somebody else. The four narrative gospels were written decades after Jesus died (ca. 30 AD). The Gospel of Mark, which was the first, was written between 75 and 80 AD (dated by Catholicism: 64 AD), whereas that of John (the latest) was composed more than half a century after the facts. It contained enough gnostic material to be rejected by second century centrist (i.e. Roman catholic) theologians.

Moreover, the Christmyth developed in these gospels is not confirmed by the Q-source they used and incorporated.The original teachings of Jesus stand next to inventions and mythological constructions which were derived from a variety of sources, foremost Jewish (like Philo of Alexandria) but also pagan of origin (Greek philosophy, mystery-cults and Persian religions). The Didache (the first catechesis probably written in Galilea at the turn of the first century) proves that the Jewish Christians of the first century held different views than those expressed in the narrative gospels.

Both the Greco-Romans as well as the Hellenized Jews were far more civilized than the Arab Muslims of the first hour and could therefore easily turn for inspiration to the cultures around them to elaborate their own fancy superstructures. In fact, some Jewish Christians doubted whether Christ had come to save the gentiles (as Paul claimed). They were all circumcised, continued this practice among them and went to the temple of Jeruzalem to offer and pray. Moreover, in the Didache, prophecy played an important role. It directly influenced the making of Christian theology as well as its first liturgy (the practice of the eucharist).

These Christians believed that Jesus would return in their lifetimes (the "parousia"). Hence, their theology was not the same as that developed by those second century Christians who were confronted with a variety of Christianities and sects. False prophets are mentioned in the Didache, but the notion of heresy emerged only mid-second century (to reject gnosticism, Montanism and other forms of Christianity besides the Roman catholic centrists). However, as early as the first century, gnostic currents were active (cf. Gospel of Thomas). And these elaborated a different metaphysical outlook on Christ.

These differences increased. In the middle of the second century, various Christian sects propagated non-centrist views, each proposing a different Christ... (in some sects, the function of the spiritual leader of the community, the overseer or bishop changed in every service and was determined by chance). Hence, at the end of the second century an enormous contradictory Christian literature had been composed. When these different views are compared, we can only conclude that the teaching of the historical Jesus (as expressed in the earliest layer of the Q-source, called Q1) had been largely replaced by the conflicting theologies of the believers. Only after the canonical view was implemented in the West "de manu militari" and motivated by the politics of Constantine, did Europe become catholic... and the conflicting texts were burned and/or forced to go underground (cf. the Nag Hammadi library).

It is true that shortly after Muhammad had died, different fractions rose (they had already been present before, but had been kept at peace by virtue of the charisma of the living prophet). But their differences were largely theopolitical and did not touch the core of Quranic theology, namely the unity of ALLAH. Nobody doubted that ALLAH was One and that there was no deity next to him (the question whether Jesus was God or not continued to trouble Christianity for many centuries after Jesus physically disappeared). None of these Muslim fractions reintroduced the "daughters of ALLAH". Indeed, the conflict between Sunnites and Shiites had everything to do with the status of the leader of the community, not with the major theological issues (unity of ALLAH, angels, last day, heaven and hell, prayer, alms, pilgrimage, fast, etc.). Indirectly, however, the status of the leader did influence the interpretation of the Quran.

For the Shiites, the inspired leader had the last word in everything, whereas the Sunnites stressed the importance of the Sunna of the prophet and the consensus arrived at by the Muslims. Consider the differences of opinion regarding Christ between for example the Gospel of Mark and the works of the Christian gnostic Valentianus. They are huge compared with the variations evidenced by the different collections and the canonical text of the Quran. Hence, the revelations given to Muhammad have come to us without that their existing variations substantially clouded their original Quranic meaning. But this original meaning is not a priori the celestial one!

5

Quranic Critique of Islam

A revelation is a Divine sign which is sent down by ALLAH from heaven to earth. This does not arrive here directly from ALLAH, for nobody witnesses the Face of ALLAH. ALLAH created the worlds by writing with His Pen on the Table. Hence, the origin of everything created is found in the Divine Names of ALLAH. The scope of the metaphysics involved is suggested by the following hermeneutical table. The three registers (Divine, angelical, human) incorporate the fact that the interpretation of the Quran belongs to ALLAH alone. The first major step being the assimilation of the sense of the guarded tablet by Gabriel.

Even he did not know its absolute interpretation (i.e. its sense in the light of all possible revelations and their co-relative books, to be attributed to ALLAH alone). He did grasp the sense of the guarded tablet and transmitted this as such to Muhammad. This extraordinary ability being Gabriel's Divine side, especially related to the fact of revelation as such. As Muhammad was a human, as were all prophets, his revelatoric propensities were angelical (not archangelical). So in the Quran, Muhammad is called the "messenger", but Gabriel "rasul karim" or perfect messenger (suggestive of the major arch role played by Gabriel in the transmission of the sense of ALLAH's guarded tablet and probably of other spiritual texts out of the Divine library as well).

The extraordinary fact of Muhammad's capacity to read the Arabic words revealed to him by Gabriel and the subsequent maturation of this capacity (between 610 and 632 CE), being the distinguishing factor here. During the 22 years of Muhammad's prophetic life, the dynamical features of the contents of the recital brought by Muhammad became apparent. The later Quran evidences this in many places. The distinctions between guarded tablet and recital, essence and allegory, in effect and abrogated mark the extend of this movement and the complexity of the matter. Ancient Egyptian, Judaic, neo-Platonic and Christian streaks are present, distinguishing it from the inspired (read: jinn-possessed) poetry of pre-Islamic Arabia.

An extraordinary austere and radical monotheism is developed. This being the backbone around which all the various movements of the revelation revolve. Austere, because all positions eventually have to bring us back to the Oneness of the Absolute, in which the Face (or essence) of ALLAH is only for ALLAH. Radical, because no other divinities are accepted next to ALLAH. The Quran often allows the deities to exist story-wise, so that they may end up saying to their worshippers: "We never told you to worship us. For we submit to ALLAH. But you did not listen." The same figure of speech is used regarding Iblis and his demons. At the end of the day (i.e. on the day of doom) they laugh with those who revered them, for only ALLAH is worthy of worship (as they know). So they only fooled themselves.

The signs brought by Muhammad to his people were not collected and gathered together in one book. Muhammad never ordered his secretaries to write down and collect his many revelations in one book. Such an act would in a way "close" the revelation, which was apparently ongoing as long as Muhammad was alive. Muhammad himself was the "unity" around which the Muslim community was erected. When he died, his word inevitably became that "unity", which prompted the redaction of the many signs. If we may believe tradition on this, some signs were inscribed on various materials (original texts) but also in the "hearts of men" (memory).

The legendary redaction of Zaid under Abu Bakr was meant to be a collection of the original writings, for to find experts to recite the Quran was not as difficult as "removing a mountain". However, to collect all the original texts (written in the presence of Muhammad but never collected into one book) was not an easy task. The idea however that a complete text existed "in memory" and not in writing (so that all the compositional structures such as the sûras, their titles and contents are original) is left by critical scholarship. The basic Quranic unit of revelation is therefore the "sign" or thematic set of "verses".

Quran: sûra 27, the Ant, verses 36-39

North African Text in Maghrebi-Script, 12th CE

Perhaps the redactions made after Muhammad died, did bear his "nihil obstat" seal. The fact that fifteen primary codices exist, indicates the contrary. The schisms in Islam did also not improve the situation, nor do the actual divisions. One of the solutions out of this, being each believer's honest experience of the Quran and its Author. In the latter case, one must be aware of the possibility of interpolation, especially when the issue is not repeated in different chapters and other contexts. Indeed, the fact that Muhammad had 22 years to recite, his "original" (of memory) contained the essence over and over again intermixed with issues which were important at hand.

Hence, if extremely important matters are only mentioned once (or conflict with other signs or general themes), chances are high that they do not belong to the arabesque structure of the "original" recitation and might be put there either as a safeguard or trap, or perhaps later for political reasons, such as the consolidation of horizontal power.

Vertical Approach of the "Fact of Spirituality"

Some General Considerations

All human beings are, at some point in their existence, confronted with the unconditional and the unbounded. This need to transcend limitations has been understood since Plato as one of the major characteristic of the human race. It is true that we share this with other living beings, who under the pressures of evolution- are forced to battle with the boundaries imposed to them by nature. Moving beyond borders is essential to life as a whole to win this war with evolution and erect strong architectures in the process.

However, only the human is able to transcend in a way which defies the possibilities of the other creatures on this planet. In fact, highly intelligent systems only survive as the result of growth-through-conflict, and the ability to autoregulate their internal structures and operators in the light of changed environmental circumstances. The human forms of transcendence, i.e. the different roads taken by humanity (as a whole or in part) to arrive beyond the treshold of crisis, turbulence and catastrophe and attain relative stability are multiple, the two fundamental ones being language (the ability to communicate knowledge) and culture. But they are many. To study these forms is one way to understand the many civilizations this planet has carried.

Since the French Revolution, the organs of power of the Western world have been radically secularized in order to free Europe from the chains of Christian fundamentalism. The so-called "religious forms of transcendence" have been distinguished from other modes, ways or means to be in touch with the "beyond", like science, art, humanism, erotism and the short trills offered by consumerism. Atheist forms of religiosity were also developed. These secular forms are contrasted with religious forms precisely because their fulfillment does not reach beyond physical death but instead stress the importance of individual freedom and expression within the framework of democracy and human rights and obligations right here on Earth and possibly today. Because of this secularization, the intolerable forms of religious oppression and coercion have dwindled in the West.

As a result every individual has received his or her religious freedom and nobody can be discriminated on the basis of their adherence to any of the numerous faiths. The traditional and systematic forms of transcendence proposed by many religions, however, never limit their scope to a good life lived on Earth only, but instead connect the post-mortem state of a human consciousness with his or her activities during life here. This means that eternity is considered to be more important than temporality, although our life here is truly transient. This also implies that human responsibility is transferred from today to the Last Day... Those who have sowed good deeds will reap good fortune, while those who do evil will see the little that they have being taken away from them, perhaps in this life, but certainly in the next. Poverty and a denial of this world are considered essential to transcend the conditions of our life on Earth.

Realizing the spiritual truths of heaven and hell is seen as essential to be able to transcend the world and find salvation "for ever and ever". In the same line of thinking, the life of an individual is considered to be less important than the community of believers. The traditional religious forms of transcendence promote the collective, which shows their political rather than their spiritual origin. In Judaism, Christianity and Islam these kind of considerations are often heard. As explained above, most collective religious forms of transcendence are superstructures which elaborate the revelations of their founding mystic.

As such, they are limited by the same conditions and limitations which pertain to superstructures in general. But, as mystical experiences have degrees of maturity, it is very likely that some religious forms of transcendence are less a genuine expression of the Will of the Absolute than others.

Instead, they reflect the ideosyncratic features of this incomplete, imperfect experience of the Divine. Hence, any superstructure raised upon these immature forms, will undoubtedly show identical weaknesses and thus at times draw spiritually irrelevant conclusions. This is of course unacceptable.

No human soul is the plaything of another human soul, especially not when its salvation in the light of eternity is at stake. At this point, let me distinguish between individual and collective forms of spirituality. The religions "of the book" are clear examples of forms of transcendence which a priori involve a collectivity. The Jews exhalt their race, the Christians revere the "mystical body of Christ" and the Muslims live according to the "sunna" of their prophet, considered to be a model for all of humanity to follow and dream of the "umma" or unity of all Muslims. In these forms, the individual is submerged in an existing tradition, and supposed to find his or her place in the community by adhering to the tenets of its theology, soteriology, ethics and the like.

Alternative mystical revelations are of course shunned and if they occur, they are marginalized or persecuted. Individual spirituality can never outlaw the established pathways, and if it does, it is considered as heretical and should if possible be destroyed. Is individualized spirituality an alternative? In Hindu yoga, the yogin/pupil relationship is essential. The interactions taking place there, may serve to discover the spiritual imperative. In some immature cases, unconditional surrender is expected from the disciple (cf. "bhakti" yoga), leading to other forms of abuse, but this is not a conditio sine qua non, quite on the contrary.

For in the so-called all-comprehensive "royal" yoga of Patañjali, surrender is but one aspect of the spiritual technology of enlightenment (or mystical experience) and when it occurs, it is directed towards the Supreme Being only. The worse that may happen (if he or she is not able to comply) is to be expelled from the "ashram" or spiritual community. But as there are many teachers around, one may always try again... The yogi/pupil relationship is emancipatoric (the pupil is called to become a teacher). What we know about classical yoga is a historical reference for a postmodern approach and reconstruction of the early stages of spiritual technology or orthopraxis on the basis of a universal spiritual imperative assuring that each human being should be protected against spiritual abuse.

Furthermore, because of the dangers involved, large yogic communities are out of the question. The genuine yogin has but a few pupils, the true "ashram" is not unlike a small family, a spiritual cell in the mystical body of spiritual humanity (humans seeking the direct experience of God)... This brings us to the core of the message of this paragraph: genuine XXIth century spirituality does not emerge from collectivities and their fossilized traditions, but is the sole responsibility of the individual. In other words, the horizontal, intersubjective dimension is only important in the earliest stages of spiritual awakening. Its structures should be emancipatoric only (a kind of universal spiritual growth technology) and organized in a decentralized way. Hence, the horizon of initiative and initiation is put in place to stimulate and help to open up the vertical inner dialogue between the Absolute and every individual.

In other words: explain to people the importance of having mystical experiences and assist them in such a way that they may reach, elaborate and sustain their vertical experiences to attain genuine spiritual maturity and as a reflection of this live a life in a permanent (horizontal) state of compassion and charity. Only after this vertical contact has been realized (cf. "ascendat oratio, descendat gratia"), will one's individual horizon be filled with the hidden treasures received as a result of this exclusively individual experience (which may or may not have been prepared in small spiritual cells, providing shelter to the individual's mystic intent). Hence, the spirito-social dimension is given shape on the basis of individual spiritual merits. The fossilized remains of earlier builders of superstructures are left behind and understood as collective forms of religiosity which do not necessarily please God.

Hence, it is clear that the combination of a collective religious form with a soteriology projecting the ultimate goal of human existence beyond physical death (or in abstractions like a chosen people, a mystical body of Christ or a Muslim "umma"), is likely to demonize other expressions of human civilization and hence, at times, find pseudo-reasons to destroy the lives of innocent human beings. The history of Jewish, Christian and Muslim fanatics have proved this point with great clarity and this was and remains unacceptable. These collective forms of ignorance are the negative example par excellence which has made the return of a horizontal, political organization of religious communities (as theocracies) impossible in genuine democracies. They confirmed the importance of consequent secularization.

The Case of Islam

Each of the three religions "of the book" developed different theopolitical perspectives: Judaism teaches that the people of Israel are chosen by God to lead the world in the future Messianic age. They are the best of the best, a kind of spiritual master race... This fraudulent notion has been the cause of most of their suffering and this kind of arrogant fundamentalism continues to thrive even today. The Christian is called to give to Caesar what belongs to Caesar, for the ultimate is not found in this world but in the next. The rejection of this world together with its "prince of darkness" and the dogma of primordial sin, make of any work in this world a forteriori a confrontation with the adversary. Charity is based on the love for Jesus Christ, believed to have given his life for the children of Israel (to complete the revelations) and for the whole world (in Paulinian theology). What is given to the smallest, is given to Christ himself.

The establisment of a just society is an integral part of Islamic theology. The Quran is very clear regarding this and it repeats the importance of the just redistribution of wealth over and over again. The presence of poverty and the fact that weak and needy people are forced to suffer because of the cruel neglect of the rich, is deemed unacceptable and an insult of ALLAH, who is Master on the Day of Justice and who gives to everybody their just wages. His main distributive principle being the righteous equilibrium between strong and weak, between rich and poor... Commerce, trade and the adjacent notion of profit are not rejected as such, except if they lead to criminal disparities in the world and to a forgetfulness of ALLAH. And as the Quran teaches this neglect of ALLAH is more likely to befall wealthy people than poor.

For wealth is a distraction given by ALLAH to test the soul, and most are unthankful and hence fail. The rich are called to eliminate suffering, not to cause it... But most of them corrupt the world, make others suffer and are unable to manage their own souls, leading to their eventual downfall. Let us, to help this critical investigation, distinguish between, on the one hand, the Quranic message and, on the other hand, the Islamic traditions which saw the light after the prophet died. This distinction is warranted by the fact that shortly after this death, the conflicts between the many fractions rose. These differences had as object the different collections of the Recital, the fundamental question of leadership and the ways to regulate and organize the rapidly expanding community (in the first decades of the 8th century, Islam had already crossed the French Pyrenees).

The Quran contains both general and specific judical regulations. One of these general laws prescribes that Muslims should give alms. No beggar should be refused. Giving alms became one of the so-called "five pillars of Islam", together with the declaration of unity, the daily prayers, the fast during the holy month and the pilgrimage to Mecca. The specific regulations involve laws organizing marriage, inheritances, position of women, rules for retaliation and the like. It may well be that these specific laws are largely historical and thus valid for the original Muslim community only (although traditionalists will argue otherwise). But surely this is not the case for the general law, repeated often in the Quran and regulating the righteous distribution of wealth in the community and eventually in the world.

Indeed, poverty and social injustice have to be taken out. The natural egoism of people and their need to dominate their fellow human beings lead to injustice and the differences between rich and poor. Although this distinction is unavoidable, due to the natural differences between people, each Muslim is called to help the poor and the needy and to eliminate the excesses caused by the unthankful. Trade and commerce (the major origin of wealth) have to be submitted to extensive controls and regulations which make sure that the gap between rich and poor does not become outrageous (as it is for example today). The "free" market, the principle par excellence of neo-capitalism, is therefore in conflict with the Quran.

For the traditionalists, this noble goal can only be achieved if all Quranic laws are used to give form to the Islamic state. This implies democracy and a free market, but not without the controls in the hand of religious authorities able to veto any rule which is in conflict with the Quran. As democrats, we can not limit the wish of a community to organize their lives according to religious laws, except if these are in conflict with the universal declaration on human rights (like the Taliban interpretation of Islam were women were humiliated and forbidden to study).

Like Tibetan Buddhists or Zionists, Muslims have the right to form a community and live according to laws derived from the Quran. But if people choose for this, then clearly the endeavor has to be (locally) in accord with the majority (everybody being able to make a free choice in favour of an Islamic state) and (globally) with the dignity of human beings. Unfortunately, at least four Quranic laws do not satisfy these conditions, namely the punishment for adultery (100 lashes of the wip in public), theft (severing of hands), the beating of women and the explicit acceptance of slavery. In a more general way, the ontological differences proposed between men and women should also be criticized...

"Men are the managers of the affairs of women for reason of the qualities with which ALLAH has elevated the one over the other, and because men expend of their property to them. Righteous women are therefore obedient, guarding, when their husbands are absent, that what ALLAH ordered to conserve intact. And those you fear may be rebellious admonish, banish them to their own couches, and beat them. If as soon as they obey you, look not for any way against them. ALLAH is All-high, All-great." (2:38)

Does the conflict between these verses and the universal declaration on human rights not show that these specific rules do not belong to the essence of the Quran? Is it possible that certain regulations (like those occuring only once) were actually added after Muhammad died? How to be absolutely sure that this did not happen? Surely ALLAH does not want us to erect a society on analogical and circumstancial teachings? Were they put in there to test the believers after their point of reference vanished? Or are they inventions sanctified by the Ommayads (the role played by the founder of this first Islamic dynasty, Mu'awiyah, can be compared with that of Constantine in Europe)?

Critical investigations evidence that the history of the emergence of the Recital does not eliminate the possibility of later additions, quite on the contrary. And as the book itself does not provide us with the keys to decide which verses are essential and which are allegorical, no unambigeous moral system applicable to a collective can be safely rooted in them. This explains the need to introduce scholarly interpretations to "solve" this problem (the consensus of the learned Sunnites) or to deify the (Shiite) leader. This strategy was followed several times in the course of 15 centuries of Islam. The result being that even today terrorists are able to justify their vile actions through uncritical, fideist Medieval interpretations of the Recital.

These groups represent the laws of the fractions, cutting the Recital into pieces to sell it or to make their own sacred text out of it to justify their own petty politics... In the Quran, the consensus of the learned is not mentioned (neither is the circumcision which the Sunnites consider essential). And nowhere is Muhammad, the proto-type of all possible Muslim leadership, deified or considered as infallible. Quite on the contrary ! Nobody except ALLAH knows the interpretation of the Quran. No consensual view is therefore a priori the view of ALLAH (as is the case in Catholicism were the decisions of the body of bishops is automatically considered to be "sealed" by the Holy Spirit). In fact, one may ask whether the Recital did not descent to make an end to this practice of people to decide for God ! If this is the case, then surely many followers of Muhammad fell into the same trap as did Buddhists and Christians.

Superstructures became more important than the actual mystical experience upon which they are erected. The horizontal structures put in place to organize the community of believers became more important than the vertical relationship between ALLAH and the individual believer, which should be the prime focus. Polytheism, which indeed vanished from Arabia, was thus replaced by a variety of collections, readings, traditions and interpretations. These distinctions continued to exist till today. Hence, the relative and historical opinions of Muslim scholars or Muslim leaders are always situational and tained by their own limitations. No universally valid system of governement can thus be erected upon their consensual views. Unlike the Christianity of Paul, the Quran does not teach that the elect may "seal" their personal opinions with the Holy Spirit. The spirit of holiness may inspire, but nobody can bear the load of another soul and each one of us will be individually addressed on the Last Day, the Day of Doom.

The Personal Spiritual Message of the Quran

It goes without saying that the emergence of a genuine spiritual community was part of the Quranic message. Togetherness characterized the believers, and together they tried to establish the world ALLAH wants, if necessary with the sword. But as the Quran alone did not suffice to organize everything, analogical thinking was called in to invent laws considered Quranic. One is forced to conclude that the horizontal dimension of Islam did not receive form as a reflection of the vertical one. Instead, extra-Quranic elements were introduced (like the Hadîth). They were deemed prescribed because reputed to be done or said by Muhammad. The Quran indeed stipulates that the prophet is to be listened to, but the problem is not Muhammad's authority in this, but the genuineness of the reports and the stories told.

For example, the fact that, when Muhammad's life had arrived in its final stage, a lot of believers could not accept that he would really die, proves the point: the prophet (although mortal) was considered by a lot of people around him to be a kind of superman. It is this unQuranic projection which makes most superstructures introduced by the companions and the followers doubtful. Is it not dangerous to accept these stories if historical truth is sought? Personal preferences creep in and the historical situation is distorted to the point of mythogenesis. The narrative gospels of the centrist Christians are another good example: the Roman traditionalists claims that they represent four perspectives on Christ but in truth these different stories contain flagrant contradictions and lead to a fundamentally irrational view on Jesus the Christ.

In fact, this plurality of Christian gospels proves the principle: most people color the colorless water of mysticism with the color of the glass of their own vessel. This brings us back to the importance of the original elocutions... Hence, one may understand why some scholars reject the hadîth's and stories attributed to Muhammad. And what about the "consensus catholicus"? "Ijma'", or universal agreement, probably the most important factor in defining what the Quran and the straight path imply, has itself remained the least clearly formulated religious institution of Islam. Modern criteria for communicative actions (cf. Habermas) show that a symmetrical discourse implies that nobody is coerced or limited (to say or not to say something). Democratic principles add to this that universal agreement reflects the will of the majority, so that in representational systems it has to be proved that those making the decisions really represent the community of believers.

The Taliban conclave called together to decide whether Bin Laden would be given over or not is a good example. This conclave has not been assembled using democratic means and so nobody knew what the majority really wanted. The decision was made "top/down". Clearly, this is in conflict with the notion of a universal agreement, except if "universal" is only put in for rhetorical justication, and actually stands for the majority of those who detain political power, i.e. able to enforce their ideas "de manu militari". In Roman Catholicism, the same happened. Although Vaticanum II stressed the importance of common believers to participate in the leadership of their church, the latter have no direct influence on who is their leader (this was not the case in early Christianity, appointing their overseers democratically). However, the Roman Church never introduced universal agreement as a way to erect the Christian empire. It was totally dogmatic from the start and remains the only imperial order in existence today...

So, instead of thinking that the first Muslims (after Muhammad died) were better informed regarding how to organize their community than later believers (cf. the "isnads" of each "hadîth"), politicians had better focused on the direct contact between ALLAH and each individual believer. This would have resulted in a permanent reformation of the horizontal dimension as a function of the vertical one. Believers today would have the Quran and their personal spiritual experience of the signs of ALLAH instead of thousands of pages of laws considered holy (the Islamic "deposit of faith"), the dictates of Islamic authorities and the danger implied by fundamentalism and islamized terrorism.

Only in Sufism is direct spiritual experience considered as essential. But Sufism was regarded by traditionalists as the cradle of heretical anti-islamic ideas and rituals. Furthermore, it was elitist, for common mystical experiences were excluded. The advanced mystic was a superior being, one who stood at the top of the pyramid of society... This superiority-complex of some Islamic mystics (cf. Ibn'Arabî claiming to be the "seal of the saints") has sidetracked the original goal of Sufism: to serve ALLAH as perfectly as possible. So, as had been the case in Buddhism, Judaism and Christianity, the Islamic spirito-communal horizon determined the ways and modalities put at the disposal of the believers. This explains also why in Islam heresy saw the light and why some mystics were persecuted and even executed for having said or done things which were in conflict with the tenets developed by jurists and theologians. The latter rejected the self-manifestation of the Divine Names and hence transformed the "no second" theology into a fanatical, unQuranic view, acting even against those who annihilated themselves in ALLAH!

A good example of a doubtful superstructure is circumcision. Although nowhere mentioned in the Quran, no uncircumcized person is allowed to enter Mecca and perform the duties asked for by ALLAH in His Recital. This means that laws which are not part of the Recital were made to condition the performance of essential Quranic prescriptions! If ALLAH considers circumcision a condition sine qua non to enter Mecca and to walk the circumambulations, would the Recital not have mentioned this? How can the general association of circumcision with the convenant of Abraham lawfully block the uncircumcized believer from going to Mecca and visit the Ka'aba? Does this not show that these post-Quranic teachings were actually aiming at politically consolidating the emergent sense of community in the Arabic consciousness?

The history of Islam proves that its "deposit of faith" (traditions, laws, specifics of liturgy, philosophy, etc.) became nearly as important if not more important than the genuine adherence to the message of the Quran by each individual Muslim... The same problem rose in early Christianity, but Paul was able to convince the pillar apostles of the church of Jeruzalem that gentile Christianity and circumcision were incompatible (did the fact that the gentile churches would pay the church of Jeruzalem help to convince the latter?). In its first centuries, Islam too did not consider itself to be the religion of humanity. Just as it was claimed that Jesus only came for "the lost children of Israel", Muhammad was said to be the prophet of the Arabs, and not, as the Quran teaches, of the whole of humanity!

The most important prescription given in the Quran is to remember ALLAH. He or she who does this will be remembered by Him and this will radically change one's life. This remembrance is not a collective event, but part of one's individual piety. To pray daily is the prescribed Quranic standard for this remembrance. But besides these prayers, (which are obligatory) the believer may remember ALLAH as much as he or she likes or is able to. Hence, the daily prayers (the number of which is not mentioned in the Quran) are a minimum minimorum. In fact, the five pillars of Islam are not defined in terms of the spirito-communal but as the activity of the individual (who may be assisted in this by others but this is optional).

The declaration of unity, the prayer, alms, pilgrimage

and the fast testify that the aim of ALLAH is to transform every individual (vertical) automatically resulting in a more just communal sense (horizontal). So the house of Muslim faith is built on individual spirituality. The biblical notion of a church (cf. the New Testament on the "mystical body of Christ") is hence absent in the Quran, stressing that each person will receive his or her wage, for ALLAH knows what is in the hearts of His believers and He will always recompense humans for what they have done... That this spiritual activity may incite believers to come together is not rejected, quite on the contrary. The Quran teaches one to communicate, assist each other and work to establish a peaceful community, living in harmony with its neighbours.

Characteristics of Ritual, Liturgic Recitation

The history of liturgic recitation starts in Ancient Egypt and was further developed in Judaism. It contrasts with the Summerian and Greek approach of the Divine. The latter was based on conjuration (words mostly the name of a god or goddess forcing the deities to act in accord with the will of the magus) and not on recitation (words re-enacting the original, mythical time of creation so that this original power may merge with and be helpful in the situation of man here and now). For example, as late as the 4th century A.D., Greek magicians (the "magoi") would invoke the Moon goddess and command her as follows:

"Tu feras quelque chose, que tu le veuilles ou non,

parce que je connais ta lumière dans ses détails infimes

et que de tes actions belles je suis le célébrant, le serviteur et le témoin, ô vierge.

Ce qui doit être, il n'est pas possible de la fuir.

Cette chose, tu la feras, que tu le veuilles ou non, je te conjure..."

In the religion of the Egyptians, rituals did not mediate between humanity and the gods, for the latter abided in the sky. Ritual action only took place between the gods themselves. As Pharaoh was the sole god living on Earth, he was the only one able to "face" the deities directly. Hence, all rituals were performed in his name. Pharaoh allowed the ritualists to assume the form of the local deity and recited certain words of power enabling this god or goddess to send its double ("ka") and/or soul ("ba") to dwell in the ritualists, the statues of the deities prepared beforehand and the place of worship.

These words of power brought all ritual action back to the "first time", the mythical time of the creation of the world. The importance of intelligent (Sia) creative speech (Hu) able to produce extraordinary, magical (Heka) effects which fashion justice and truth (Maât) is clearly attested in the Pyramid Texts and in the Memphis Theology. The former evidence that both Re and Pharaoh possessed the Great Word. After insightful planning (Sia, taking place in the heart, i.e. the mind) they uttered this word of command (Hu) which is inherently protected against all resistances because of its supernatural, magical power (Heka) able to break all resistances and annul them.

Without answering the question whether Judaism has been influenced by Ancient Egyptian thought (in particular New Kingdom theology), it should be noted that the notion that certain spiritual words give (eternal) life was not uncommon in Jewish spirituality. When a Jew blessed, he did so unlike a neo-Platonist or a (Persian) magician. For the "berakah" the Jewish prayer, unlike the magical prayers of Babylon or Greece, has a particular intentional structure. The Old Testament claims that the Divine revealed Its being to Moses by speaking Its Name in a Holy Fire. Hence, Israel "knows" (cf. "Daath") the Divine (YHVH the Elohîm), for He made a covenant the Torah with His chosen people, the Israelites.

Because of this link forged between the Divine and His chosen ones (in the mythical time of the new beginning of the Israelites after its liberation), we may understand the "berakoth" as an expression of their mutual relationship sui generis. Hence, ideally Jewish prayers do not liberate "divine energy" trapped in the form of a sacrificial animal, nor command the "gods" by knowing their name, but form a continuous reply to the original Divine speech, using the Words of the original speech, and thus re-enacting the experience initiating the Mosaic covenant.

Another characteristic of the "Great Word" in Judaism is its immediacy. Not only is this Word action (as it was in Ancient Egypt), personal intervention (the Divine letting Himself known), and Divine Presence, but, being the Word of Elohîm, it produced by its own virtues that which it announced. By uttering the Divine Word its meaning is realized. This characteristic is akin to "Heka", also automatically realizing the authoritative command based on insightful planning. So the "berakoth" answer YHVH Elohîm, directly manifesting the Divine intent of what has been said. They are more than supplications, invocations or magical commands, but immediate, direct and eternal Divine actions (theurgy) realizing the Plan of the Divine within the physical realm (containing Kether in Malkuth).

So these prayers are theurgical acts. They constitute a deifying elocution of the abstract order of the Divine Word by those wise enough to answer their personal experience of the Divine by means of the Words given by the Divine.

So the following stages are noted:

1. The Divine reveals Himself in original Words;
2. The Presence of the Divine is experienced by the individual (or the collective);
3. Prayers answer the Divine Presence using these original Divine Words;
4. The elocution of these Words immediately create what they intent: spiritualization.

The Quran is called "a Recital" because it is not to be

read as an ordinary text. To recite this Book, is, at best, a return to the original moment when a sign was brought to Muhammad by Gabriel. Tradition recorded the extraordinary state of mind he was brought in everytime a revelation was sent to him. Identical stories are told about the prophets of Israel. Comparative cultural anthropology too attested the trance-like states of Shamans and wizards. However, the Quran itself makes a clear distinction between pre-Islamic poets (inspired by jinns) and the revelations of Muhammad.

"Shall I tell you who the Satans inspire? They inspire the liar, he who is plunged into sin. Those who teach what they have heared: but most of them are liars. It is the poets that the perverse follow. Have you not seen how the poets like madman wander in every valley? How they say what they do not do? Save those who believe, who do righteous deeds, and who repeat the name of ALLAH without cease. The Quran has not been brought down by the Satans." (28:210).

His distinction defines the major difference between Divine revelation and inspirations coming from other sources. These "poets" were the authors of pre-Islamic literature, and they too went into trance to utter their extraordinary words. However, they were not necessarily Muslims, i.e. believers in the unity and uniqueness of ALLAH. Their inspirations could therefore stem from evil jinns or Satans. Then they are like madmen, uttering words which are not backed by their own way of life. The same criterion can be found in the Didache, the first Christian catechesis, were the distinction between a false and genuine prophet is established on the basis of the correspondence between his words and his deeds.

In the Quran however, this is not considered to be a sufficient reason... Genuine poets repeat the Name of ALLAH constantly and by doing so they repell the Satans able to give pseudo-revelations. Hence, not the state of trance or for that matter any other extraordinary state of consciousness or paranormal feat is sufficient proof of the genuineness of spiritual inspirations. Only the spiritual intent of the poet, the fact that he or she refers everything to ALLAH, is a sufficient reason to guarantee its Divine source. And because trance-states are an open invitation to the Satans, they are mostly considered as rejectable. In that line of reasoning, we find the rejection of alchohol or, for that matter, any substance altering the normal waking state.

Muhammad himself was considered mad by those adhering to the pre-Islamic polytheism of the "daughters of ALLAH". For them, he was another crazy poet, bringing a dangerous revelation, one rejecting the existence of divinities next to ALLAH. In Sufism, these states are common, but as Al-Junayd so eloquently explained, he who is his own teacher in these matters has taken Satan as his guide. And this will eventually lead to perdition (not for Satan, for he will reject this affiliation on the Last Day). The highest state is "trance-in-sobriety". In this sense, liturgical recitation stands between reading genuine spiritual poetry and having a direct revelation of the Divine.

When a genuine revelation is recited, no insane poetical elements can creep in. And if, after a lot of practice, this recitation is well performed, another liturgically induced state of consciousness may emerge. During as well as after this ritual recitation, actual themes, situations and problems can be approached in this particular state of mind and solutions may be revealed. Finally, let us distinguish between recitation in spirit and truth versus recitation with sacrifice. In Ancient Egypt, the recitation of ritual texts was always accompanied by sacrifice, going from the libation of fresh water and incense to the sacrifice of hundreds of animals during the major festivities.

This because the deities were supposed to exist in the sky. Their doubles (ka's) and souls (ba's) could dwell on Earth but this only if they were fed. Hence, liturgy without sacrifice was deemed totally useless, for no god or goddess would accept the requests if its subtle bodies had not received nourishment. In pre-synagogal Judaism, the holocaust of animals was part of the bloody temple service held in Jeruzalem. It was not enough to recite the Torah, for YHadonaiVH was pleased with these sacrifices.

The notion of feeding the deity was absent. The reason for sacrifice was the fact that by slaughtering and offering his animals, the Jew proved his ability to relinquish his precious earthly goods for Adonai (cf. the story of Abraham and his son). In this way it became obvious that He and only He was the Lord. The roasted meat was eaten by the priests and the participants. After the destruction of the second temple, this sacrificial ritualism was abandoned because it was considered too sacred an act to be performed outside the temple. In synagogal liturgy, the service of the word stands alone and a recitation in spirit and truth prevails.

Occasional sacrifices still occur, but not in the synagogal context. Suppose that Israel would be able to rebuild its temple (a very unlikely event). Would the ancient practice of the bloody holocaust of animals be reestablished? Informed sources confirm that this would be the case. Hence, synagogal Judaism is not the next stage of Jewish spiritual practice, but only one which awaits the return of the Messiah who will reaffirm the ancient ways... When asked why this kind of sacrifice is necessary, the pious Jew responds that it was commanded by the Creator, i.e. a justification based on a literal, uncritical reading of the Torah and other so-called "sacred" texts.

However, it is beyond doubt that parts of the texts which were organized, edited and rewritten after the Israelites returned from their Babylonian captivity (Jeruzalem was looted in 587 BCE) and came under Persian rule (587 - 331 BCE) were of an earlier date (parts of Exodus and Deuteronomium were probably composed ca.1250 BCE). But how to know for sure which texts go back to the original (oral) composition? What part of this oral original was already lost after the Babylonian capitivity? Also, which contemporary influences were allowed to play a role in the redaction which took place at the time of Ezra? What about the absence of punctuation? Clearly Mozes could not have written about his own death and funeral? Scholars agree that we do not know which sources were used.

The fact that several editors were responsible is also very likely. Moreover, traces of the myths recited at Ur can be found in Genesis (cf. the parallel with the Babylonian poem of creation, the Enuma Elisj). And the influence of the literature of the New Kingdom of Ancient Egypt on some of these writings can also be established (cf. Genesis, Psalms, Proverbs). Under Persian rule, the Old Testament as we know it did not exist. In the Septuagint (the Alexandrian translation into Greek), the Name of God (YHadonaiVH Elohim) was badly translated and hence in the Greek Old Testament, a crucial theological nuance was lost (the plural "ALHYM" became the singular "Theos", and "YHVH" became "Kyrios", eclipsing the ineffable bi-polar nature of the Divine). Although Philo of Alexandria (a contempory of Jesus) thought that this translation was divinely inspired, it nevertheless shows the corrosive influence of Hellenism on original Judaism, forcing traditional Jews outside the walls of Jeruzalem and triggering more than one rebellious, desert fraction or fundamentalists avant la lettre.

The presence of the Qumrân Scrolls (Dead Sea) shows that textual inventivity continued to grow (the first Qumrân text is dated ca.150 BCE) and that different opposing fractions (with their texts) existed. After the destruction of the second Tempie (29th of August, 70 CE) all important elements of Jewish faith were recorded and after Rabbi Akiba (who was ca. twenty when Jeruzalem fell) the "final" redaction (incorporating different spelling and ornamentation of certain letters) became a sacred Temple of its own, treated with a reverence as if the Supreme had been personally at work here. Unfortunately, after the execution of Akiba by the Romans, only thousands of little pieces of paper found in a synagogue in Caïro was all that what was left of the Hebrew Bible as it existed in the centuries after Akiba's death.

In Catholic Christianity, the notion of sacrifice has been transformed in a very special way. It was believed that Christ, as the sole son of God, sacrificed himself for those who adhere to him (Paulinian thesis). During the eucharist, the officiating priest acts "in persona Christi" and repeats the original sacrifice in a bloodless way. Hence the priest (as Christ) sacrificed Himself again during each eucharist. Transsubstantiation added a realistic element to this, for by uttering the words spoken by Christ at the last supper (before being killed) over the bread and the cup, the priest (as Christ) changes the offerings of bread and wine into the body and blood of Christ... After this epiclesis (the exact moment of which remained a matter of dispute between the Western and Eastern churches), the fact that Christ died but was resuccitated is affirmed.

Although during Mass, the role of the "service of the word" is an important preliminary, it can not be said that the ritual recitations of the "Great Prayer" (after the Offertory) are devoid of sacrificial connotations. Quite on the contrary. Take away the sacrifice of Christ and Paulinian theology collapses. Later Protestant interpretations show that it is possible to remove the sacrificial component. The result being a "service of the word" which resembles synagogal practices, except for the verbal affimation of Christ's sacrifice and resurrection, which remained unaltered and can be seen as the heart of Christian faith.

The Quran prescribes occasional sacrifices, but the activities in the Mosk have always been devoid of it. Not unlike synagogal Judaism, Islamic liturgy is wholly verbal. The believers come together to perform their prayers and to listen to the liturgical recitation of some Quranic verses by the imam, the person who leads the prayers. After this, the imam pronounces his sermon, intended to explain and actualize the meaning of the recited texts. No sacrificial elements creep in. Although the Quran prescribes certain occasional sacrifices, they do not belong to the "pillars" of Islam. On a grand scale they were introduced for a stated term only, namely for the Jews of the "ancient house" (22:34). Unlike Judaism, Islam never indulged in elaborated sacrificial practices. The most important obligation for the Muslim is to remember ALLAH and this through the repetition of His Name.

"Be pure of faith. Do not associate anything with Him. For those who associate anything with ALLAH are like him who has fallen from heaven and the birds snatch him away, or the wind sweeps him headlong into a far away place. It shall be like this. He who venerates ALLAH's waymarks does a deed that belongs to the piety of the heart. In the sacrificial animals are many things which are profitable to you for a stated term. Thereafter their lawful place of sacrifice is by the ancient house. We have appointed for every nation a holy rite, so that they may mention ALLAH's name over such beasts of the flocks as provided by Him. Your ALLAH is the unique ALLAH. So to Him surrender. And you, Muhammad, give good tidings to the humble." (22:32-35)

Is this good tiding the fact that mentioning ALLAH's Name is all that matters? If the slaughter of animals is considered essential to please ALLAH, then surely the Lord would be limited by the fire of the holocaust. This would be in contradiction with His oneness and uniqueness... Sacrificial activity indeed only serves the purpose of being an important object (to the believer) over which His Name may be mentioned. It is also part of the obligation to feed the poor, for instead of burning everything, the sacrificed animal should be used to aleviate the situation of the needy.

For the true believers, an external sacrificial object is not really necessary, for all that matters is the remembrance of ALLAH. Of course, the Quran does not deny that for some people such an object of sacrifice may been important, but is it surely not considered essential in the same way as the sacrificial activity of the Ancient Egyptians, the pre-synagogal Jews or the Christians.

Elements of the Arabesque

In the Quran we read:

"It is He who let the two seas come near, the one with sweet water which is grateful to taste, and the other with salt water, which is bitter to the tongue. Between them He set an insurmountable barrier." (25:55)

"The two seas are not equal. The one is sweet, grateful to taste, delicious to drink, and the other is salt, bitter to the tongue. Yet of both you eat fresh flesh, and bring forth out of them ornaments to wear. You may see ships cleaving through it, so that you may seek of His bounty. Perhaps you will be thankful. He makes the night to enter the day and the day to enter the night. He has subjected the sun and the moon, each of them running a stated term. That is ALLAH, your Lord. To Him belongs the kingdom and those you call upon, apart from Him, possess not so much as the skin of a date-stone." (35:13-14)

"He separated the two seas that touch each other. Between them is a barrier so that they do not overpass." (55:19-20)

The logic of the arabesque is an example of the "coincidentio oppositorum" discovered in mystical discourses all around the world. In Muslim thought however, it became the core of their superstructure. All divisions, also those between the Divine and creation, are ruled by this arabesque logic, or the symbolization of the fundamental dialectic apparent everywhere in creation and even beyond. Indeed, in Sufism, the Divine itself is a dual-unity of the essence of ALLAH (His Face) and His most beautiful Names. Ibn'Arabî distinguished between the "most holy emanation" (the Essence revealed as Divine Names) and the "holy emanation" (the Divine Names creating the worlds).

The Divine Names (the "hidden treasure") themselves form an arabesque between the noble and the base Names. In creation too the same dialectic is witnessed, for all created objects are a mixture of light and darkness, good and evil, truth and falsehood. In Muslim theology, only the Face of ALLAH is free from all possible duality, and represents the ineffable, unsaying transcendence beyond all possible affirmations and denials (cf. the "hypertheos" of ps.-Dionysius the Areopagite). Hence, only ALLAH is the truth and the real. He is the absolute neutral in which all equations, positive as well as negative, are rooted. Besides this syntax, the arabeque has definitely semantical intentions. Although everything except ALLAH's Face is organized as a dialectic, its "arabesque" nature is exemplified by the fact that both sides of the spectrum are put there by ALLAH and kept there by Him too. He divides the spectrum by means of an unsurmountable barrier.

The fact that this barrier is there, shows that both sides need to be distinguished. But the fact that He makes it unsurmountable evidences the fact the He alone rules all divisions in a way no creature is able to supercede. The interplay of the two sides of the arabesque is only possible because ALLAH is the Lord of all divisions. The caleidoscopic dynamics unfolding when the divisions are maintained but put into motion allows every Name to find its locus of Self-expression. Everything tasteful and tasteless has its function and role to play. There is no division or ALLAH controls it. We have to accept that some of the water can not be drunk, although it is only tasteless from our perspective.

The arabesque of the two commands springs into mind. Firstly, ALLAH creates everything by His command "Be !". Chaos and order alike depend on this generative command, which is the expression of His Will. This is suggestive of the two seas, the sweet and the bitter. Both are under His command. Nothing happens in creation or ALLAH wills it to happen. Even what we would call the greatest misery is part of His Will. Secondly, ALLAH sends His messagers to inform humanity about the specific task ALLAH has prescribed for them, which is the expression of His Wish. Many revelations came down, a holy rite for every nation. This is the prescriptive command: "Be yourself !", implying for the human that he or she has to realize the Divine Names which make them exist so as to realize the perfection ALLAH has intended for them.

The prescriptive command is the sweet sea, and suggests that humanity should leave part of creation untouched (the salt sea). Only ALLAH is able to divide both and so He alone is the arbiter that decides which evil befalls man. The Quran teaches that if a human decides to leave the bitter untouched, s/he will be given the sweet and protected from the bitter by the barrier of ALLAH. The division is therefore a test, a way to observe whether a creature endowed with the freedom to choose for those aspects of ALLAH's Will (like unjustified violence, corrupting the land, lack of respect for others, gross and rejectable attitudes, etc.) which are not His Wish (for that creature) will stick to what ALLAH knows (of that creature), for indeed ALLAH only does what He knows.

If somebody goes against the Divine Wish, then the taste of the salt sea will make the person go astray and leave it unprotected. Surely the forces of darkness will encompass it and the final outcome of the process is destruction and damnation. Once the crooked path has been entered, the freedom to choose is hampered and no return is possible (except if ALLAH decides otherwise). But, as some people are the expressions of the Base Names, their infernal terminus is in accord with what they are, namely expressions of the Divine Wish to put upon the face of the Earth humans which are evil and corrupted (like Hitler, Stalin, Pol Pot etc.)... For them, the tortures of hell are as natural as the bliss of the inhabitants of the heavens.

Religious experience, mystical experience and religion are three different answers to the call of the unconditional, i.e. the absolute in all its possible forms of absoluteness (as in number: infinity; length: limitlessness, time: eternity, knowledge: omniscience and will: omnipotence). Some never notice the call or try in vain to construct an "absolutely" relative model of being. They are either atheists or agnostics. The former fight against any notion of "divinity" (they say: "nothing is absolute" or "there is no Supreme Being"). The latter confess no to know and so leave the matter open (they say: "it is possible that the absolute exists but even so that it does not exist").

We must try to understand that universals may act as the deities of old. In this perspective, atheism is impossible, for it entails the worship of univeral ideas proposed by a limited group of people. If the absolute is negated because of some universal, then clearly this idea is actually the "absolute" used to deny the absolute. Hence, atheist logic contains a "contradictio in actu exercito" (a contradiction in the act). How to deny the absolute with the absolute (How to maintain democracy if everything is decided by the majority, also majority-ruling? What if the majority decides to kill the minority?). In its humanistic form, atheism is thus forced to wrongly elevate the human to the status of God.

It goes without saying that arabesque logic is highly effective in mystical and poetical discourses intended to arouse religious feelings and point to the basic tenets of mysticism, namely the fundamental unity of the Divine veiled by the infinite multiplicity of Divine Names emanating from the infinite source. As the context of the arabesque is an absolute consensus and never a majority rule alone, it is dangerous to use this kind of logic to organize groups of people (politics and law). Hence, to mirror its vertical features socially (creating a spiritual elite) runs against mystical principle that nobody is or is able to claim to be or represent God (for the finite never grasps the infinite).

Final Remarks:

Allow me to articulate a few final remarks:

1. Muhammad, peace with him, was a genuine mystic. His mysticism being that of the "unity of being", in particular, the unity and oneness of ALLAH, The God, or the One Absolute Divine Being. To affirm the fundamental unity of ALLAH is the hallmark of Muhammadan mysticism. This "declaration of unity" (or "tawhîd") is the actual affirmation (performance) of two distinct adhesions, each in two parts:

- say: 'there is no god only The God' or
  - a. 'there is no god' ("la ilaha");
  - b. 'only The God is' ("illa-Allâh");
- say: 'and Muhammad is the Prophet of The God'.

As a mystic, he was very "noetic" (cf. "say:"), implying that the aforesaid unity unveiled itself in a cognitive structure, a book with the truth sent by ALLAH to humanity. Muhammadan mysticism shares this feature with other mystics before him, such as Akhenaten, Moses and Jesus. But in the case of Muhammad, this revelatoric form ("word" or elocution) is an answer to the command of Gabriel, the perfect messenger: "Read !" Tradition describes the extraordinary state he was in when a Divine sign "came down" in his heart. And there were many witnesses, believers as well as unbelievers. Some of the latter compared his state with that of the mad poets of old. Nevertheless, the Quran makes a clear distinction between poetry and Divine revelation.

Muhammad never claimed divinity for himself as had done Akhenaten and the Christians with Jesus, son of Mary. He did not see ALLAH face to face, for His Face is essentially His Alone (i.e. apophatism and radical unsaying). The "noetic" and "revelatoric" nature of Muhammad's mysticism may eclipse the fact that he was truly a mystic of un-knowing (apophasis), for ALLAH knows and we do not. To return everything to ALLAH, is the golden treat enabling the reader to read through the complete text of the Quran several times.

2. Muhammad was a prophet. Not all mystics are prophets, but all prophets are mystics. The revelation brought to Muhammad came to radically reaffirm Divine unity and the fact that the Absolute is all-comprehensive and all-inclusive, excluding all possible associated things next to it. It also claimed to be the final word, because it was the first to include all other possible revelations, which are all from ALLAH. Indeed, the Quran states that no distinction is made between any messenger of ALLAH! If with Christianity salvic access had become generalized (Judaic circumcision abrogated), with Islam revelation itself was universalized (through the Muhammadan form).
3. The Quran states that its interpretation is known to ALLAH alone. It distinguishes between a guarded tablet and a book to be recited sent by ALLAH. If during Muhammad's lifetime, collections of the revelations existed, then it is probable that he himself had his own set of chapters in which he arranged the verses which descended in his heart or spiritual recipient. Was this original also 114 chapters long? Was their order (according to subject-matter and not chronology) also fixed? Critical scholarship doubts this. In their minds, Muhammad did not order a single book and the work of subsequent redactors was considerable.

   As no original texts seem to subsist, the argument is undecided. But where are the fragments used by Zaid? It is probable that Muhammad had his "memory" copy of the "recitation", with its own original arrangement. It is also likely that the later redactions of Zaid are "worked" copies. The rather large number of original codices proves the point. On the other hand, it is also likely that these copies somehow used the original form (scattered around in texts and living memory), of which a part was lost (for the original recitation was larger). By itself, this editorial history is remarkable. Compared with what had happened in Judaism, Buddhism and

Christianity, the difficulties are smaller and the final reliable text larger.

Critical views about the revelations of the prophet assailed Islam from the very beginning. Already in the late eighth century there were those who doubted that the Quran was the "uncreated" and eternal word of God. Under the Caliph al-Ma'mun (813-833) the heretical view was adopted that the Quran was created gradually. By the end of the tenth century the opposite view, that of the inimitability of the Quran, was taken and adhered to. As a result the mainstream Muslim understanding is that the Quran is the literal and uncreated word of God. There is even a day of festivity to celebrate the event of the holy book descending from heaven.

The reputation of the Quran as God's word would be irreparably damaged if it could be proven that unjust teachings and rules were part of the culture and custom of Arabia in the 7th century. Christianity has a long history of exegesis and literary criticism of the Bible. Not so in Islam. Scholars and writers in Islamic countries who have ignored warnings have sometimes found themselves the target of death threats and violence.

The fatwa on Salmon Rushdie is well-known:

- When Arab scholar Suliman Bashear maintained that Islam developed into a religion gradually, instead of coming fully formed from the mouth of the Prophet, he was injured after being thrown from a second-story window by his students at the University of Nablus on the West Bank.
- In 1992 the Egyptian journalist Farag Foda was assassinated by Islamists for his critical writings about Egypt's Muslim Brotherhood.
- In 1994 the Nobel Prize-winning novelist Naguib Mahfouz was stabbed for writing "heretical" conceptions of God and the Prophet Muhammad.
- Egyptian scholar Abû Zayd had to terminate his

academic career as a result of judicial inquiry and persecution for apostasy. He is living in exile in the Netherlands as a lecturer now.

- Egyptian blogger Abdel Karim Suleiman was sentenced to four years inprisonment for offending the Islam, prophet Muhammad and president Hosni Mubarak in februari 2007.
- In August 2004 the highest religious authority in Egypt, the Al Azhar university, ordered the confiscation of books of David Cook and Jamal al-Banna for violating 'islamic principles'.

Yet despite threats, a handful of experts have been quietly investigating the origins of the Quran, offering radically new theories about the roots of Islam:

- Christoph Luxenberg for one, a scholar of ancient Semitic languages in Germany, argues that the Quran has been misread and mistranslated for centuries. His work, based on the earliest copies of the Quran, maintains that parts of the text are derived from pre-existing Christian Aramaic texts that were misinterpreted by later Islamic scholars.
- John Wansbrough of the School of Oriental and African Studies in London maintains that the text of the Quran appears to be a composite of different texts compiled over dozens, if not hundreds, of years. There is no evidence of the existence of the Quran until 691 AD, being 59 years after Muhammad's death, when the Dome of the Rock mosque in Jerusalem was built, carrying several Quranic inscriptions, which are slightly different as we know them today.
- Much of what we know of the life and sayings of the Prophet is based on texts from between 130 and 300 years after Muhammad's death. Patricia Crone and Michael Cook of Princeton University have studied several non-Muslim, seventh-century accounts. In those texts Muhammad is not mentioned as the founder of a

new religion but as a preacher in the Old Testament tradition, hailing the coming of a Messiah. Many of the early documents refer to the followers of Muhammad as "Hagarenes" and the "tribe of Ishmael" as descendants of the Jewish patriarch Abraham and Hagar, the slave girl and their son Ishmaël.

- During restoration of the Great Mosque of Sana'a in Yemen, fragments of Qurans were discovered that are among the oldest we know of. German scholar Gerd R. Puin who studied the manuscripts found that some scriptures differed from the accepted autorized version and that part of it was even inscribed over an earlier text so indicating that the present-day Quranic text is not from the time of Mohammad.
- According to Islamic tradition the Ka'ba in Mecca was built by Abraham and Ishmaël but Islamic scholar Snouck Hurgronje has shown that Muhammad invented the story to give his religion an Arabian origin.
- Incidentally, a group of archeologists led by Zev Herzog of the university of Tel Aviv stated in October 2003, after seventy years of research, that there is no historical evidence for the biblical stories. Abraham and Ishmaël may be figures of a legend.

Fundamentalism

The humiliation of westernization evoked counterforces. Fundamentalist movements had already been in existence from the ninth century. Modern fundamentalist aspirations date from the '30s and '40s. Hasan al-Bannâ became a proponent of the Muslim Brotherhood. This brotherhood called in 1920 for an Islamic form of nation-state, a state where Islamic law, the shari'a, would be the law of the land. In particular in Saudi-Arabia: in law schools of Sunni-Islam a return is preached to the purity of the letters and an imitation of the Salaf, the ancients of Medina and the model-life of the prophet. Thereby forgetting that Medina was scarred by a bloody civil war waged by these 'ancients' at the time.

Ibn Taymiyya (1263-1328), a Syrian theologian, made corporal punishment the very criterion of the Shari'a. Flagellation, chopping off of hands and feet, stoning and even crucifixion were the cruelties he recommended. It is still the basis of Wahhabism, the movement named after Abd-al-Wahhab (1703-1792) practised in Saudi-Arabia. Fundamentalism is the curse that haunts any budding religion, whether it be Islam, Christianity, Hinduism, or Buddhism. Fundamentalists aspire to regain power. The same power as their opponents, the Western governments, with the difference that in Islam it is used to coerce mankind into obeying Allah's commands, the advent of the Kingdom of God.

Islam fundamentalism has a political as well as a religious component. It is a messianic dream, anti-modern in ideology, narrowed down to an overly concern with the hereafter. Its recent extreme form: terrorism, is encouraged by the instilled belief that martyrs await a heavenly reward. Admittedly, to die for one's religion pre-existed in Judaism and Christianity, but there it was no excuse to hurt or kill non-believers and so bring one's faith into discredit.

On Losing Faith / Apostasy

Losing faith in Islam is an excruciating process. Not only by the threat of punishment upon defecting. In Islamic society it may mean banishment from social life. As Islam is more a binding social network between families and groups of believers than that it is born out of a religious inclination, leaving the clan is felt as an insult. How serious the offense is may be clear from the following Hadith: "Whoever changes his Islamic religion, kill him."(Vol. 9:57).

Defective Muslims in the West have a way out to immerse in the non-religious society. Yet (s)he may feel thrown in a vacuum in picking up a new way of life without support of the family. No Allah to guide him/her, no outsiders to heap the blame on! Yet compensated by the feeling of release from oppressive social control!

The Quran and the Prophet toward Knowledge

Islam is a religion based upon knowledge for it is ultimately knowledge of the Oneness of God combined with faith and total commitment to Him that saves man. The text of the Quran is replete with verses inviting man to use his intellect, to ponder, to think and to know, for the goal of human life is to discover the Truth which is none other than worshipping God in His Oneness. The Hadith literature is also full of references to the importance of knowledge. Such sayings of the Prophet as "Seek knowledge even in China", "Seek knowledge from the cradle to the grave", and "Verily the men of knowledge are the inheritors of the prophets", have echoed throughout the history of Islam and incited Muslims to seek knowledge wherever it might be found.

During most of its history, Islamic civilization has been witness to a veritable celebration of knowledge. That is why every traditional Islamic city possessed public and private libraries and some cities like Cordoba and Baghdad boasted of libraries with over 400,000 books. Such cities also had bookstores, some of which sold a large number of titles. That is also why the scholar has always been held in the highest esteem in Islamic society.

The Pre-Islamic Sciences

As Islam spread northward into Syria, Egypt, and the Persian empire, it came face to face with the sciences of antiquity whose heritage had been preserved in centers which now became a part of the Islamic world. Alexandria had been a major center of sciences and learning for centuries. The Greek learning cultivated in Alexandria was opposed by the Byzantine who had burned its library long before the advent of Islam. The tradition of Alexandrian learning did not die, however. It was transferred to Antioch and from there farther east to such cities as Edessa by eastern Christians who stood in sharp opposition to Byzantine and wished to have their own independent centers of learning. Moreover, the Persian king, Shapur I had established Jundishapur in Persia as a second great center of learning matching Antioch. He even invited Indian physicians and mathematicians to teach in this major seat of learning, in addition to the Christian scholars who taught in Syriac as well as the Persians whose medium of instruction was Pahlavi.

Once Muslims established the new Islamic order during the Umayyad period, they turned their attention to these centers of learning which had been preserved and sought to acquaint themselves with the knowledge taught and cultivated in them. They therefore set about with a concerted effort to translate the philosophical and scientific works which were available to them from not only Greek and Syriac (which was the language of eastern Christian scholars) but also from Pahlavi, the scholarly language of pre-Islamic Persia, and even from Sanskrit. Many of the accomplished translators were Christian Arabs such as Hunayn ibn Ishaq' who was also an outstanding physician, and others Persians such as Ibn Muqaffa', who played a major role in the creation of the new Arabic prose style conducive to the expression of philosophical and scientific writings.

The great movement of translation lasted from the beginning of the 8th to the end of the 9th century, reaching its peak with the establishment of the House of Wisdom (Bayt al hiLmah) by the caliph al-Matmun at the beginning of the 9th century. The result of this extensive effort of the Islamic community to confront the challenge of the presence of the various philosophies and sciences of antiquity and to understand and digest them in its own terms and according to its own world view was the translation of a vast corpus of writings into Arabic. Most of the important philosophical and scientific works of Aristotle and his school, much of Plato and the Pythagorean school, and the major works of Greek astronomy, mathematics and medicine such as the Almagest of Ptolemy, the Elements of Euclid, and the works of Hippocrates and Galen, were all rendered into Arabic.

Further more, important works of astronomy, mathematics and medicine were translated from Pahlavi and Sanskrit. As a result, Arabic became the most important scientific language of the world for many centuries and the depository of much of the wisdom and the sciences of antiquity. The Muslims did not translate the scientific and philosophical works of other civilizations out of fear of political or economic domination but because the structure of Islam itself is based upon the primacy of knowledge.

Nor did they consider these forms of knowing as "un-Islamic" as long as they confirmed the doctrine of God's Oneness which Islam considers to have been at the heart of every authentic revelation from God. Once these sciences and philosophies confirmed the principle of Oneness, the Muslims considered them as their own. They made them part of their world view and began to cultivate the Islamic sciences based on what they had translated, analyzed, criticized, and assimilated, rejecting what was not in conformity with the Islamic perspective.

The Mathematical Sciences and Physics

The Muslim mind has always been attracted to the mathematical sciences in accordance with the "abstract" character of the doctrine of Oneness which lies at the heart of Islam. The mathematical sciences have traditionally included astronomy, mathematics itself and much of what is called physics today. In astronomy the Muslims integrated the astronomical traditions of the Indians, Persians, the ancient Near East and especially the Greeks into a synthesis which began to chart a new chapter in the history of astronomy from the 8th century onward. The Almagest of Ptolemy, whose very name in English reveals the Arabic origin of its Latin translation, was thoroughly studied and its planetary theory criticized by several astronomers of both the eastern and western lands of Islam leading to the major critique of the theory by Nasir al-Din al-Tusi and his students, especially Qutb al Din al-Shirazi, in the 13th century.

The Muslims also observed the heavens carefully and discovered many new stars. The book on stars of 'Abdal-Rahman al-Sufi was in fact translated into Spanish by Alfonso X el Sabio and had a deep influence upon stellar toponymy in European languages. Many star names in English such as Aldabaran still recall their Arabic origin. The Muslims carried out many fresh observations which were contained in astronomical tables called zij. One of the acutest of these observers was al-Battani whose work was followed by numerous others. The zij of al-Ma'mun observed in Baghdad, the Hakimite zij of Cairo, the Toledan Tables of al Zarqali and his associates, the Il-Khanid zij of Nasir al-Din al-Tusi observed in Maraghah, and the zij of Ulugh-Beg from Samarqand are among the most famous Islamic astronomical tables. They wielded a great deal of influence upon Western astronomy up to the time of Tycho Brahe.

The Muslims were in fact the first to create an astronomical observatory as a scientific institution, this being the observatory of Maraghah in Persia established by al-Tusi. This was indirectly the model for the later European observatories. Many astronomical instruments were developed by Muslims to carry out observation, the most famous being the astrolabe. There existed even mechanical astrolabes perfected by Ibn Samh which must be considered as the ancestor of the mechanical clock. Astronomical observations also had practical applications including not only finding the direction of Makkah for prayers, but also devising almanacs (the word itself being of Arabic origin). The Muslims also applied their astronomical knowledge to questions of time keeping and the calendar.

The most exact solar calendar existing to this day is the Jalali calendar devised under the direction of 'Umar Khayyam in the 12th century and still in use in Persia and Afghanistan. As for mathematics proper, like astronomy, it received its direct impetus from the Quran not only because of the mathematical structure related to the text of the

Sacred Book, but also because the laws of inheritance delineated in the Quran require rather complicated mathematical solutions. Here again Muslims began by integrating Greek and Indian mathematics. The first great Muslim mathematician, al-Khwarazmi, who lived in the 9th century, wrote a treatise on arithmetic whose Latin translation brought what is known as Arabic numerals to the West.

To this day guarismo, derived from his name, means figure or digit in Spanish while algorithm is still used in English. Al-Khwarazmi is also the author of the first book on algebra. This science was developed by Muslims on the basis of earlier Greek and Indian works of a rudimentary nature. The very name algebra comes from the first part of the name of the book of al-Khwarazmi, entitled Kitab al-jabr wa'l-muqabalah. Abu Kamil al-Shuja' discussed algebraic equations with five unknowns. The science was further developed by such figures as al-Karaji until it reached its peak with Khayyam who classified by kind and class algebraic equations up to the third degree.

The Muslims also excelled in geometry as reflected in their art. The brothers Banu Musa who lived in the 9th century may be said to be the first outstanding Muslim geometers while their contemporary Thabit ibn Qurrah used the method of exhaustion, giving a glimpse of what was to become integral calculus. Many Muslim mathematicians such as Khayyam and al-Tusi also dealt with the fifth postulate of Euclid and the problems which follow if one tries to prove this postulate within the confines of Eucledian geometry. Another branch of mathematics developed by Muslims is trigonometry which was established as a distinct branch of mathematics by al-Biruni. The Muslim mathematicians, especially al-Battani, Abu'l-Wafa', Ibn Yunus and Ibn al-Haytham, also developed spherical astronomy and applied it to the solution of astronomical problems.

The love for the study of magic squares and amicable numbers led Muslims to develop the theory of numbers. Al-

Khujandi discovered a particular case of Fermat's theorem that "the sum of two cubes cannot be another cube", while al Karaji analyzed arithmetic and geometric progressions such as:

1**3+2**3+3**3+...+n**3=(1+2+3+...+n)** 2

Al-Biruni also dealt with progressions while Ghiyath al-Din Jamshid al-Kashani brought the study of number theory among Muslims to its peak. In the field of physics the Muslims made contributions in especially three domains. The first was the measurement of specific weights of objects and the study of the balance following upon the work of Archimedes. In this domain the writings of al-Biruni and al-Khazini stand out. Secondly they criticized the Aristotelian theory of projectile motion and tried to quantify this type of motion. The critique of Ibn Sina, Abu'l-Barakat al-Baghdad), Ibn Bajjah and others led to the development of the idea of impetus and momentum and played an important role in the criticism of Aristotelian physics in the West up to the early writings of Galileo.

Thirdly there is the field of optics in which the Islamic sciences produced in Ibn al-Haytham (the Latin Alhazen) who lived in the 11th century, the greatest student of optics between Ptolemy and Witelo. Ibn al-Haytham's main work on optics, the Kitab al-manazir, was also well known in the West as Thesaurus opticus. Ibn al-Haytham solved many optical problems, one of which is named after him, studied the property of lenses, discovered the camera obscura, explained correctly the process of vision, studied the structure of the eye, and explained for the first time why the sun and the moon appear larger on the horizon.

His interest in optics was carried out two centuries later by Qutb al-Din al Shirazi and Kamal al-Din al-Farisi. It was Qutb al Din who gave the first correct explanation of the formation of the rainbow. It is important to recall that in physics as in many other fields of science the Muslims observed, measured and carried out experiments. They must be credited with having developed what came to be known later as the experimental method.

The Medical Sciences

The hadiths of the Prophet contain many instructions concerning health including dietary habits; these sayings became the foundation of what came to be known later as "Prophetic medicine" (al-tibb al-nabawi). Because of the great attention paid in Islam to the need to take care of the body and to hygiene, early in Islamic history Muslims began to cultivate the field of medicine turning once again to all the knowledge that was available to them from Greek, Persian and Indian sources. At first I the great physicians among Muslims were mostly | Christian but by the 9th century Islamic medicine, I properly speaking, was born with the appearance of the major compendium, The Paradise of Wisdom (Firdaws al-hilmah) by 'All ibn Rabban al Tabari, who synthesized the Hippocratic and Galenic traditions of medicine with those of India and Persia.

His student, Muhammad ibn Zakariyya' al-Razi (the Latin Rhazes), was one of the greatest of physicians who emphasized clinical medicine and observation. He was a master of prognosis and psychosomatic medicine and also of anatomy. He was the first to identify and treat smallpox, to use alcohol as an antiseptic and make medical use of mercury as a purgative. His Kitab al-hawi (Continens) is the longest work ever written in Islamic medicine and he was recognized as a medical authority in the West up to the 18th century.

The greatest of all Muslim physicians, how ever, was Ibn Sina who was called "the prince of physicians" in the West. He synthesized Islamic medicine in his major masterpiece, al-Qanun fi'l tibb (The Canon of Medicine), which is the most famous of all medical books in history. It was the final authority in medical matters in Europe for nearly six centuries and is still taught wherever Islamic medicine has survived to this day in such lands as Pakistan and India. Ibn Sina discovered many drugs and identified and treated several ailments such as meningitis but his greatest contribution was in the philosophy of medicine. He created a system of medicine within which medical practice could be carried out and in which physical and psychological factors; drugs and diet are combined.

After Ibn Sina, Islamic medicine divided into several branches. In the Arab world Egypt remained a major center for the study of medicine, especially ophthalmology which reached its peak at the court of al-Hakim. Cairo possessed excellent hospitals which also drew physicians from other lands including Ibn Butlan, author of the famous Calendar of Health, and Ibn Nafis who discovered the lesser or pulmonary circulation of the blood long before Michael Servetus, who is usually credited with the discovery.

As for the western lands of Islam including Spain, this area was likewise witness to the appearance of outstanding physicians such as Sa'd al Katib of Cordoba who composed a treatise on gynecology, and the greatest Muslim figure in surgery, the 12th century Abu'l-Qasim al-Zahrawi (the Latin Albucasis) whose medical masterpiece Kitab al-tasrif was well known in the West as Concessio. One must also mention the Ibn Zuhr family which produced several outstanding physicians and Abu Marwan 'Abd al-Malik who was the Maghrib's most outstanding clinical physician. The well known Spanish philosophers, Ibn Tufayl and Ibn Rushd, were also outstanding physicians.

Islamic medicine continued in Persia and the other eastern lands of the Islamic world under the influence of Ibn Sina with the appearance of major Persian medical compendia such as the Treasury of Sharaf al-Din al-Jurjani and the commentaries upon the Canon by Fakhr al-Din al-Razi and Qutb al-Din al-Shirazi. Even after the Mongol invasion, medical studies continued as can be seen in the work of Rashid al-Din Fadlallah, and for the first time there appeared translations of Chinese medicine and interest in acupuncture among Muslims. The Islamic medical tradition was revived in the Safavid period when several diseases such as whooping cough were diagnosed and treated for the first time and much attention was paid to pharmacology. Many Persian doctors such as 'Ayn al-Murk of Shiraz also traveled to India at this time to usher in the golden age of Islamic medicine in the subcontinent and to plant the seed of the Islamic medical tradition which continues to flourish to this day in the soil of that land.

The Ottoman world was also an arena of great medical activity derived from the heritage of Ibn Sina. The Ottoman Turks were especially known for the creation of major hospitals and medical centers. These included not only units for the care of the physically ill, but also wards for patients with psychological ailments. The Ottomans were also the first to receive the influence of modern European medicine in both medicine and pharmacology.

In mentioning Islamic hospitals it is necessary to mention that all major Islamic cities had hospitals; some like those of Baghdad were teaching hospitals while some like the Nasiri hospital of Cairo had thousands of beds for patients with almost any type of illness. Hygiene in these hospitals was greatly emphasized and al-Razi had even written a treatise on hygiene in hospitals. Some hospitals also specialized in particular diseases including psychological ones. Cairo even had a hospital which specialized in patients having insomnia.

Islamic medical authorities were also always concerned with the significance of pharmacology and many important works such as the Canon have whole books devoted to the subject. The Muslims became heir not only to the pharmacological knowledge of the Greeks as contained in the works of Dioscorides, but also the vast herbal pharmacopias of the Persians and Indians. They also studied the Medical effects of many drug, especially herbs, themselves. The greatest contributions in this field came from Maghribi scientists such as Ibn Juljul, Ibn al-Salt and the most original of Muslim pharmacologists, the 12th century scientist, al Ghafiqi, whose Book of Simple Drugs provides the best descriptions of the medical properties of plants known to Muslims. Islamic medicine combined the use of drugs for medical purposes with dietary considerations and a whole lifestyle derived from the teachings of Islam to create a synthesis which has not died out to this day despite the introduction of modern medicine into most of the Islamic world.

Natural History and Geography

The vast expanse of the Islamic world enabled the Muslims to develop natural history based not only on the Mediterranean world, as was the case of the Greek natural historians, but also on most of the Eurasian and even African land masses. Knowledge of minerals, plants and animals was assembled from areas as far away as the Malay world and synthesized for the first time by Ibn Sina in his Kitab al-Shifa'(The Book of Healing). Such major natural historians as al-Mas'udi inter twined natural and human history. Al-Biruni likewise in his study of India turned to the natural history and even geology of the region, describing correctly the sedimentary nature of the Ganges basin. He also wrote the most outstanding Muslim work on mineralogy.

As for botany, the most important treatises were composed in the 12th century in Spain with the appearance of the work of al-Ghafiqi. This is also the period when the best known Arabic work on agriculture, the Kitab al-falahah, was written. The Muslims also showed much interest in zoology especially in horses as witnessed by the classical text of al-Jawaliqi, and in falcons and other hunting birds. The works of al-Jahiz and al Damiri are especially famous in the field of zoology and deal with the literary, moral and even theological dimensions of the study of animals as well as the purely zoological aspects of the subject. This is also true of a whole class of writings on the "wonders of creation" of which the book of Abu Yabya al-Qazwini, the 'Aja'ib al-makhluqat (The Wonders of Creation) is perhaps the most famous.

Likewise in geography, Muslims were able to extend their horizons far beyond the world of Ptolemy. As a result of travel over land and by sea and the facile exchange of ideas made possible by the unified structure of the Islamic world and the hajj which enables pilgrims from all over the Islamic world to gather and exchange ideas in addition to visiting the House of God, a vast amount of knowledge of areas from the Pacific to the Atlantic was assembled. The Muslim geographers starting with al-Khwarazmi, who laid the foundation of this science among Muslims in the 9th century, began to study the geography of practically the whole globe minus the Americas, dividing the earth into the traditional seven climes each of which they studied carefully from both a geographical and climactic point of view.

They also began to draw maps some of which reveal with remarkable accuracy many features such as the origin of the Nile, not discovered in the West until much later. The foremost among Muslim geographers was Abu 'Abdallah al-Idrisi, who worked at the court of Roger II in Sicily and who dedicated his famous book, Kitab al-rujari (The Book of Roger) to him. His maps are among the great achievements of Islamic science. It was in fact with the help of Muslim geographers and navigators that Magellan crossed the Cape of Good Hope into the Indian Ocean. Even Columnbus made use of their knowledge in his discovery of America.

Chemistry

The very name alchemy as well as its derivative chemistry comes from the Arabic al-kimiya'. 'The Muslims mastered Alexandrian and even certain elements of Chinese alchemy and very early in their history, produced their greatest alchemist, Jabir ibn Hayyan (the Latin Geber) who lived in the 8th century. Putting the cosmological and symbolic aspects of alchemy aside, one can assert that this art led to much experimentation with various materials and in the hands of Muhammad ibn Zakariyya' al-Razi was converted into the science of chemistry.

To this day certain chemical instruments such as the

alembic (al-'anbiq) still bear the original Arabic names and the mercury-sulphur theory of Islamic alchemy remains as the foundation of the acid-base theory of chemistry. A1-Razi division of materials into animal, vegetable and mineral is still prevalent and a vast body of knowledge of materials accumulated by Islamic alchmists and chemists has survived over the century' in both East and West. For example the use of dyes in objects of Islamic art ranging from carpets to miniatures or the making of glass have much to do with this branch of learning which the West learn completely from Islamic sources since alchem was not studied and practiced in the West before the translation of Arabic texts into Latin in the 11th century.

Technology

Islam inherited the millennial experience in various forms of technology from the peoples who entered the fold of Islam and the nations which became part of Dar al-islam. A wide range of technological knowledge, from the building of water wheels by the Romans to the underground water system by the Persians, became part and parcel of the technology of the newly founded order. Muslims also imported China and whose technology they later transmitted to the West. They also developed many forms of technology on the basis of earlier existing knowledge such as the certain kinds of technology from the Far East such as paper which they brought from metallurgical art of making the famous Damascene swords, an art which goes back to the making of steel several thousand years before on the Iranian Plateau. Likewise Muslims developed new architectural techniques of vaulting, methods of ventilation, preparations of dyes, techniques of weaving, technologies related to irrigation and numerous other forms of technology, some of which survive to this day.

In general Islamic civilization emphasized the harmony between man and nature as seen in the traditional design of Islamic cities. Maximum use was made of natural elements and forces, and men built in harmony with, not in opposition to nature. Some of the Muslim technological feats such as dams which have survived for over a millenium, domes which can withstand earthquakes, and steel which reveals incredible metallurgical know-how, attest to the exceptional attainment of Muslims in many fields of technology. In fact it was a vastly superior technology that first impressed the Crusaders in their unsuccessful attempt to capture the Holy Land and much of this technology was brought back by the Crusaders to the rest of Europe.

Architecture

One of the major achievements of Islamic civilization is architecture which combines technology and art. The great masterpieces of Islamic architecture from the Cordoba Mosque and the Dome of the Rock in Jerusalem to the Taj Mahal in India display this perfect wedding between the artistic principles of Islam and remarkable technological know-how. Much of the outstanding medieval architecture of the West is in fact indebted to the techniques of Islamic architecture. When one views the Notre Dame in Paris or some other Gothic cathedral, one is reminded of the building techniques which traveled from Muslim Cordoba northward.

Gothic arches as well as interior courtyards' of so many medieval and Renaissance European structures remind the viewer of the Islamic architectural examples from which they originally drew. In fact the great medieval European architectural tradition is one of the elements of Western civilization most directly linked with the Islamic world, while the presence of Islamic architecture can also be directly experienced in the Moorish style found not only in Spain and Latin America, but in the southwestern United States as well.

6

Influence of Islamic Science

The oldest university in the world which is still functioning is the eleven hundred-year-old Islamic university of Fez, Morocco, known as the Qarawiyyin. This old tradition of Islamic learning influenced the West greatly through Spain. In this land where Muslims, Christians and Jews lived for the most part peacefully for many centuries, translations began to be made in the 11Ith century mostly in Toledo of Islamic works into Latin often through the intermediary of Jewish scholars most of whom knew Arabic and often wrote in Arabic.

As a result of these translations, Islamic thought and through it much of Greek thought became known to the West and Western schools of learning began to flourish. Even the Islamic educational system was emulated in Europe and to this day the term chair in a university reflects the Arabic kursi (literally seat) upon which a teacher would sit to teach his students in the madrasah (school of higher learning). As European civilization grew and reached the high Middle Ages, there was hardly a field of learning or form of art, whether it was literature or architecture, where there was not some influence of Islam present. Islamic learning became in this way part and parcel of Western civilization even if with the advent of the Renaissance, the West not only turned against its own medieval past but also sought to forget the long relation it had had with the Islamic world, one which was based on intellectual respect despite religious opposition.

The modern Spanish school of scientific historians is not favourably disposed towards the legacy of Islam. A hundred years ago the importance of 'the Moors in Spain' was unduly exaggerated; today the subject is out of fashion among serious workers and apt to be despised by intelligent readers. This attitude may be regrettable, but there arc reasons for it, and not all of them are bad reasons. The inaccuracies in Conde's Historia de la dominacion de los drabes en Espana, the somewhat unfortunate conclusions reached by Dozy regarding the Cid conclusions which subsequent research has proved to be fallacious, and lastly the tendency emanating from French and American universities to trace everything, if possible, to a Latin origin, have led Hispanists to regard oriental studies with a certain feeling of distrust, from which not even the solid achievements of an Asin or a Ribcra have altogether been able to save them.

Other influences also have been at work, as a result of the social and political conditions of modern Spain. An idea has gained ground that oriental studies, and Islamic solutions for the problems of Spanish history, philology, and art, belong to that romantic but disastrous tradition, which, after a nineteenth century of invasion, civil war and unrest, ended in the Spanish-American conflict of 1898. The movement for reform and recuperation, begun by 'the generation of 1898' and encouraged by the inspired teaching and blameless life of Francisco Gincr, led to the development of that sense of accurate scholarship which is so conspicuously manifest in the work of Professor Mcnendez Pidal. Yet it was singularly unfortunate that wherever Pidal turned to the old ballads, to the poem of the Cid, to the origins of the Spanish language he found a body of ill-supported assumptions concerning 'Moorish origins', assumptions which had to be cleared away before any real progress could be made.

Menendez Pidal was so much better equipped than any of his contemporaries that the conclusion was drawn that a

Romance philologist must inevitably be more reliable in Spain than an orientalist, and a Romance explanation of any phenomenon in Spanish philology or Spanish art intrinsically more probable than a solution derived from oriental studies. Pidal himself, however, had no illusions as to the value or necessity of the study of Arabic in Spanish philology; and in the first number of the Revista de Filologia Espanola, founded by him in 1914, the leading article was by Professor Miguel Asin.

Effects of Islam on Political and Economic History

Yet there is another line of opposition in Spain to the legacy of Islam: that the Muslims were the cause, directly or indirectly, of all the evils which afterwards befell the country. 'Without Islam' (writes one of the best of the younger Spanish medievalists) 'Spain would have followed the same course as France, Germany, Italy and England; and to judge by what was actually accomplished through the centuries, Spain might have led the way. But it was not to be. Islam conquered the whole of the Peninsula, distorted the destinies of Iberia and allotted to it a different part in the tragicomedy of history a role of sacrifice and vigilance, of sentinel and teacher, a role which had enormous importance in the life of Europe, but which proved extremely expensive to Spain.'

The first result of the Muslim conquest of 711 was that Iberian particularism sprang once more to life. All along the mountain chains which cross northern Spain from the Atlantic to the Mediterranean arose nuclei of resistance to the Muslim invaders; and these nuclei became ire time the kingdoms of Asturias and Navarre and the 'counties' in the Pyrenees. The new states led a separate existence for something like eight centuries, with nothing in common except their faith and the fact that the dialects they spoke had once been a form of Low Latin. They had begun as Christian points of resistance, like the Balkan states, and so they continued. When at length Islam ceased to be a dangerous neighbour, each of the Christian states turned its gaze in a different direction; they fought with one another again and again, and in their isolation created different dialects, different traditions.

The most vital of these new kingdoms was the kingdom of Castille; but even that, owing to its prolonged contact with Islam, was some three centuries behindhand in the development of those institutions which are characteristic of medieval Europe. Meanwhile the reconquest advanced southwards, and the Christian kings replenished their resources by the occupation of immense territories inhabited by Muslim agricultural labourers, while their Christian subjects tended to become more and more an exclusive military caste. The economic consequences of the reconquest were disastrous. It was not that the influence of Islam was directly harmful, but it certainly retarded the economic development of the Christian states. Christian Spain revolved for five centuries in the economic orbit of the Islamic South; commerce was monopolized by Muslims and Jews.

For nearly four hundred years the Christian kingdoms in Spain used no money except Arabic or French, and for two hundred more the kings of Castille had no gold coinage of their own. Among the 'Old Christians' there was no impulse towards economic activity; the reconquest, whether it was a conscious ideal or not, absorbed all men of action in military adventure. When the reconquest was interrupted, as it was from the middle of the thirteenth century until the fifteenth, the spirit of adventure led Aragon to seek hegemony in Italy and the East, and Portugal to exploration in Africa and the Atlantic, while Castille, having no outlet to the sea, consumed its energies in dynastic quarrels and barons' wars.

The union of Aragon and Castille in the persons of Ferdinand and Isabella, which led to the capitulation of Granada and the end of the reconquista, in 1492, coincided with the discovery of America; and this once more drew away, on the greatest adventure in history, the most vigorous part of the Spanish population. The banishment of the Jews, which also took place in that year, had not been unpopular with the 'Old Christians'; but the expulsion of the Moriscos (the Spanish Muslims who by one means or another had been converted to Christianity) never had the support of the majority of the Christian inhabitants; and when, at the beginning of the seventeenth century, the country was suddenly deprived of all its skilled workmen and several hundred thousand agricultural labourers by this measure, the decline of Spain was inevitable.

Yet the fact of living in contact with a Muslim people had had at least one advantage. It had created in the small cultivated minorities of the Christian kingdoms a spirit of toleration rare in Europe in the Middle Ages. The French crusaders who had helped Alfonso VIII to win the battle of Las Navas de Tolosa (1212) deserted him in disgust when they saw how mildly he treated the conquered Muslims, while Pedro II of Aragon died fighting for the Albigensian 'heretics', and several monarchs of Castille and Aragon surrounded themselves with learned Moors and Jews. They employed Muslim architects, listened to Muslim musicians, and enjoyed the refinements of Muslim culture. But at the same time the fact of constant 'holy wars' against Islam at length produced an exacerbation of religious sentiment.

In no country in Europe did the clergy reach a position of power and influence comparable with that achieved in Spain; and the country came to be governed by an ecclesiastical minority with whom the true interests of Spain took second place: 'Spain sacrificed to Catholicism both liberty of spirit and greatness as a nation. 'Islam, while it died out in al-Andalus, ended by poisoning Spain. Ferdinand and Isabella soon fell victims, and with innocent hands administered the draught to their own kingdoms.

In the first place they abandoned the traditional toleration of the houses of Castille and Aragon; they allowed themselves to be overruled by the ideas and sentiments of the ecclesiastical minority, and tried to achieve the fusioa of their ill-united kingdoms by' converting the national unity into a unity which was less political than religious... Philip II, urged onward by the ideas which had been imprinted on his mind by the ecclesiastical minority, denaturalized the policy of Ferdinand and Isabella to the limit of intolerance and absurdity; and the prosecution of this line of conduct by the successive Philips ruined in a few generations that marvellous flower of Hispanic thought, the only favourable legacy which Islam had bequeathed.'

Races and Languages in Muslim Spain

Such is the indictment of a modern Spanish historian. Yet it cannot be denied that while Europe lay for the most part in misery and decay, both materially and spiritually, the Spanish Muslims created a splendid civilization and an organised economic life. Muslim Spain played a decisive part in the development of art, science, philosophy, and poetry, and its influence reached even to the highest peaks of the Christian thought of the thirteenth century, to Thomas Aquinas and Dante. Then, if ever, Spain was 'the torch But who were the torch-bearers? It was formerly the custom to call them 'Moors' or 'Arabs', but such a statement is far too sweeping. The leader of the first successful expedition into Spain, Tariq, was not an Arab but a Berber, and so were a large proportion of his followers: the actual figures given arc 300 Arabs and 7,000 Berbers.

The forces brought over in the following year, 712, by Musa ibn Nusair were also a mixed force of Arabs (from different parts of Arabia), Syrians, Copts, and Berbers. Study of ancient records and modern place-names (particularly in the kingdom of Valencia) makes it possible to arrive at an approximate tribal distribution of Arabs in Spain, both directly after the invasion and later: and besides their tribal names, the invaders brought their tribal quarrels, which were fought out in Spain with as much bitterness as in the land of their origin. Many families of Christians living in Spain were converted to Islam, and the more important of them, and some who remained Christian, left their names also, with the Arabic prefix Banuy or Barii y 'sons of. There was much intermarriage between Muslims and Christians.

The son of Musa ibn Nusair and other leaders of the expedition married into the family of Witiza, the last legitimate king of Visigothic Spain; and throughout the country the mothers of the next generation, whether Muslim or Christian, were all Spanish. The Muslims of succeeding generations preferred the mothers of their children to be those fair-complexioned slaves captured in the north of Spain, rather than, or in addition to, their own womenfolk. Professor Ribera has studied the records of the slave-market at Cordoba at various periods.

The purchase of a slave was not so simple a transaction as is often imagined. It had to be concluded in the presence of a notary, and the purposes for which a female slave was required, as well as her capabilities and treatment, were carefully considered. Women enjoyed more freedom and more consideration under the Umayyads in Spain than under the f Abbasids of Baghdad; yet it was thought highly desirable that those destined to become the mothers of children in good families should be fair-skinned, and, if possible, Galicians. The result was that, although their descendants bore the names of their ancestors in the male line only, the purity of the Arab race was diminished by crossing with Spanish strains in each successive generation, and the more Arab names a man bore the less Arab blood he had in his veins.

It is wrong, therefore, to assume that all Muslims in Spain were Arabs, and all Christians Romans or Goths; that all of these fled to the north for refuge at the time of the conquest, or that the 'reconquest' was a war lasting eight centuries between the 'Latino-Goths' in the north and the Andalusian 'Arabs' in the south. From the third or fourth generation after the conquest, most Spanish Muslims were bilingual, both those of Arab descent (by that time a small minority) and those of Spanish Christian origin. Besides Arabic, which was the official language, they used a Romance patois, which was also spoken by the Mo/arabcs (mustarib, 'Arabized' or 'would-be Arab') the Christians still living under Muslim rule.

Al-Khushanl (Aljoxani), in his history of the qadis of Cordoba, 1 brings out clearly how general the use of this Romance dialect was. It seems to have been used in Cordoba by all classes, even in courts of law and in the royal palace. There were, in fact, four languages in use in Muslim Spain:

1. Classical Arabic, the language of men of letters;
2. Colloquial Arabic, the language of administration and government;
3. Ecclesiastical Latin, a merely ritual language associated with a particular form of worship; and
4. A Romance dialect, mainly derived from Low Latin, but destined to become one of the great international languages of the world, by the side of English, and Arabic.

It was difficult at first for the illiterate people of Peninsular origin to learn to express themselves in Arabic of any kind; and in the first centuries after the conquest there were many newly- converted Muslims in Spain who were too ignorant of the Arabic language to be instructed in the fundamental laws of Islam. Even in later times it caused no great surprise when a man who spoke no Arabic was appointed qddi. 'Abd al-Rahman III and his courtiers made jokes and rimes about the odd-sounding words employed by the people.

He only spoke in Romance (al-ajamiya 'the outlandish speech'), but he was so esteemed for his honour and sincerity that his testimony was accepted without question in legal and judicial proceedings. He was much beloved in Cordoba for his virtues and his orthodox professions of the Muslim faith; and one day the officers invited him to give evidence in a case against a certain qddi. 'The old man replied in ajamiya: "I do not know him, but I have heard the people say of him that he is a little."

Mozdrabes and Muslim Culture

Yet in spite of the fact that many Muslims in Spain were of Spanish origin, and that the Arabic language was by no means universally understood nor spoken very well even in the ninth century the Arabic of Spain was described by a traveller from the East (al-MuqaddasI) as being 'obscure and difficult to understand' still the legacy of Islam continued to make progress. If cultivated Mozarabes were bilingual, the majorities were illiterate; the few who could read and write preferred to do so in Arabic rather than in Latin. Latin was a clumsy language to write compared with Arabic, and the Latin literature available was of no great interest; so we find paper and books were more quickly and cheaply produced in Arabic than in Latin.

Cordoba in the tenth century was the most civilized city in Europe, the wonder and admiration of the world, a Vienna among Balkan states. Travellers from the north heard with something like fear of the city which contained math; yet whenever the rulers of Leon, Navarre or Barcelona needed such things as a surgeon, an architect, a dressmaker or a singing-master, it was to Cordoba that they applied. Queen Tota of Navarre, for instance, brought her son Sancho the Fat to be cured of his corpulence. She was referred to a famous Jewish physician; and not only was the treatment successful, but the government made use of the doctor to negotiate with the Queen an important treaty.

But what most struck the imagination of travellers were the reports of the summer palace of Madmatu-1-Zahra, situated about three miles to the west of Cordoba, which even in the sober pages of al-Maqqari writing long afterwards seems more like a dream-palace of the 'Thousand and one Nights' than a group of buildings of which modern excavators can find little except the drains. But the fall of the Caliphate meant that its culture or, at any rate, some of it became 'available to the conquerors. The tenth century is the period of Muslim city states or 'party-kings'; and though

Seville under the 'Abbadite dynasty (e.g. Mu'tamid, the poet) was no less brilliant than Cordoba had been the century before, the Muslim states were now more open to the Christians of the north, and cultural influence spread as their political power declined.

The expansion of Muslim culture to the north was still further encouraged by the emigration of the Mozarabes during the persecution which took place under the Berber dynasties, Almoravides (al-Murdbituri) and Almohades (al-Muwakhiduri), especially between 1090 and 1146. For the first time in Spanish history intolerance had appeared; but it is curious that it should have appeared almost simultaneously in both camps, being introduced by the Berber fanatics in, the south and the Cluniac monks in the north. The Mozarabes of Valencia found it impossible to live under the Almoravides; when Jimena abandoned the city in 1102 after the death of the Cid, all the Mozarabes were expatriated to Castille.

This mass emigration was followed by others; and under the Almohades (1143) the position of the Mozarabes grew worse. 'Abd al- Mu'min decreed the expulsion f all Christians and Jews who refused to turn Muslim. The deported Mozarabes had carried with them certain ways of building and styles of dress, certain Muslim customs and expressions, but the legacy of practical Muslim civilization as it had existed in Spain was spread all over the country by the Christian conquests and by Jewish intermediaries in the first half of the thirteenth century, which brought large numbers of Muslim craftsmen under Christian rule.

The way to Muslim learning had been thrown open to the whole of Europe by the capture of Toledo (1085), and with the fall of Cordoba (1236) and Seville (1248) it spread rapidly. With the conquest of Granada (1492) the legacy might be said to have come to an end, except for pottery and some of the minor. The Arabic renaissance, which had been preceded by a French renaissance, was followed by the Italian renaissance, and the period of Arabic influence was ended.

Architecture: Mozarabe and Mudejar

Muslim architecture has been dealt with in another chapter. The periods of the emirate and caliphate are represented by the great mosque of Cordoba; a memorial (one of the very few) of the 'party-kills' are the scanty remains of the Aljaferia (al-Jaffariya) at Saragossa. The Almohade period is illustrated by the Giralda cover and the oldest part of the Alcazar (the patio del yeso) at Seville; while the art of the Nasrite dynasty of Granada is represented by the Alhambra and the Generalifc (frontispiece). There are, however, two other styles, both characteristically Spanish, which deserve attention: the Mozarabic and Mudcjar. Mozarabic architecture is in some ways a reaction against Islam, but it had to submit to influences from its more powerful and more civilized neighbour in the south.

Originating in a style practised in Spain before the invasion of 71 1, it became the typical style of the Christian kingdoms of the north between that period and the introduction of the Romanesque style towards the end of the eleventh century. As *a distant outpost of Byzantine art', it shows certain features which appear in Muslim architecture also, such as the paired animus windows (al-shamas) and the horseshoe arch. The history of this 'Moorish' arch is a very pretty problem, for it is found not only in Muslim buildings but in Mozarabic churches also. It has been suggested that Christian emigrants from Cordoba, especially monks, brought with them ideas of a higher culture than any known in the north, including new methods of building.

The unpretending churches which date from this epoch, though they show certain features of Byzantine origin, betray the influence of Cordoba in the structure of the arch and in the system of vaulting (e.g. San Miguel dc Escalada, built by monks expelled from the Muslim capital in 913). Cordoba made the 'Moorish' arch known to the Christians and Muslims alike, but did not originate it, for it undoubtedly existed in Spain before the date of the conquest, and is even found on late Roman tombstones. The Spanish Muslims, however, quickly realized its possibilities, both structural and decorative, and adopted it generally, exaggerating the 'pinch' in the sides and eventually half filling the hollow of the arch.

The influence of Cordoba, including the horseshoe arch, is also to be seen in Mozarabic illuminated manuscripts (such as the commentaries of Beatus of Liebana); while other Latin manuscripts are known which actually have marginal notes in Arabic explaining the meaning of the Latin words. But the most original contribution of Cordoba to architecture was the system of vaulting based on intersecting arches and visible intersecting ribs, a system which attacks the main problem of architecture that of covering space with a roof in much the same way as the system of Gothic vaulting which developed two centuries later.

The architectural forms developed at Cordoba were carried to Toledo and Saragossa, where they are beautifully exhibited in brickwork. The exquisite 'Cristo de la Luz' at Toledo, originally a Visigothic church, was turned into a mosque at the time of the Muslim occupation, and was restored by a Muslim architect in 980, as is stated in an inscription on the front of the building. Inside, the walls are lined with 'blank arcading' rows of 'dummy' arches leading nowhere. This is said to be the earliest instance of its use, the next being the cathedrals of Durham and Norwich (1119). Decorative intersecting arcading became a favourite device with the Muslim workmen after they had submitted to the Christians.

These men, known as Mudejares (mudajjanln\ were the creators of the Spanish national style, perhaps the most characteristically Spanish contribution to the art of Europe, and their work is to be seen all over Spain. But its real home is Toledo. There we find those beautiful brick church-towers with constantly varying courses of blank arcading, the principle of decoration being one of tiers of arches, one above the other in rows, while each story has windows of different form. In Aragon, the Mudejar towers arc separated from the churches, like minarets, and is sometimes decorated with brightly-coloured tiles as well as brickwork. At Teruel, four of the towers arc built across the streets, with the traffic going through an arch at the bottom; at Calatayud (qafat Ayyub) the towers are octagonal.

The brick apses of the Mudejar churches in Toledo arc also particularly beautiful examples of brickwork, while the north wall of the older of the two cathedrals at Saragossa is a splendid example of this kind of decoration. Mudejar workmen were employed all over Spain for the decoration of churches and private houses, e.g. the fantastic courtyard of the Infantado palace at Guadalajara (wddi-l-hijdra). They were particularly in request for the canopies of tombs, and also for synagogues, as may be seen in the buildings at Toledo now known as E1 Transito' and 'Santa Maria la Blanca'. The Alcazar at Seville was built by Mudejar workmen for King Pedro the Cruel entirely in the Muslim style, and is still used as a royal residence.

Woodwork, Ceramics Textiles and Music

The Mudejar workmen excelled above all in the minor arts: woodwork, pottery, textiles. The Spanish coffered (artesonado) ceilings have no parallel in Europe if we except that of the Capella Palatina at Palermo, which is also Muslim work. Their inlaid doors are no less beautiful and individual, and to this day the technical Spanish words of the carpenter's trade are largely Arabic. The various kinds of coloured tiles (azulejos), so familiar today in Spain and Portugal, are a legacy from the Muslims, as the name implies.

After the re-conquest the geometrical patterns and inscriptions of earlier times were replaced by pictures, or even by vast frescoes composed of tiles. In Seville, tiles were used for altars, balustrades, fountains (where the water was arranged so as to trickle slowly over the rim of the basin and keep the tiles below it wet and shining); and in public gardens they are used for seats and bookshelves (the free library in a public garden is a peculiarly Spanish institution). In Portugal coloured tiles and tile-pictures are used to an even greater extent: there is a church in Evora, the interior of which is completely covered with blue and white tiles. The highest level of Mudejar workmanship was reached in Hispano-Moresque lustre pottery, which, in the eyes of collectors, ranks only below Chinese porcelain.

The earliest mention of it is in the eleventh century, while Idrisi describes its being made at Calatayud before 1154. Two other places in Spain, widely separated, were famous for this ware: Malaga and, above all, Manises in the kingdom of Valencia. The earliest existing pieces date from the fourteenth century, though fragments which must have been four hundred years older were found during the excavations of Madinatu-1-Zahra. Typical Hispano-Moresque ware has a shimmering metallic golden lustre varying from ruby to mother-of-pearl and greenish yellow.

The earliest forms of decoration are Byzantine, but the square Kufic characters were soon introduced for decoration; while later, a favourite inscription was al-'dfiya, good health (Sp. alafia, prosperity, fate, or blessing). This formula was popularly supposed to have been adopted by the potters as a substitute for the sacred name of Allah, so that there might be no chance of the piece with that name being broken and the potter consequently losing his soul. The Valencian potters, however, invented other schemes of decoration based on the wild bryony a plant familiar in their district. Vine-leaves were also employed, and, latterly, heraldic devices, from which it has been proved that Hispano-Moresque pottery was manufactured for popes and cardinals and the greatest families of Spain and Portugal, Italy and France.

'They lack our faith', Cardinal Ximencz remarked of these heretical craftsmen, but we lack their works. Spanish-Moorish silks were hardly less in demand than Spanish-

Moorish pottery. They were particularly treasured in Christian churches; even at Canterbury Cathedral several of the little silk bags which held the seals of documents, dating from 1264 to 1366, were found to be made of pieces of ancient Spanish silk, the patterns being unmistakable and unequalled for their intricacy and fineness of workmanship. The best surviving pieces probably date from the end of the twelfth and beginning of the thirteenth centuries.

With the fourteenth century, new designs appeared with still more elaborate interlacings, and these outlasted the Muslim dominion in Spain and are one more manifestation of the Mudejar art of the fifteenth and sixteenth centuries. Cordoba became famous for its leather, known as 'Cordovan' or 'Cordwain', so that the Cordwainers' Company, or at least the name, might be considered part of the legacy of Arabia. In later years fine and characteristic work was done by Mudejar bookbinders. The Muslim-Spanish goldsmiths also achieved renown; and the workers in other metals took no less pains with such things as enamelled and inscribed sword-hilts, as with such everyday objects as iron keys, the wards of which often take the form of interlacing letters and words in the square Kufic script to which their shape is admirably adapted.

It is difficult to do justice to the industrial arts of the Spanish Muslims; in music, on the contrary, their influence has probably been exaggerated. The superficial resemblance between popular music heard in the south of Spain and that heard in Morocco and other Muslim countries has led many observers astray. Though in the dances and dance-rhythms there is undoubtedly a relationship between modern Spain and modern Morocco, and although certain melodies in the repertory of musicians at Fez are said to have been brought from Granada, in other music the likeness lies in the manner of performance rather than in the modes and forms of the music itself.

There are other instruments in the Peninsula with names derived from Arabic, such as the tambourine; while the 'jingles' round the edge are known in Spain as sonajas. The old Spanish trumpet anafil is the Arabic al-nafir; while the word 'fanfare', a piece of music played by several trumpets, is derived by Dr. Farmer from a plural form ofnafir anfdr. The Spanish bagpipes gaita are the Arabic al-ghaifa (hautboy), known in West Africa as 'alligator', the nearest English word to the colloquial pronunciation of the Arabic. There is also the old Spanish instrument known as albogue, and albogon. This has long been a mystery; but it has recently been described and illustrated as played today in the Basque provinces.

Finally (as pointed out in another chapter) the words 'troubadour' and trobar are almost certainly of Arabic origin: from tarraba to sing, or make music. During the persecution and gradual expulsion of the Moriscos during the sixteenth century, the Gipsies (who are first reported as landing at Barcelona in 1442) gradually came in and took their place, some even settling down in the abandoned quarters of Granada, and giving up their wandering habits. Though they sometimes plied the trade of tinker or farrier, they had no arts or crafts, and were in every way a bad substitute for the Moriscos; but they gradually became the musicians of the people, performing music which they had heard in the course of their wanderings, but performing it with a dash and fire that was all their own.

The manner of performance, which is known to the initiated as a zambra (Ar. zamara) and still more, the manners of the audience, breaking in with cries of Ole! Ok! (walldhi?) kept up a likeness to what had been in Muslim times. The guitar-player began alone, playing a long prelude until the spirits of the audience and the other performers were worked up to the proper pitch; and then, when the singer at last entered, he or she would begin with a long way for the same purpose to try the voice or (as was heard as lately as 1922) with a wild wailing leli, leli, which may be nothing else than a memory of the Muslim creed, or perhaps 'my night, my night!' There is, however, a distinct possibility that European musical theory, like cover other branch of learning in medieval Europe, was^ influenced by Muslim writers.

Between the eight and eleventh centuries many Greek treatises on music were translated into Arabic, and important original works were written in Arabic by Al-Kindi, Al-Farabi, Avempace, Avicenna, and others. When students from the north began to visit Toledo, these Arabic works gradually became known in Europe in Latin translations, and it is a curious coincidence that this period (the first half of the twelfth century) is the period in which a new principle appears in northern music the principle that the notes have an exact time-value or ratio among themselves, instead of the fluid time-value of plain-song.

The inventor of this 'measured music' is sometimes stated to have been Franco of Cologne; but he himself speaks of measured music as a thing already in existence, and it seems to have been known to Al- Khalil as early as the eighth century, as well as to Al-Farabi (tenth century), who, under the name of Alpha rabius, was translated into Latin and widely read among northern musicians. Walter Odington, the greatest musician of the thirteenth century, spoke with enthusiasm of the Arabic masters; and another English musician of the time, a writer on the theory of music, goes so far as to call the new note-values by Arabic names: thus he speaks of 'elmuahym' and 'clmuarifa'.

Medieval music is, at present, a subject in which too much is known about the theory, and too little about the practice; the chapter on the 'Social aspects of music in the Middle Ages' in the introductory volume of The Oxford History of Music (1929) broke entirely new ground. Yet the practical value of the system of 'measured music' was immense, for it enabled music to be composed and written down in a legible form for several voices singing together.

Such music would probably have been completely unintelligible to 'Alpharabius' and the other Muslim theorists, and they might never have understood that the northern musicians were applying a principle which they themselves had been the first to enunciate. 'Sumer is icumen in', the great 'round' for six voices composed about 1240 by a monk of Reading, is in advance of any music of its time; and is in a different world altogether from the songs of the Troubadours and the Cantigas of the Spanish king Alfonso the Sage (c. 1283) which probably arose under direct Muslim influence.

Arabic words in Spanish and Portuguese Nothing in Spain gives care evidence of the debt to Islam than the Spanish language. Yet here particularly it is important to avoid exaggeration and to estimate as accurately as possible what the debt amounts to. By the time of the Muslim invasion of 711, a Romance dialect was already in process of formation from the Low Latin which had once been spoken in the Peninsula, and it is known to have been used (as we have already seen) by the Christians under Muslim rule, and, as time went on, by numbers of Muslims themselves.

A considerable number of Arabic words made their way into this Romance dialect; and the reason is to be found, not so much in the direct borrowing of Arabic words, as that the Spanish dialects themselves were in an uncertain and fluid state while there were Arabic-speaking people in the Peninsula. The borrowed Arabic words are in most cases nouns, and they are the kinds of objects and ideas which had (and in many cases still have) Arabic names in modern Spanish, e.g. Jondu hotel (Ar. funduq), tahona bakery (Ar. tdhuna mill), tarifa tariff (Ar. tarlf notice, definition). As a rule, however, the Arabic word was taken over into Spanish with the Arabic definite article joined to it, and then the Spanish article was added in front of that, e.g. la alhaja the jewel (Ar. al-hdja), el arroz the rice (al-ruzz), la acequia the canal or dyke (al-sdqiya), el anacalo the baker's boy (al-naqqdl the carrier.)

The really cultivated Spaniard still takes pleasure in words of mixed Spanish-Arabic origin, no less than in those of Spanish- Latin origin which can be traced back to Mozarabic times. The wandering minstrels who recited the Toem of my Cid' and the older Spanish ballads, the poems of Gonzalo de Berceo and the Archpriest of Hita, the prose of Alfonso the Sage and Don Juan Manuel all these drew upon 'a well of Castilian undefiled' which, from its Low Latin origins and Arabic borrowings, had become a possession peculiarly characteristic of the Spanish people. Nevertheless the influence of minds which cannot conceive of any good thing which does not come from Paris is leading to the introduction of colourless Gallicisms in their place.

No one in Spain under forty, perhaps, would have taken pleasure in explaining to a foreigner the exact nature of the leather bindings still known by the Berber name of tajllete or have referred to the exactions of the Corunna fish-wives (who seize on the luggage of passengers arriving from America) as an almojarifazgo, a kind of customs duty. What has been said of the destructive effects of cosmopolitan 'Latin' journalism is no less true of Portuguese.

A number of oriental words passed into that language, but they came rather from the Portuguese colonies in India, East Africa, and the Far East than from the Muslim occupation of Portugal. Yet it is curious that some of the Arabic words which have survived there from that time have either died out in Spain, or seem never to have become naturalized there at all. Many of the Spanish words in the foregoing list are also found, under one form or another, in Portugal.

Arabic Place-names in Spain and Portugal

Place-names are unaffected by journalism, and the map of Spain and Portugal is of extraordinary interest to a student of Arabic. Though some of the names are Arabized forms of older Iberian and Phoenician names, and many are of characteristically mixed origin, Arabic and Romance, they form when taken together a striking demonstration of the mark which the Islamic peoples left on the Peninsula.

Mountains and hills, capes and islands, sand-banks, rivers, lakes, and hot springs; plains, fields, woods, gardens, trees, and flowers; caves and mines; colours; and works of man such as farms, villages, towns, markets, mosques, paved roads, bridges, castles, forts, mills, towers, have all become geographical names. Thus jabal (mountain) appears in Monte Jabalcuz, in Jabalcon, Jabaloyas, Jabalquinto, Javaleon and the Pico and Sierra de Javalambre; there is also the Sierra de Gibralbin, Gibraleon, Gibralfaro (mountain of the pharos), while Gibraltar (mount Tariq) is named after the Berber chief who led the first successful Muslim expedition into Spain.

Al-kudya (the hill) appears in the nine or ten places known as Alcudia, as also in Cudia Cremada (Burnt Hill) in Menorca; al-qur (plural of qdra, hillock) in Alcor and Alcora; while al-mudawwar (round, from ddra, turn) is the name of the hill-towns Almodovar del Rio and Almodovar del Campo, and others. The port of Almeria is named from al-mariyya the watch-tower. From al-manara (beacon) are named the heights Cerro de Almenara, Sierra de Almenara, and the harbour Puerto de la Almenara; the Spanish word almena y however (battlement), is not al-mana, but a Latin word minae to which the Arabic article has been added; while in Aragon the word almenar (al-manbar) is connected with irrigation.

Taraf (cape) has given Trafalgar, taraf al-gh dr, cape of the cave; al-jazira, the island, appears in Algeciras and Alcira. Kallff anchorage (from halo? a, protect) is found separately as Gala (beach), and in combination, such as Cala Barca, Cala Blanca, Gala de San Vicente, Cala Santany, Punta de la Cala, Torre de la Cala Honda, La Caleta. The sand-banks at the mouth of the Ebro are known as Los Alfaques, perhaps from al-fakk, jaws. Ramla a sandy river-bed, recalls the origin of La Rambla, the principal street of Barcelona; but the Arabic word most familiar in Spain in connexion with a river is wddi, which in Spanish is spelt guady though still often pronounced with a w.

The School of Toledo

Place-names and common words which have survived show how the Spanish language was affected by Arabic at the most tender period of its growth. By the tenth century the whole basis of life throughout Spain was profoundly influenced by Islam: with the capture of Toledo that influence spread to the rest of Europe. Since the destruction of Cordoba by the Berbers at the beginning of the eleventh century, Toledo had gradually become the centre of Muslim learning in Spain, and it maintained that position after the Christian conquest in 1085.

The court of Alfonso VI, though nominally Christian, was as much imbued with Muslim civilization as the court of Frederick II at Palermo nearly two hundred years later, and Alfonso proclaimed himself 'Emperor of the two religions'. The schools of Toledo attracted scholars from all parts of Europe, including England and Scotland. Among them were Robert 'the English- man', Robertus Anglicus, the first translator of the Quran, Michael Scot, Daniel Morlcy, and Adelard of Bath. Their adventures and activities, the shifts and subterfuges to which they resorted in order to obtain Latin translations of the works of Aristotle, Euclid, and other books which were only to be read in Arabic, have been vividly described in another volume of this series, and there is no need to repeat them here.

The greatest contribution of the Muslims in Spain to European thought was (as has been pointed out in another chapter) the work of the philosophers. Though they had adopted the narrowest and most orthodox forms of Muslim theology, they gave free rein to philosophic speculation; and although the Berber rulers Almoravides and Almohades were inclined to fanaticism, they not only tolerated the speculations of the philosophers but even encouraged them, with certain reservations, so that the philosophers were left free and unhampered in their work of teaching, provided that that teaching was not spread abroad amongst people in general.

The great thinkers of Muslim Spain do not belong to the brilliant age of the Caliphate of Cordoba, but to the ages of political confusion which followed. They rediscovered Greek philosophy, and above all the works of Aristotle. The historians and the dramatists were apparently unknown to them, but they introduced Aristotle to the West centuries before the revival of Greek scholarship which directly preceded the Renaissance and was one of the causes of the Reformation. They seem hardly ever to have known the Greek texts at first hand or to have translated from them directly; their translations were made as a rule from intermediate versions in Syriac; so that an English or Scottish student, if he wished to become further acquainted with the works of Aristotle than was possible from the meagre Latin versions at his disposal, found it convenient to travel to Toledo and learn to read his Greek authors in Arabic.

The transmission of Greek learning to the West began at Baghdad, whence it was forwarded by Jewish or Muslim intermediaries to the Muslims in Spain; and thence, by Jewish intermediaries again, it was conveyed to wandering scholars from Christian Europe, Arabic influences on early Spanish literature The administrative, economic, and artistic aspects of Muslim civilization in Spain have already been mentioned, while its effects on European literature have been discussed in another chapter.

Something more, however, remains to be said concerning the influence of Muslim thought on the literature of Spain. In the age of heroic poetry (c. 1050-1250) the influences are French and Teutonic rather than Arabic. The national epic of Castille, the Toem of my Cid', has the form of a chanson degeste, though the hero himself was very nearly contemporary with the first minstrel who sang of his doings, and was not (as in the case of Roland) a semi-mythical hero who had perished hundreds of years before.

The date of the poem is about 1 140, and Ruy Diaz de Bivar, the Cid, died in 1099. His title, of course, is Arabic:

saiyyid (colloquial sld), lord; and the mixture of languages prevalent at the time could not be better shown than by the usual form under which the Cid was addressed by his men: Ya mio Cid. An Arabic-speaking vassal would have said: Yd sidi. The second period (c. 1250-1400) is one in which the chief foreign influence on Spanish literature was Arabic.

The gates of oriental learning and story were opened both to Spain and to the whole of Europe by the capture of Toledo (1085), which became a school of translation from oriental languages. As early as 1 120 Petrus Alfonsi, a Spanish Jew who was baptized and whose godfather was Alfonso VII, introduced Indian fable into Spain by the celebrated collection of stories known as Disciplina Clericalis. The Spanish translation of the 'Indian tales' of Calila e Dimna made directly from the Arabic text dates from 1251: it is the earliest attempt at story-telling in the Spanish language.

The romance of the Seven Sages (Sindibad or Sende-bar) was translated from the Arabic for the Infante Don Fadrique about 1253, under the name of Libra de los engannos e asayamientos de las mujeres (Book of the Wiles and Deceptions of Women). From the second half of the thirteenth century, collections of aphorisms and moral tales become numerous in Spain. They include a lost version of the Buddhistic legend of Barlaam and Josaphat, the Libra de enxemplos for ABC collected by Clemente Sanchez de Vercial, and the oddly-named Libra de los gatos, 'Book of Cats', which is probably a misreading for Libra de los qetos (quentos), 'Book of Stories' and is derived from an Arabic source through the Narrationes of the English monk Odo of Cheriton.

The greatest apostle of Muslim learning in Christian Spain was Alfonso X, el Sabio, king of Castille and Leon from 1252 to 1284. Under his patronage and indeed under his immediate supervision a number of vast works were undertaken, many of them being compiled from Arabic sources, which were made available to him by Jewish assistants? His prose works and his naive, semi-oriental prose is one of the great delights of medieval Spanish studies include a code of laws, Las siete partidas, which is a mine of curious information on Spanish life and customs of the time; the Cronica general, in which chapters 466 to 494 are devoted to a strange life of the Prophet Muhammad; and the Grande e general Estoria, a 'great and general history' on a vast scale which is now in process of being printed for the first time.

The astronomical studies of Alfonso the Sage include the famous 'Alfonsine Tables' a collection of observations taken at Toledo, which were in use throughout Europe for some centuries; he also compiled a Lapidario, a treatise on the virtues of precious stones, and a 'Book of Games', Libra i.e. los juegos, including dice, backgammon, and several varieties of chess played on boards of different shapes and sizes. Chess is so characteristic a product of the legacy of Islam that it deserves more than a passing mention. Modern European chess is the direct descendant of an ancient Indian game, adopted by the Persians, handed on by them to the Muslim world, and finally borrowed from Islam by Christian Europe.

In most European languages the game is named after the king (Persian shah; Medieval Latin scad, chessmen); but the Spanish word ajedrez, (formerly axedrez or acedrex), and the Portuguese xadrez arc derived from the Arabic name for the game itself: al-shatranj, a word borrowed from Persian and ultimately from Sanskrit. Several of the terms still used in chess are Persian: 'checkmate', for instance, shah mat, which does not necessarily signify that 'the king is dead', but that he is dishonoured or defeated.

The Castle or Rook is the Spanish roque, and the Persian rukh the dreaded 'roc' encountered by Sindbad the Sailor. It has been discovered, however, that this word was in use among the Muslims in Spain for a chariot, and the idea of a chariot seems to explain at once the straight move and devastating power of the Rook in modern chess. In an early set of chessmen, reputed (but only since the seventeenth century) to have belonged to Charlemagne, the Rook is actually a chariot with a man in it; while the triumphal car used in certain religious festivals at Valencia is still known as the roca.

The Bishop, again, is known in Spain as el alfil (Ar. al-fil, the elephant), the French fou (when it refers to chess) being a corruption of the same word, and in no way connected with the moves or powers of a dignitary of the church. Spain provides the earliest certain references to chess in Europe; there are bequests of chessmen in the wills of two members of the family of the Counts of Barcelona, dating from 1008 (or 1010) and 1017.

The first description of the game in a ' European language is that of Alfonso the Sage. His book is obviously compiled from Arabic sources and the miniatures usually show players in oriental dress. Sometimes they are accompanied by oriental musicians, while now and then the musicians may be seen having a game by themselves, holding their instruments ready in the left hand, in case they are suddenly called upon to play them. The description of the game given by Alfonso has been found to be not altogether in accordance with Muslim practice, but the problems he gives are almost exclusively Muslim, for the chess-problem is a kind of mental activity which is characteristic of the legacy of Islam to Europe.

His pieces, with one exception, are the same as ours. There is no Queen; her place is taken by the piece which Chaucer called the Ters' and Alfonso ell alferza. The Fers could move one square diagonally; but for his first move he could jump to the third square either diagonally or straight. He is the ancestor of the modern Queen, and the development of his powers in that direction is chiefly due to two Spanish players: Lucena (1497) and Ruy Lopez (1561). Alfonso X's games of chess on a larger number of squares than usual are of peculiar interest at the present time, when suggestions for improving the game (and reducing the chances of a draw) are being made by such masters as Sr. Capablanca.

One of these suggestions is a board of 100 squares instead of the usual 64; while another is a kind of double chess, played on a board with 16 squares at each end and 12 at the sides. It is curious that the name of Alfonso el Sabio has never been mentioned in the discussion of these projects; for he knew of a game played on a board of 100 squares, with two additional pieces (which he calls ' judges') on each side, and two additional pawns. A game which interested him more, however, was 'great chess' played on a board of 144 squares, with 12 pieces and 12 pawns. Next to the King stood a Gryphon; and then, on each side, came a Cocatrice, a Giraffe, a Unicorn, a Lion, and a Rook.

The King moved, as in the modern game, to any adjacent square; and although 'castling' had not yet been invented, he could leap to the third square for the first move. The Gryphon (Sp. aanca, Ar. 'anqa) moved one square diagonally and then any number straight. The Cocatrices moved like modern Bishops, though the large board gave them a far greater range and power. The Giraffes had a move resembling that of the modern Knight, except that their leap was longer; for while the Knight moves one square diagonally and two squares straight, the Giraffes moved the one square diagonally and four squares straight. The Unicorns also had a complicated move, and were regarded as the most powerful pieces on the board, after the Gryphon; they began like a Knight and went on like a Bishop, with the proviso that they could not take another piece until the move was completed.

The Lion could leap to the fourth square in all directions; while the Rook moved as usual: straight, in any direction. The pawns moved as in the ordinary game: one square forward at a time. They had no right of moving two squares for the first move, but in compensation for that, they started on the fourth row instead of the second, and if they reached the twelfth square of their file and 'queened', they took the rank and powers of the piece on whose file they had started. Alfonso the Sage has one more connexion with the legacy of Islam to Spain. He was responsible for one of the greatest collections of medieval poetry, the Cantigas de Santa Maria, preserved, with contemporary musical notation, in two manuscripts in the Escurial and one at Madrid.

The language of these poems is not Castilian but the Galician dialect of northern Portugal, which, in the thirteenth century, was the language of court poetry in Castille and Aragon as well as Portugal, and continued to be so until Castilian Spanish became sufficiently ductile for refined lyrical expression. The music has been claimed by Professor Ribera to be Andalusian music of Muslim origin, a claim which historians of music are not very ready to admit. Yet many of the instruments shown in the miniatures, and even some of the performers, are obviously of Muslim origin; while the poetic form is peculiar to Muslim Spain, consisting almost entirely of stanzas of the type of the muwasbshah and zajal first- employed by Ibn Quzman (Abencuzman) and described in another chapter.

It has been urged that these poems are of exclusively Christian inspiration, and are therefore unlikely to be tainted with any suspicion of Islamic artifice. But the forms of muwashshah and zajal developed into the typically Castilian popular verse form of villancico which was extensively used for all kinds of Christian poetry, including Christmas carols; and the subject the praise of the Virgin Mary is a logical development of the troubadour's idealization of the lady of the manor; while the poems of the troubadours are, in matter, form, and style, closely connected with Arabic idealism and Arabic poetry written in Spain.

Don Juan Manuel and, the Archfriest of Hita

The period of translation and compilation from oriental sources represented by the school of Alfonso the Sage was succeeded by a brilliant period of original work, in the prose of the Infante Don Juan Manuel (1282-1349?) and the poetry of the Archpriest of Hita (d. before 1351). Both had learnt from Eastern story, not only how to employ fables for teaching a moral lesson, but also how to set them in a suitable framework. In Don Juan Manuel's Conde Lucanor the Count asks the advice of his Councillor, Patronio, on certain questions of life and government, and Patronio replies in each case by telling a story to illustrate the point.

The stories have in many cases been traced to an Eastern origin, and on two or three occasions they contain phrases in the colloquial Arabic of the time, written out phonetically in Spanish. The moral tone is uniformly high, and the author, a nephew of Alfonso the Sage, is clearly conscious that by writing he is performing a public duty. Juan Ruiz, Archpriest of Hita, is a man of the people, with no sense of public duty or personal obligation to society and still less with any religious vocation. Yet he is a true poet, among the greatest in the Spanish language. His Libro de buen amor ('The Book of True love' buen amor as contrasted with earthly love, loco amor) is a satirical autobiography in which he tells with disarming candour the tale of his love-affairs.

There is no possibility of an allegorical intention. The love that leads the Archpriest is earthly love, though in lyrics of passionate sincerity he protests his devotion to the Virgin Mary. Not all his desires end in fulfillment; but some of the ladies, e.g. Dona Endrina, are vividly and enchantingly portrayed, and the go-between, Trotaconventos (the direct ancestor of La Celestina and Juliet's nurse), is already one of the great characters in fiction. The Archpriest moved on the margins of society; he ministered to outcasts and wantons, and such despised subjects as musicians and Moorish dancing-girls. He reports conversations and sometimes transcribes answers which were given in Vulgar Arabic.

The form of his work is to a certain extent oriental, a framework on which numerous fables and apologues are hung, and the vocabulary is a store-house of words borrowed from Arabic; but the Archpriest also availed himself of subjects borrowed from French and from Medieval Latin. He employed every metre known to him in a masterly fashion, not excluding the characteristic zajal, with the thought ever present in his mind that a minstrel might one day sing parts of his book in the street as indeed is known to have actually happened during the half-century after his death.

For a distracted scribe, copying a chronicle in his cell, one day made notes of the performance of a wandering minstrel in the street outside; and the man, in the midst of a string of anecdotes, rhymes, and a somersault or two, was heard to catch the flagging attention of the audience by exclaiming: 'Now we begin from the v book of the Archpriest!'

Contemporary with the Infante Don Juan Manuel and the Archpriest of Hita was the author of the earliest Spanish book of chivalry, the His tor ia del Cav oiler o Cifar which was probably composed between 1299 and 1335. Like all books of chivalry, it was said to have been taken from a 'Chaldean' (i.e. Arabic) original, and the underlying idea is that of a story in the 'Arabian Nights', though the detail is a strange mixture of the 'Golden Legend', Arthurian romance, and Oriental fable.

The name Cifar is Arabic (safar, a journey; or sifara, an embassy), so that 'Caballero Cifar' is equivalent to 'Knight-Errant'. His wife is named Grima (Karima, a common name among Muslim women and signifying 'precious thing', 'nobly-born', or 'daughter'). Other Oriental features have been noticed.

Spanish Written in Arabic Characters

Another contemporary of the Archpriest was the author of the Poema de Tusuf an anonymous poem based on the legend of Joseph. Its peculiarity is that although the words are Spanish (Aragonese dialect) and the verse-form French, it is written in the Arabic character; and the poem is derived from the Qur'dn and other Muslim sources. It is an example of what is known in Spain and Portugal as literatura aljamiada, 'ajama meaning to speak bad Arabic, whence' 'ajami a foreigner, and al-ajamiya the outlandish language.

In Spain it was originally used by Arabic-speaking Spaniards to designate Spanish, and afterwards applied to the writings of the Moriscos who employed the Arabic character for Spanish words. Manuscripts of this kind are fairly numerous. Some time ago a collection was found hidden under the floor of an old house at Almonacid de la Sierra in Aragon, where they must have been placed to keep them out of sight of the 'familiars' of the Inquisition: they are now in the library of the Junta para Ampliacion de Estudios at Madrid.

They include important legal documents, verses in praise of the Prophet written in muwashsbah form in the fourteenth century, sermons, legends, stories, and superstitions of the fifteenth and sixteenth centuries; while one of the most instructive manuscripts of the time is a pastoral epistle from the mufti of Oran advising the persecuted Moriscos in the century following the conquest of Granada to what extent they should conform to the conquerors, who seemed to regard every decency of Muslim life even washing as heresy and therefore a capital offence. The use of the Arabic character, even after the fall of Granada, shows how the conquered Muslim Spaniards clung to the handwriting of their religion, even when they spoke a Romance dialect and were (in many cases) of Christian Spanish descent.

The method of transcribing the Spanish sounds in Arabic character offers many points of interest, and is especially valuable as an indication (confirmed by Pedro de Alcala's transcription into Roman type of the colloquial Arabic of Granada as spoken about 1500), of how the Muslims in Spain pronounced the languages of the country, Spanish and Arabic. The after-effects of Morisco pronunciation are still perceptible today.

The pitiful story of the expulsion of the Moriscos need not be repeated here. They were not driven out finally until 1614, so that Arabic was still spoken in the Peninsula during the lifetime of Cervantes, and it could not have struck his contemporaries as fantastic or impossible when, remembering that the romances of chivalry had usually been stated to have been taken from a book in Arabic or 'Chaldean', he declared that the original of Don Quixote was the work of a Moor called 'Sidi Ham'ete ben Engeli', and that it too had originally been written in Arabic.

Plato according to al-Mubashshir

Plato is known to Arab authors according to the different ways in which his genuine works or those erroneously attributed to him were read and studied in the Greek sections of the Roman Empire during the centuries preceding the Arab conquest of Hellenized lands in the Eastern Mediterranean. Most Arab thinkers did not consider Plato the main representative of Greek thought as St. Augustine e.g. had done but subordinated him to Aristotle; they were however like e.g. Porphyry, Ammonius and Simplicius aware of an identity of purpose and a basic agreement between the two great philosophers. Just as commentaries on Aristotle written outside the Neoplatonic schools survived in Arabic translations and, partly, in Arabic translations only (as in the case of certain writings of Alexander of Aphrodisias and Themistius, etc.), interpretations of Plato, untinged by Neoplatonism, found their way to the Arabic philosophers and were studied by them.

Part of Galen's Platvnikn dialgvn sinociw in eight books, lost in the Greek original but still partly accessible to Hunayn b. Ishaq and his school, has been traced and recently published, viz. the summary of the whole of the Timaeus, with many verbal quotations, a fragment of his paraphrase of the Republic, a fragment of his summary of the Laws and a reference to his summary of the Parmenides. Fragments of his medical commentary on the Timaeus have been recovered from Arabic medical writers. Many quotations from Plato and references to him reached the Islamic world through translations of other works by Galen. As had happened in the case of Aristotle, late Greek philosophers tried to arrange Plato's dialogues in systematic order. An otherwise unknown work of this type, completely free from Neoplatonic influence and still fully aware of the political aspects of Plato's thought, was used and partly reproduced by al-Farabi.

The author of the Greek treatise, who had even regarded this systematic ordering of the dialogues as a chronological arrangement by date of composition, is unknown. A commentary on the Republic of similar provenience was widely used by al-Farabi; it constitutes the main part of Ibn Rushd's commentary which is available in a Hebrew translation and a 16th century Latin one. A summary of Plato's Laws, of a similar type, was used by al-Farabi in his compendium of the work. Al-Razi commented on Plutarch's commentary on the Timaeus and Yahya b. 'Adi copied Plutarch's book. But, in general, Arabic philosophers look at Plato through the eyes of his Neoplatonic interpreters, Plotinus, Porphyry, Proclus and others. In the preface to his translation of a fragment of Proclus' commentary on the Timaeus 89E-90C: E. Pfaff, Corpus Medicorum Graecorum, Supplementum, iii, p. xlii, 1941) Hunayn b. Ishaq says: 'Galen is the standard interpreter of Hippocrates, and the man who is best entitled to explain the meaning of Plato's words is Proclus the most famous of scholars'.

An instructive example of this Proclean interpretation of Plato is to be found in Miskawayh's al-Fawz al-Asghar, in the section on the immortality of the soul, based probably on Proclus' work On the immortality of the soul according to Plato, in three books, which was known to the Arabs. A tradition of this kind is followed by al-Kindi, in whom the Platonic element is strong not only in psychology but also in his extremely orthodox neoplatonic metaphysics of the One and in his ethics. The Plato to whom al-Farabi (with the exception of his theory of the ideal state), Ibn Sina, Ibn Badhdha and Ibn Rushd refer is, whether explicitly or implicitly, always the Plato of Plotinus and his followers.

Yahya b. 'Adi had Olympiodorus' (6th century A.D.) commentary on the Sophist (lost in the Greek original) in his library in the translation of Ishaq b. Hunayn. We find an interesting account of Plato's metaphysics, cosmology and psychology, derived from an unknown but valuable neoplatonic source, in al-Shahrastani, t83 ff. On the whole, since Neoplatonism claims to be a reinterpretation of Plato, influential Neoplatonic writings deserve to be mentioned here as well, the Theology of Aristotle, in which Aristotle is supposed to have become a Platonist in his old age, the Liber de causis based on Proclus' Elements of Theology, the new Plotinian text discovered by P. Kraus and the Arabic Plotinus source discussed by F. Rosenthal. A new development starts with al-Suhrawardi al-Maqtul [q.v.] and the Ishraqis [q.v.], who, criticizing al-Farabi and Ibn Sina, emphasize the mystical aspects of Platonism, or rather Neoplatonism, and make Plato the mystic the chief authority in philosophy. The 'ufis now become the true followers of Plato (cf. e.g. al-Suhrawardi, Opera Metaphysica et Mystica.

An anonymous book On the Platonic Ideas, written probably in the 14th century, depends on al-Suhrawardi's strange interpretation of the Platonic ideas. Another special tradition of Platonism is represented by Muhammad b. Zakariyya' al-Razi [q.v.], who also claims to follow Plato as his main authority. His Platonising ethics may be connected with his study of Galen, and his rejection of the eternity of the world with the interpretation of the Timaeus put forward by Plutarch and Galen, but his five eternal principles are of Neopythagorean provenience, although he considered them to be Platonic.

His theory of the atomic structure of matter may go back to Plato's lecture On the Good, it is certainly found in a neopythagorean version of Plato's metaphysics. The Arabic bibliographers list the titles of all the dialogues to be found in the Greek Corpus Platonicum, but give little information about Arabic translations. They mention a commentary on the Republic (translated by Hunayn b. Ishaq); translations of the Timaeus by Yahya b. al-Bitriq, Hunayn b. Ishaq and Yahya b. 'Adi. (Hunayn wrote also a treatise that which ought to be read before Plato's works.) Ibn al-Nadim also mentions a copy of the Crito in Yahya b. 'Adi's handwriting. Part of Proclus' commentary on the Phaedo (lost in the Greek original) was translated from the Syriac by Ibn Zur'a.

No manuscripts of these or other Arabic translations of a Platonic dialogue have so far been traced. A verbal quotation from the Republic (apart from the more or less verbal references in Ibn Rushd's paraphrase and references to its contents in works of other philosophers) occurs e.g. in the Rasa'il Ikhwan al-'afa', Cairo 1347, iv, 134. Al-Kindi wrote a treatise on the Platonic number. Quotations from the Timaeus occur frequently, but it is difficult to decide whether they are taken from Plato or from some intermediary. For the quotations from the Laws to be found in al-Biruni's India cf. F. Rosenthal, 359 f. and F. Gabrieli, Plato Arabus, iii, p. xii, n. t. There are numerous quotations from the Phaedo in the same work.

The closing section on Socrates' death is to be found e.g. in Ibn al-Kifti, t00-6 and Ibn Abi Usaybi'a, i, 45. A Persian version of the dialogue exists in Brusa. The Alcibiades-speech from the Banquet has been traced by F. Rosenthal in Istanbul, Kkprülü 1608, fol. t16. Persistent research will no doubt trace more quotations of Platonic dialogues in Arabic philosophical and non-philosophical writings. Among the pseudepigrapha of a philosophical kind can be mentioned: the neophythagorean treatise Plato's Exhortation of young men, probably of Greek origin, a letter by Plato addressed to Porphyry about the banishment of grief, depending on a treatise on consolation by al-Kindi and Plato's will addressed to Aristotle.

But the Arabs are acquainted not only with the different interpretations of Plato's thought which are familiar to the student of Greek philosophy but also with a Plato who had been associated with the superstitions which had become an integral part of the teaching of most of the neoplatonic schools: magic, astrology and alchemy (Olympiodorus and other late Neoplatonists had dabbled in alchemy and made Plato their patron). The Arabs went aqstep further and made Plato the author of alchemical works. Dhabir quotes a Musahhahat Aflatun in which Plato initiates his disciple Timaeus in the secrets of alchemy; but the passages of the Timaeus referred to by Dhabir have nothing to do with the original dialogue of Plato.

Another work of a similar character, a philosophical alchemical book attributed to Plato is the Rawabi' Aflatun known to the West as Liber Quartorum and preserved in two Arabic MSS. It contains a dialogue between Ahmad b. al-Husayn b. Dhahar Bukhtar and the well known Harranian mathematician and astronomer habit b. qurra. Another alchemical treatise, the Liber Platonis de XIII clavibus, is supposed to have been translated from the Arabic into Latin in A.D. 1301. Cf. also Kraus, op. cit., 51, n.

Among the magical treatises ascribed to Plato the al-Nawamis, which deals with artificial generation, appears to be worth mentioning (P. Kraus, op. cit., 104 and n. 1t), as well as al-Sirr al-khafi (ibid., 5t).

The Arabic 'Lives of Plato' do not add anything substantial to the material to be found in the Greek tradition as represented by Diogenes Laertius, book iii, Olympiodorus, and the Prolegomena to the Platonic philosophy by an anonymous Neoplatonist. There is, however, no direct connection between them and any of the Greek texts known. Part of the Arabic tradition can be traced back to an introductory work by Theo of Smyrna, referred to by the Fihrist, t45, and quoted at length by Ibn al-qifti, 17-9.

Al-'Amiri, a philosopher of the 4th/10th century (quoted

in the Abbreviation of Abu Sulayman al-Mantiqi's 'iwan al-Hikma, introduction), probably following some lost Greek tradition, made Plato one of the five pillars of wisdom, the others being Empedocles, Pythagoras, Socrates and Aristotle (Anbaduqlis, Futhaghuras, Suqrat, Aristutalis [qq.v.]); these philosophers derived their wisdom from the Prophets. According to him Plato retired in old age into solitude and prayer. He also gives an account of Plato's solution of the Delian problem.

On him depends 'a'id al-Andalusi, tabaqat al-Umam, t3; 'a'ids life was used, as a minor source, by Ibn al-qifti, passim. The life in Mubashshir b. Fatik's Mukhtar al-Hikam was copied by Ibn Abi Usaybi'a, i, 50 ff. He made both Plato's parents descendants of Asclepius, probably misinterpreting the epigram to be found in Diog. Laertius, iii, 45. Alone among the Arab biographers he mentions Plato's supposed stay in Egypt. For the physiognomical section cf. F. Rosenthal, loc. cit., 38. Ibn al-qifti based his long and detailed life (17-t7) on the Fihrist, on Theo of Smyrna (cf. above) and on an unidentified Greek source (19 line 16-t5q1. 3).

There are Greek parallels to almost everything mentioned. Stories similar to the discussions reported to have taken place at Dionysius' court (t1) are to be found in Olympiodorus' Life and in Plutarch's Dio. There are a very few confusions, such as the story of Socrates' stay in Sicily and the introduction of Plato's two female disciples as his wives and the inclusion of Proclus among his pupils. The section t54-t614 is taken from al-Farabi; t615-t714 reproduces 'a'id al-Andalusi, 19. Plato's prayer in neoplatonic language (t715-7) is worth mentioning. Al-Shahrazuri's account of Plato's life in his Nuzhat al-Arwah (in MS) is based on Mubashshir. In later centuries Plato's tomb could be visited at qonya.

The main source for the various compilations of sayings of Plato is H unayn b. Ishaq's Nawadir al-Falasifa wa 'l-Hukama'. Another primary source is Ibn Hindu, al-Kalim al-

Ruhaniyya fi 'l-Hikam al-Yunaniyya, Cairo 1318. The life in the Abbreviation of Abu Sulayman's 'iwan al-Hikma contains only sayings. Ibn Abi Usaybi'a, i, 517-5316, reproduces the section on sayings to be found in Mubashshir. Sayings attributed to Plato occur very often in Arabic literature.

Although Prodicus was also one of those philosophers with the reputation of speculating 'about the heavens' (above), this was not his main claim to fame. In fact, his ideas were much more radical as, according to Philodemus, he maintained 'that the gods of popular belief do not exist nor do they know, but primitive man, [out of admiration, deified] the fruits of the earth and virtually everything that contributed to his existence'. The highly stylised character of the language suggests that this passage reflects rather closely Prodicus' very words. But what did Prodicus actually mean? Renewed attention to the fragmentary papyri that are our best source for Prodicus' ideas has shown that Prodicus proposed a two-stage theory of the origin of polytheism.

First, primitive man started to call 'gods' those elements of nature on which he was most dependent, such as sun and moon, rivers and fruits. Subsequently, those humans who had been the main benefactors as inventors of the proper usage of the fruits of the earth, viz. bread and wine, Demeter and Dionysos, were likewise called 'gods' and worshipped as such. Evidently, there had been a time without gods yet for Prodicus, even though man was already there. Comparison with other cultural theories of his time suggests that Prodicus located the beginning of religion in agriculture. Now the advent of Demeter and Dionysos with their gifts of bread and wine was part of Attic mythology. In fact, Athens prided itself as having given agriculture to the Greek world.

Prodicus may well have heard about this claim on his island Keos, which was in easy reach of Attica, but he may also have been influenced by his frequent stays in Athens, where he did not forget his own interests while being ambassador of his island. The fact that he appeared before the Athenian Council and had impressed them by his eloquence almost certainly guarantees that he had well prepared his case by studying Attic mythology. In addition to Prodicus, the only other fifth-century intellectuals in whose work clear atheistic statements can be found are Euripides and Critias. Unfortunately, ancient biographical evidence for Euripides' atheism is based primarily on inferences from his poetry, which were elaborated, often with a degree of malice, by writers of the fourth century and after tradition of Euripides' trial for atheism is probably either derived from comedy or invented in analogy of the trial of Socrates.

On the other hand these inferences had some material to work from. In the end, though, there is only one passage with a clear atheistic content and it pays to quote it in full. In a fragment that has been handed down in Christian times from the Bellerophon, a tragedy that was probably performed around 430 BC, Bellerophon himself states early in the play:

Does someone say there are indeed gods in heaven? There are not, there are not, if a man is willing not to rely foolishly on the antiquated reasoning. Consider for yourselves, do not base your opinion on words of mine. I say myself that tyranny kills very many men and deprives them of their possessions; and that tyrants break their oaths to ransack cities, and in doing this they are more prosperous under heaven than men who live quietly in reverence from day to day. I know too of small cities doing honour to the gods that are subject to larger, more impious ones, because they are overcome by a more numerous army. I think that, if a man were lazy and prayed to the gods and did not go gathering his livelihood with his hand, you would [here is a lacuna in the text] fortify religion, and ill-fortune.

The statement is a radical expression of a feeling encountered more often in Euripides that the irreligious prosper, whereas the pious suffer. Consequently, the gods have no power and religion is imaginary. Such a radical stance must be one of those that elicited Aristophanes' scorn, but at the end of the play the traditional order was re-established and Bellerophontes' atheistic declaration more than outweighed by his pitiable lot. In other words, the statement is the expression of a character in the play, not the opinion of the playwright himself There could be a second passage, but its authorship is highly debated. It used to be ascribed to the sophist Critias (ca. 450-403 BC), who was one of the most unscrupulous members of the Thirty Tyrants, a group of aristocrats that had seized power at the end of the Peloponnesian War and was remembered for its rule of terror.

As such, the cynical tone of the piece seemed to fit perfectly the image of its author in the historiographical tradition. On the other hand, Critias is mentioned only once as the author of this passage, whereas Euripides is mentioned twice. In fact, several recent studies have persuasively argued that it is completely out of character of the genre of the satyr play that a character would develop here a highly provocative theory for the very first time instead of parodying it, as indeed seems to be the case here – the more so when the passage does not reflect the opinion of just one philosopher but those of several. Moreover, a character that tries to persuade somebody that a crime without witnesses will remain unpunished fits a satyr play much better than a tragedy.

Finally, the passage contains a number of words that occur only in Euripides. Consequently, the passage could have belonged to either Euripides' Sisyphus (415 BC) or, perhaps more attractively, his Autolykos A (date unknown). Yet the recent authoritative edition of Euripides' fragments has not accepted these arguments and once again ascribes the fragment to Critias. This is probably correct, since the new edition of Philodemus' On Piety (519-41) shows that Epicurus already concluded that what Critias himself had said about the gods 'made it impossible for them as generally conceived to exist'; in fact, lines 539-40 and 1185-1217 of On Piety exhibit vestigial echoes of the Sisyphus account. In other words, Critias' reputation as an atheist predates the Hellenistic biographers.

In this long passage, which most likely was pronounced by Sisyphus, the cleverest Greek in mythology, we see the first occurrence of the theory that religion (here: the gods) was invented to ensure good behaviour of humans. It is unique in its time, but it is hardly imaginable that a playwright would put forward such a theory in a play meant to entertain his audience without any previous knowledge of it among its spectators. Now it is clear that several aspects of this passage must have been familiar to the audience. First, the picture of an animal-like situation at the beginning of humankind was a recurrent topos in descriptions and parodies of the primeval situation by contemporaries of Euripides.

Second, the opposition between public assent to laws but private freedom from restraint can be paralleled in the work of the contemporary sophist Antiphon, who stated that justice would be most advantageous to a man if 'he were to regard the laws as great in the presence of witnesses, but nature as great when deprived of witnesses'. Third, Democritus' (A 75 DK) institutors of religion relied on human fear of celestial phenomena and, fourthly, Prodicus had also advanced a two-stage theory of the development of religion (above). Yet the theory espoused in our passage goes further and is more cynical than anything proposed in our surviving texts. Critias' (or Euripides') drama well illustrates a gradual change in mood regarding the gods in Athens in the later fifth century.

There was worse to come. In 415 the Athenians undertook a major expedition to Sicily to conquer Syracuse, and our sources still enable us to observe the nervous mood of the Athenian population at that time. It was at this precarious moment that the highly guarded secrecy of the Eleusinian Mysteries twice came under attack. One morning, shortly before the Athenian fleet was due to sail to Sicily, it was discovered that nearly all the images of the god Hermes in public places had been mutilated. Those denounced were also accused of having profaned the Eleusinian Mysteries. Whereas the mutilators had parodied the Mysteries (if they actually had done so) in private circumstances, around the same time Diagoras, a citizen of the island Melos, mocked the Mysteries openly after the Athenians had treated his home island badly.

Consequently, as the eleventh-century Arab Mubashshir, whose account - directly or indirectly - seems to derive from the erudite Athenian Apollodorus (ca. 180-120 BC), notes:' When he [viz. Dhiyaghuras al-mariq, or "Diagoras the heretic, or apostate"] persisted in his hypocrisy [or "dissimulation"], his unbelief and his atheism, the ruler, the wise men [or philosophers, hukama] and leaders of Attica sought to kill him. The ruler Charias the Archon [Khariyus al- Arkun (415-4)] set a price on his head [literally: "spent money", badhal] and commanded that it should be proclaimed among the people: "He who apprehends Diagoras from Melos [Maylun] and kills him will be rewarded with a large sum [badra, traditionally a leather bag containing 1000 or 10,000 dirhams]".

This is a pretty exact report of the events, since the Athenians promised one talent of silver to anyone who killed Diagoras, and two to anyone who caught him alive. Now Diagoras is already mocked in Hermippus' comedy Moirai (fragment 43 Kassel-Austin), which was written before 430. In Aristophanes' Clouds (830), which even in its revised version cannot be later than ca. 418 BC, Socrates is called the 'Melian' for espousing 'atheistic' views. This must mean that Diagoras had been living safely in Athens for many years despite his irreligious views - a fact which also shines through in the Arab report. However, his mocking went too far, and Epicurus already mentions Diagoras together with Critias and Prodicus as the arch-atheists. In that capacity Diagoras would remain notorious all through antiquity More famous than Diagoras, if less for his atheism, was Socrates (469-399 BC).

It is clear from Arisptophanes' portrait of Socrates in the Clouds that already in that time the latter was considered to be something like an atheist; this is also suggested by his frequent association with Euripides in comedy. It is therefore not wholly surprising that in 399 BC the Athenians charged Socrates as follows: 'Socrates does wrong by not acknowledging the gods the city acknowledges, and introducing other, new powers (daimonia). He also does wrong by corrupting the young'.

The process of Socrates still poses many questions, but it is certain that for many Athenians Socrates had moved too close to those who questioned the traditional gods. It is only about a decade after Socrates' death, in Plato (ca. 429-347 BC), that we start to find the Greek word atheos, which originally was used in the meaning 'godless, without gods, godforsaken', denoting intellectuals who denied the gods of the city or any form of deity. This particular meaning may of course be slightly older, but its date fits our impression of the intellectual climate of the last decades of the fifth century. The increasing criticism of the gods by philosophers and poets had eroded the traditional beliefs in the gods and some intellectuals drew the inevitable consequence. Yet the combined power of traditional belief and Plato's influential theism made that 'real' atheists would always remain a rare phenomenon in the Greek world. The Hellenistic period The death of Socrates constituted the end of an era.

Most philosophers had got the message and remained pretty careful in expounding their views. There was the occasional exception, such as Theodorus of Cyrene (ca. 340-250 BC), who is mentioned most with Diagoras as the atheist par excellence. However, our evidence mainly exists of anecdotes, and it is hard to reconstruct his theology. In the Hellenistic period two important developments are noticeable. First, we now start to find a listing of atheists in an index atheorum. The earliest example is by Epicurus (341-270 BC) in the twelfth book of his On Nature, which must have been written around 300 BC. He probably included his criticisms of Protagoras, Prodicus, Critias, and possibly

Diagoras, as 'raving lunatics' in the context of how men first came to believe in and worship the gods. Epicurus himself was not an atheist, but later philosophers, probably the Stoics, attacked the premises of his physical system, inferred that the gods had no necessary place in his system and happily labelled him as an atheist.

After Epicurus, at the end of the second century BC, the list was extended by the Academic sceptic Clitomachus in his treatise On atheism. He was an adherent of the most important representative of the sceptical Academy, Carneades (ca. 214-128 BC) who probably had alleged that Epicurus did not really mean what he said about the gods. In turn he was followed by Cicero in his De natura deorum (I.1.63), Pseudo-Aëtius (ca. 50-100 AD), and, towards the end of the second century AD, by Sextus Empiricus (Adversus Mathematicos 9.50-8).

The second development was the instant success of Prodicus' theory about the gods, witness its reflection after Euripides (above) in later poets and historians. Yet his most famous follower lived a good deal later. In the first quarter of the third century BC, the Alexandrian Euhemerus wrote his Sacred Record in which he turned the Hesiodic succession of Ouranos, Kronos and Zeus into a dynasty of mortal kings that inhabited a fictitious island called Panchaea. It was the aim of Euhemerus to keep the gods but to present them in a form in which sophisticated people could believe.

7

Geography and Commerce

Were we to draw a map of the political condition of Europe, Africa, and western Asia about the middle of the tenth century of our era, we should see that by far the greater part of that 'inhabited world', which the Greeks called the 'oikoumene', was occupied by countries possessed of an Islamic government and an Islamic civilization. They no longer constituted a strict political unity, but they were connected by such strong ties of common religion and culture that their inhabitants and not only their Muhammadan inhabitants felt themselves citizens of one vast empire, of which Mecca was the religious, and Baghdad the cultural and political centre. This vast empire had grown in the three foregoing centuries from a series of conquests that started originally from Medina. Arabia was its centre.

To the west it comprised Egypt with the entire northern coast of Africa, including the Atlantic coast as far as the Anti-Atlas and, further, nearly the whole of Spain (with the exception of Asturia), and the islands of Sicily and Crete. Sardinia and Cyprus, too, were constantly exposed to Muhammadan attacks; so was also the southern Italian coast, where some towns, like Bari, were actually under Islamic rule, while others, like Amalfi, belonged to its sphere of influence. To the north of Arabia, Syria with Armenia and the south-east of the Caucasus belonged to the permanent possessions of Islam; and, farther to the east, Mesopotamia with 'Iraq, followed by the whole of the territory of modern Persia with Afghanistan. Northward of these countries, again, Transoxania belonged to Islam, including in the west the delta region of Khwarizm, and, in the east, the valley and the mountains of Farghana.

The Indus had been crossed already in the eighth century; the regions on its lower course belonged, with Sind, to the Islamic Empire. Only in the southward direction did the territorial extension of Islam in Africa scarcely exceed the latitude of Aswan in Egypt. 'The length of the Empire of Islam in our days extends from the limits of Farghana, passing through Khurasan, al-Jibal (Media), 'Iraq and Arabia as far as the coast of Yaman, which is a journey of about four months; its breadth begins from the country of the Rum (the Byzantine Empire), passing through Syria, Mesopotamia/Iraq, Fars and Kirman, as far as the territory of al-Mansura on the shore of the sea of Fars (the Indian Ocean), which is about four months' travelling. In the previous statement of the length of Islam I have omitted the frontier of the Maghrib (northern Africa) and Andalus (Spain), because it is like the sleeve of a garment.

To the east and the west of the Maghrib there is no Islam. If one goes, however, beyond Egypt into the country of the Maghrib, the lands of the Sudan (the Black) lie to the south of the Maghrib and, to its north, the Sea of Rum (the Mediterranean) and next the territory of Rum.' These are the words of the geographer Ibn Hauqal, writing about A.D. 975. Although the regions enumerated above do not coincide at all with, and are even smaller than, the countries now inhabited by a Muhammadan population, the fact that they constituted not only a religious but also a politically powerful block, brought together and kept together by force of arms, enabled them to hold the position of a strong central power in the world then known.

If we consider, on the other hand, the geographical and political conditions of the Christian European world of those days, we immediately realize to what extent in reality the latter must have been dependent on the huge Islamic Empire. To the south the Mediterranean, at that time under the domination of the rulers of the Muhammadan shores, formed an insurmountable barrier; to the east the Byzantine Empire stood face to face with Islam in Armenia; the northern Caucasus and eastern Europe were the home of half-civilized nations that were at least as much under Muhammadan as under Christian influence.

Only in the north of Europe the heathen Northmen were at the beginning of their powerful extension, which was largely to contribute, in the twelfth century, to the annihilation of the political and economic hegemony of Islam. The relative geographical position of the pilgrimage centres of the two rival religions was quite different. Jerusalem, the ideal religious centre of Christian Europe, had since A.D. 638 been under the control of the Muhammadans, but the Muhammadan conquest had not put an end to the pilgrimages undertaken by European Christians to the Holy Sepulchre.

The first pilgrims of whose travels accounts have come down to us, were the Frank Arculf (c. 680), the Saxon Willibald (c. 725) and a certain Bernard, who started c. 870 from Rome on a pilgrimage. No doubt they were not the only ones that contributed to the maintenance of knowledge about the countries conquered by Islam. The relations of the Christians in the Byzantine Empire with their co-religionists in Egypt, Syria, and Mesopotamia must have been very important in this respect. In the Islamic world matters were quite different. Mecca, the centre of pilgrimage, occupied a central geographical position in Islam itself.

The pilgrimage or 'hajj' to Allah's house was one of the five 'pillars of Islam', according to the Sacred Law, and Muhammadans from all parts of the Islamic Empire met at that place. So the 'hajj' became not only a powerful factor in promoting religious unity, but it also materially assisted in strengthening the ties of commerce between all Muhammadan countries, and disseminated among Muhammadans a fairly good knowledge of all parts of their world. To the 'hajj' was due the compilation of a number of itineraries, in which the stations and stages of the roads leading from different countries to Mecca were indicated.

There was, however, a great ignorance of, and lack of interest in, the non-Muhammadan parts of the known world. Nearly a millennium has passed since 'the cultural horizon of Christian Europe was bounded in nearly all directions by Islam. In the meantime Europe has circumnavigated and pierced the barriers that separated it from the southern and eastern parts of the known world, not to speak of the unknown world. Europe owes much to its own force and initiative, but it has also largely profited by the knowledge and the experience of those who were at one time the masters of the world.

Therefore Europe ought to look upon them as its cultural ancestors in the domain of geographical knowledge, of discovery, and of world trade. The influence which Islam has exercised on our modern civilization in these spheres of action can be seen in the many terms of Arabic origin which are to be found in the vocabulary of trade and navigation. The measure of this influence can only be proved by studying the historical development of the domain over which our actual geographical knowledge extends.

For modern geography is a science so positive and independent of tradition that it all but excludes the more or less correct views of former ages; I say 'all but', for it is only just to remember the fact that, when Jaubert in 1840 edited his French translation of Idrlsl, it was thought not unlikely that this edition might increase geographical knowledge of the world, and especially of Africa. The study of the historical influence of our Islamic cultural ancestors on our knowledge of the world is not without its difficulties, because it is not always easy to ascertain how far the geographical knowledge of the Muhammadans was based on personal observation, how far they actually went on their voyages, and what the extent of their commercial relations was.

This statement may cause surprise in view of the fact that from the ninth to the fourteenth century a considerable and important geographical literature was produced in Arabic. But what the bulk of this literature has to offer us is only the official science of scholars and literary men. However observant these writers may have been of the regions and peoples which they visited, and with however much interest they may have listened to the travellers and sailors from whom they derived their information, they were still more or less captivated by ideological religious and traditional views, which prevented them from seeing certain facts in their true light, even if their opinion was much less prejudiced than that of the Christian scholars of the 'Dark Ages'.

Apart from this official and literary science there was the great naval and geographical experience of seafarers and merchants. The literary men certainly profited by their knowledge, but it appears sometimes from their own writings that the less pretentious traders and navigators were less prejudiced than themselves. Now it is this more humble kind of people whom we must consider as the principal mediators and teachers in the relations between Islam and medieval Europe. The big Arabic geographical works appear to have had practically no immediate influence on medieval geographical views, except in so far as astronomical geography is concerned.

We must not omit, however, to give a survey of the way in which the vast geographical knowledge of the Muhammadans was reflected in Arabic literature. In the first 150 years of Islam geography as a science was certainly not superior to what we observe in the Christian world. Curious opinions are reported, on the authority of contemporaries of the Prophet, concerning the length of the world and its parts, the sources of the Nile, and so on. Among them we meet with the comparison of the world to a bird, whose head is China and whose tail is North Africa. The Quran itself contains a geographical indication in the twice recurring statement that God has separated the two seas by an insurmountable barrier.

These words are interpreted by the scholars as alluding to the Mediterranean and the Indian Ocean, including the Red Sea, which interpretation is probably correct. There is little doubt that this theory of the two seas is of Persian origin, and its occurrence in the Quran has elevated the theory to a dogma, which has dominated to a great extent all Muhammadan geographical literature and cartography. The scientific study of geography in Islam began under Greek influence. One result of the widespread activity in translating Greek works, which, at the beginning of the ninth century especially in the reign of the Caliph al-Ma'mun (813-33) made the Muslims the spiritual heirs of Hellenism, was that they became acquainted with the geographical work of Ptolemy; and Ptolemy's doctrine of the prolongation of the east coast of Africa to the East fitted very well into the theory of the two seas.

We possess no early Arabic translation of the text of Ptolemy, but there exists an adaptation of this work, made about 830 by the astronomer al-Khwarizml; the map which must have accompanied his text is lost. Al-Khwarizmi's longitudes and latitudes go back for the greater part to Ptolemy, but the book gives also the geographical positions of such places as originated after the conquest of Islam. It is not certain if the latter indications are due to new astronomical observations; we only know that the Caliph al-Ma'mun had ordered the measurement of a geographical degree in the Syrian desert and that the same caliph had caused to be executed by seventy scholars amongst whom was al-Khwarizmi an 'image of the earth', of which a description is still extant in a work of rather late date.

So we may assume that al-Khwarizmi's book already contained the results of the research of Islamic scholars. It bears, moreover, traces of other influences, such as the division of the inhabited world into seven zones or climates, which does not appear in Ptolemy. Traces of the doctrine of the seven climates are no doubt to be found among Greek scholars, perhaps as early as Eratosthenes. It is probable, however, that this theory of the division of the inhabited world was of Persian-Babylonian origin and this may account for the predominant place it has occupied in much of the geographical literature of the Muhammadans, who were more receptive of Eastern traditions than the Greeks.

But the world image, that had made its entry with Ptolemy into the Muhammadan world, did not accord very well with the idea which the citizens of the new Islamic Empire must necessarily have formed of the world. They had no objection to the spherical form of the earth then denied by many Christian theologians neither did they see the necessity of affirming it. This explains the fact that very soon Islamic geography and Islamic astronomy went their own ways. The astronomers, such as al-Farghani (c. 860), al-Battani (c. 900), Ibn Yunus (c. 1000), and the great al-Biruni (c. 1030), continued to give geographical tables of longitudes and latitudes, following the division of the seven climates, but they added little or nothing to the actual knowledge of countries.

Such knowledge was gained from a description of countries and itineraries, so useful for the administration of the Empire, of which those to Mecca have already been mentioned. Thus, already in the course of the ninth century, several descriptions of countries came into existence under such titles as 'The Book of Countries', or 'The Book of Roads and Kingdoms'. The chief writers of that epoch were Ibn Khurradadhbeh (c. 870), al-Ya'qubi (c. 890), Ibn al-Faqih (c. 903), and Ibn Rusta (c. 910). In a more or less systematic form they give an administrative and topographical description of the different countries belonging to Islam, in which the itineraries occupy a prominent place.

In these works considerable attention is still paid to non-Muhammadan countries, such as the countries and islands in the Far East and also the Byzantine Empire; on the other hand they give a large place to all kinds of legendary stories. To the same period belong the accounts of the sea-captain Sulaiman of Siraf of his voyages to India and China. In the tenth century we observe the development of a literary geographical school, which was to exert a lasting influence on the geographical views of the Muhammadans. The contents of these books are based to a large extent on the earlier works, but they are enriched by the knowledge of Muhammadan countries which had been gained meanwhile; most of the authors of this epoch were travellers themselves.

This new school is distinguished from that of the foregoing period, in that it paid very little attention to countries not belonging to Islam, and in its systematic treatment of the geographical matter, accompanied by a number of maps, of which the text is meant to be a description. The first of these maps is a map of the world, circular in form, Mecca being the centre. The world is surrounded by the 'encircling ocean' and from this two gulfs enter the continent, so as to approach very close to one another at one point, the Isthmus of Suez.

These gulfs are the Mediterranean and the Indian Ocean (the Sea of Rum and the Sea of Fars), in accordance with the Quranic tradition. After the map of the world, Arabia is treated as being the centre of the world, and next North Africa, Muhammadan Spain, Egypt, and Syria; this part is completed by the description of the Sea of Rum. The second part of the geographical description treats of eastern Islam, beginning with Mesopotamia and finishing with Trans-oxania. The first author who is said to have composed a geographical treatise of this kind is Abu Zaid al-Balkhi (d. 934), who was a famous scholar at the court of the Samanid dynasty, the rulers of Khurasan and Transoxania (822-999).

Al-Balkhi stood in high favour with the vizier al-Jaihanl, who is likewise the writer of a voluminous geographical treatise, of which the text is not yet known in Europe. Balkhi's book itself is not preserved either, but some of the principal geographical works are elaborations of the system established by him. These are the books of al-Istakhri (c. 950) and Ibn Hauqal (c. 975), and the somewhat more independently composed work of al-Maqdisi (c. 985).

It is very probable that this geographical school partly inherited older Persian traditions from the time of the Sasanids as appears, for example, from the naming of the Indian Ocean 'the Sea of Pars'. The maps certainly show a more exact notion of geographical reality than those which circulated at the same time in Europe, founded chiefly on the world-map of the Spanish monk Beatus (c. 730-98). We never find in these Muhammadan maps pictures of men and animals, owing no doubt to the prohibition against the pictorial representation of living beings.

The addition of pictures makes most European maps, such as the famous map of Hereford, appear still more fantastic. But, on the other hand, we can observe already in the Islamic maps of the tenth century a tendency to represent the coastlines and the rivers under conventionalized forms; thus many Istakhri maps show the Mediterranean in a circular or elliptical form. In other works of a geographical nature written at this period only one special region is treated.

The best known are the description of the Arabian Peninsula by al-Hamdani and the famous description of India by al-Biruni. Several works of this sort have not come down to us intact, but are known from later compilations, such as the report given by Ibn Fadlan of the embassy sent in 921 by the Caliph al-Muqtadir to the Volga Bulgarians.

A special place is held by the work of al- Mas'udi. Al-Mas'udi was a globe-trotter of the Muhammadan world and collected on his travels a large amount of geographical and ethnographical knowledge. He wrote several works, two of which, finished in 956, are preserved. In geographical matters they show a remarkable lack of system, but they are important in that they display the great difference between 'imperial Islamic geography and the independent geographical notions of travellers and sailors; thus, after giving in one place a survey of the views prevailing among Islamic scholars as to the extension of the Indian Ocean, he cannot help remarking that the seafaring people from the ports on the Persian Gulf, who are well at home in those seas, do not agree at all with the measurements given by the scholars, and that they even claim that those seas have no limits at all in certain directions.

This was totally opposed to the prevailing dogma, that the 'Sea of Pars' was a gulf of the 'encircling ocean', and that it had a rather narrow entrance, like the Mediterranean. Similarly the above-mentioned author al-Maqdisi, while discussing the shape of the Indian Ocean, says that some people represent it as a 'tailasan' (a kind of semicircular Persian coat), and other people as a bird, but that after long investigations a certain sheikh, who was one of the experts in the matter, had drawn for him in the sand the shape of this sea. It did not resemble either a 'tailasan' or a bird, but was full of irregular forms for gulfs and peninsulas.

Al-Mas'udi seems to have visited China and to have known a good deal of the east coast of Africa. On the other hand, he seems to have had little grasp of astronomical geography; for we find in one of his books the curious view that in one climate all important towns must necessarily lie on the same latitude. The eleventh century continues, but less brilliantly, on the lines of its predecessor: the best-known author of this time is the Spanish Muhammadan al-Bakri (wrote c. 1067), of whose voluminous work only the part concerning Africa has been edited. Here we find a still more elaborated knowledge of itineraries and especially of the coastline with its numerous ports and inlets.

From about the same time there is an account of the travels of the Persian Nasir-i Khusrau, who came from Khurasan and visited Egypt and Mecca; this man, while showing himself a keen observer, held very erroneous views as to the structure of the world in general. The eleventh century had witnessed events which were to deal serious blows to the ideal unity of the Islamic world. The eastern half was invaded about 1050 by the Seljuq Turks; while, in the west, the island of Sicily, a good deal of Spain, and even some places on the African coast had been conquered by Christian rulers.

At the same time Europe was preparing itself for the Crusades. This was also the time when the exclusiveness of the Islamic world towards the Christian world began to break up. By disintegration it had lost its political strength, which was to reappear, only for a short time, under the hegemony of the same Seljuqs and the Ayyubids in their fierce struggle against the Crusaders. These events did not affect the prevailing geographical views in Muhammadan literature: only a slight approach towards astronomical geography is perceptible. We find, for example, that in a later extract from Ibn Hauqal's geographical treatise of about 1164, the world map is no longer round, but elliptical, in conformity with the astronomical representation of the inhabited world.

The most brilliant author of this time is al-Idnsi, formerly called Edrisi. Al-IdrisI has, more than any other Islamic geographer, a claim on our attention, first because he worked at the court of a Christian ruler, the Norman King Roger II of Sicily (1101-54), at lever 7 meeting-point of the two big cultural areas, and secondly because he long passed for the sole representative of Islamic geographical knowledge. From the study of earlier Arabic geographical texts we know that al-Idrisi was to a great extent dependent on his predecessors. But the fact that King Roger entrusted the composition of a description of the known world to a Muhammadan scholar indicates clearly how far the superiority of Muhammadan learning was acknowledged at that time.

It is well known that the Norman court of Sicily was half oriental; Roger's desire to have a geography made for him was itself oriental in character. Since olden times it had been considered as the prerogative of great monarchs, such as Alexander the Great and some Persian kings, to have a synopsis made for them of the world that lay at their feet. A similar idea had been at the bottom of the Caliph al-Ma'mun's geographical interest, and even of the tenth-century geographical school which had started at the court of the Samanids.

According to al-Idrisi's preface, King Roger had sent in all directions for information to be incorporated in the book; he had also ordered, just like al-Ma'mun, the construction of a big world -map. Al-Idrlsi's work, too, contains maps, and the maps are in a way its most important part, as the text is a commentary on them. In the best known of its two editions there are seventy maps (actually in all manuscripts one is lacking), each representing the tenth part of one of the seven climates into which he divides the world after the fashion of the Islamic astronomers.

If put together, these seventy maps constitute an oblong quadrangle, much after the Ptolemaean pattern. But the specific Islamic conception of the two big seas is strictly maintained, whereas the details, especially the coastline of the Mediterranean, answer much better to the reality than any of the previous Islamic maps. Al-Idrisi's text shows the author's indebtedness to the earlier geographers, and the work as a whole is a good illustration of the reconciliation between descriptive and astronomical geography. It is doubtful, however, if the result of the measurements of great astronomers, such as al-Biruni, have been used.

For in the second, abridged, edition of al-Idrlsi's book, the so-called 'small Idrlsf, we find, in addition to the seven climates, an eighth climate, to the south of the equator. Moreover, the world -map, which in the 'big Idrisf precedes the other maps, is round, after the traditional fashion. It is difficult to believe that al-Idrlsi's work, composed as it was at the chronological and geographical point of contact between the Islamic and the Christian civilizations, remained wholly unknown to Christian scholars in Sicily, Italy, or other Christian countries. At present, however, there is no certain trace of its influence.

The first translation known of al-Idrisi was published in Rome, in 1619, after an incomplete abridgement of the work; the translator did not even know the author's name. The geographical literature after al-Idrisi cannot claim any great originality, except the narrations of travellers, which become more numerous about this time. Among the best known are the Spaniard Ibn Jubair, who went in 1192 to Mecca and Mesopotamia; and, more than a century later, Ibn Battuta, a man from Morocco, who journeyed all over the Muhamma Han world and farther eastward to Ceylon and the Maldives, visiting also Constantinople; his last travels brought him, in 1353, far into the interior of Africa.

Another traveller, who had left a valuable description of this part of the world, about 1250, was Ibn Fatima; we do not possess his book, but it was utilized by the author Ibn Sa'id, about A.D. 1274. The work of this last writer is of great interest, because it treats its subject in the same way as al-Idrisi and, though less detailed in description, it shows how greatly Muhammadan knowledge of Africa had grown. Moreover, it approaches still closer to astronomical geography in that it gives very exact indications of the geographical position of the principal towns and places. Ibn Sa'id, again, is one of the chief authorities for Abu'1-Fida", prince of Kama in Syria. Abu'l-Fida"s 'Table of Countries' (1327) was, about 100 years ago, the best-known geographical work in Arabic next to al-Idrisi; it is, however, a rather poor compilation of earlier sources.

A much more valuable compilation, for our purpose, is the big geographical dictionary of Yaqut (1228); it contains all geographical names in alphabetical order. This work owed its existence as much to biographical as to geographical interest, the compiler's aim being to explain the surnames of well-known people, named after their birthplace or the place where they lived. Another kind of compilation was that of al-Qazwml (c. 1275). Tk 8 write 1 has been styled the Pliny of Arabic literature; he wrote a cosmography and a geography and gave in the latter many curious and fabulous details about the places he mentioned; he has also some information about the German countries. A better and more original geographer was al- Dimashqi (c. 1325), although his general tendency is the same as al-Qazwinl's. The great number of Islamic geographers after al-Idrlsi shows clearly that the knowledge of geographical matters was still widespread at that epoch, but we can no longer speak of an Islamic school of geographers. After the Mongol invasions the Muhammadan world lost for ever its ideal and even its cultural unity.

It is true that by this time the faith of Islam had made new progress in Asia Minor and Central Asia by Turkish aggression, and in inner Africa by the more peaceful way of trade and preaching. Arabic as well as Persian literature still continues to give us much information about those countries, but the Christian peoples themselves, in the first place the Italians, were already active in travel and discovery. An Egyptian author of the fourteenth century, al-'Umari, quotes a Genoese as his authority in describing Asia Minor. We now find more specialized geographical descriptions of one country and its institutions. Thus the Egypt of the early Mamluk period was fully described by a series of authors; the best known is al-Maqrizi's voluminous description of Egypt (c. 1420).

As has already been said, literary Islamic geography does not seem to have left much direct impression on European thought in the Middle Ages. One of the few proofs of the acceptance of Muhammadan geographical views by Christian writers is the world-map to be found in the Opus lerrae

Sanctae completed by Marino Sanuto in 1321 and dedicated to the Pope. This map is round, Jerusalem being its centre, and shows clearly the two big seas derived from the ocean and the prolongation of the African coast to the east. Thus this indefatigable reviver of the crusading spirit showed himself one of the few students of the lore of the people he wanted to destroy.

Something has been said already about the geographical work of the Muhammadan astronomers. This had much more direct influence on medieval science in Europe than had geography. Some of their works were translated at an early period, such as the Zlj of al-Battani (wrote c. 900), by Plato of Tivoli (c. 1150). The chief centre where Christian scholars from all countries became acquainted with Arabic scientific literature was Toledo, after its conquest by Alfonso VII. So far as geography is concerned, these studies contributed in the first place to the keeping alive of the doctrine of the sphericity of the earth, which had been nearly forgotten in the 'Dark Ages' and without which the discovery of America would have been impossibility.

All Islamic astronomers treated geography only in connexion with the determination of the geographical longitude and latitude of a certain number of places, without ever attempting, seemingly, to draw a map. Their tables of longitude and latitude are arranged after the seven climates. Because of the more general character of this science, Christian scholars took a greater interest in it than in purely Muhammadan geography; consequently, in the twelfth century there began to appear astronomical tables in Latin, sometimes accompanied by geographical tables. Some Christian scholars accepted also the division into seven climates.

A legacy of still greater importance was the idea that the known hemisphere of the world had a centre or 'world summit', situated at an equal distance from east, west, north, and south. Al-Battani speaks of this 'cupola of the earth' as an island, but another author of his time (Ibn Rusta) already knows it as the 'cupola of Arm'. The word Arm is a misreading of the Arabic transliteration of the name of the Indian town Ujjiyaini (Ozene in Ptolemy's geography), where there had been an astronomical observatory, and on the meridian of which town the 'world sumimt' originally an Indian conception was supposed to lie.

Like the Muhammadan astronomers, their Christian disciples considered this doctrine of the highest importance; amongst the latter were Adelard of Bath, who translated in 1126 the trigonometrically tables of al-Khwarizmi, Gerard of Cremona (1114-87) and, in the thirteenth century, Roger Bacon and Albertus Magnus. The Arin (or Arim) theory was still later to be found in the Imago Mundi of Cardinal Peter of Ailly, published in 1410, and it was from this book that Christopher Columbus learnt the same doctrine, which had developed in the meantime so far as to make Columbus believe that the earth was shaped in the form of a pear, and that, on the western hemisphere, opposite the summit of Arin, there was another centre, much more elevated than the one on the eastern side, so as to form the shape of the lower half of a pear. Thus Islamic geographical theory may claim a share in the discovery of the New World.

We find the influence of the same theory in quite another domain. It is highly probable that it induced Dante, whose indebtedness to Muhammadan traditions has been established in many respects, to localize his Purgatorio, in the shape of a mountain, in the western hemisphere, by combining with it, in an ingenious way, the ancient Christian belief that the terrestrial paradise was situated in the extreme east of the world, behind the sea (as shown on the different world-maps of Beatus). Islamic navigation had already reached its widest extent in the ninth century. But, while navigation on the Indian Ocean derived its chief importance from the commercial relations with the non-Islamic coasts of Asia and Africa, commercial navigation in the Mediterranean was limited to the parts under Muhammadan rule, the relations with Christian ports being of a military and predatory character.

The Indian Ocean, consequently, was the only field of great enterprise. Its base was the Persian Gulf, where ports like Siraf and Basra, with its suburb al-Ubulla, and those on the Oman coast had been, even in pre- Islamic times, very important centres of trade and navigation. The coming of Islam, however, and especially the establishment of its political centre in 'Iraq, encouraged the spirit of enterprise. About the middle of the tenth century Muhammadan ships had already reached the Chinese town of Khanfu, now Canton.

There was then a considerable Islamic colony in that town, which had become an emporium of the trade with China. From here some Muhammadan traders and sailors went even farther north, and it is probable that they knew Corea and Japan. This early commercial prosperity seems to have been brought to an end in 878 by certain disturbances, in which the port of Khanfu was destroyed. From that time regular navigation did not extend farther than a town which the Arabic authors call Kala, famed especially for its tin mines, the position of which must be sought on the western coast of Malacca. Kala was politically dependent on the ruler of Zabaj, which name is the early Arabic rendering of the name Java.

But at that time Zabaj stood in the first place for Sumatra, and particularly for the centre of the then flourishing empire of Shrivijaya; with these regions trading connexions existed. It appears from such authors as Ibn Rusta (c. 900), Sulaiman (c. 850) and his continuator Abu Zaid (c. 950) that the Muhammadan navigators were quite at home in those seas, though the texts do not give a very clear account of the sea-routes which were followed. The ships of Islam kept up an equally lively traffic with the ports of Ceylon (Sarandib) and with the west coast of India; a prosperous Arabic colony inhabited the town of Saimur in the neighbourhood of Bombay. Daibul, situated in Sind on Muhammadan territory, was an important emporium for these regions.

On the eastern coast of Africa where, on the whole, trade was less important they reached, in the beginning of the tenth century, the country of Sufala, known for its gold. This region was on the African coast, opposite Madagascar, and the island itself was known to the Muhammadans as the isle of Waqwaq. Now the authors knew also another Waqwaq, which was opposite China, and the description of which seems best to answer to that of Japan. The result was, of course, a fatal confusion in the accounts given in geographical texts, caused, no doubt, by the geographical dogma that the east coast of Africa ran in an eastern direction to reach, somewhere in the neighbourhood of China, the mouth of the 'sea of Pars'.

The knowledge of the sea-captains was not hampered by traditional views, as has been shown; stories of their voyages are very popular in Arabic literature and were soon invested with a romantic hue which has survived in the well-known tales of Sindbad the Sailor in the Arabian Nights. The age-long seafaring tradition which centres in the Persian Gulf prepared the way for the nations that afterwards sailed and ruled those waters: Portuguese, Turks, British, and Dutch.

When Vasco de Gama, after his circumnavigation of Africa in 1498, had reached Malindi on the east coast of Africa, it was an Arab pilot that showed him the way to India. According to Portuguese sources, this pilot was in possession of a very good sea-map and of other maritime instruments. Arabic sources of that time also knew the story; they state that the pilot, whom they knew under the name of Ahmad ibn Majid, could only be induced to show the way to the Portuguese after having been made drunk.

This probably fictitious story shows that the Muhammadans fully realized the far-reaching consequences of the coming of the Portuguese. The same Ahmad ibn Majid is also known as the writer of a sailing-manual for the Indian Ocean, the Red Sea, the Persian Gulf, the South China Sea, and the East-Indian archipelago.

According to a statement of Sir R. F. Burton it even seems that Ibn Majid was venerated in the past century on the African coast as the inventor of the compass. The idea of piercing the isthmus of Suez is ascribed to some of the earlier Abbasid caliphs; it was never realized, however, and since the Crusades such an enterprise was justly considered a great danger to Islam. Islamic navigation in the Mediterranean has therefore always been isolated from that in the Eastern waters: trade in the Mediterranean was restricted to Muhammadan ports. Commercial relations with Christian countries were strongly opposed, both from the Islamic side as early as the Caliph Omar and from the Christian side.

The result was the decay of the port of Alexandria and the ruin of many other ancient seaports. Now Tunis became the new centre of the considerable traffic between North African and Spanish ports. Towards Christians Muhammadan navigators were often nothing but pirates, but it is only just to say that the same thing is true of Christian navigators. From the beginning of the Crusades the Mediterranean ceased to be the almost exclusive domain of Islamic navigation. Islam had lost a great part of Spain, the island of Sicily, and its hold on the Italian coast; at the same time the Italian seaports of Genoa and Pisa began to develop.

The traveller Ibn Jubair, in 1192, made use of a Christian ship to go from Ceuta to Alexandria. In practice this transition of maritime hegemony was much less violent. It only meant that the Christians, who had navigated before as sailors or slaves under Muslim control, now fully emancipated themselves and sailed and traded on their own account. The modern international maritime vocabulary contains not a few words of Arabic origin, which show the former Muhammadan supremacy on these seas, such words for example as admiral, cable, average, shallop (sloop), barque, and, in the maritime language of the Indian Ocean, monsoon. Mention has already been made of the compass in connexion with the pilot Ibn Majid.

This man himself supposes in his work that the inventor of the compass was King David. But it cannot even be proved that the Muhammadans were acquainted with this instrument at an earlier date than the Christians. It may be true that the Chinese knew this instrument and its use in the second century and that they transmitted it to the West. But the first indubitable indication that Islamic sea-captains knew the compass is found in an author of 1282, and this is about the same time that a knowledge of it can be traced in France and Italy. Some terms of oriental but not Arabic provenance in the terminology relating to the compass make it probable that Europe received the knowledge of the qualities of the magnetic needle from the East, but it does not appear that the Muhammadans were the predecessors of the Christians.

Their, in many respects, clumsy cartography makes us rather suppose that their ships could sail only in sight of the shore. So it is safer to assume that, even if the Muhammadans knew of the compass earlier than European Christians, their acquaintance with it does not go back beyond 1200 and that, soon after it became known to them, the knowledge of it was passed on to Christian navigators. The problem connected with the appearance of the first sea-charts of the Mediterranean at the end of the thirteenth century closely resembles the problem of the compass. The oldest known portulan was probably made by the Genoese.

The portulam give at once a much more exact image of the position of coasts and islands than all the earlier maps, and their construction was only made possible by the use of the compass. The portulans also show a very detailed design of the coastlines, and these details can hardly have been the work of one generation. Now we need only remember the exact description of the African coast in the work of al-Idrisi and his predecessors Ibn Hauqal and al-Bakri, to realize that the experience of the Islamic navigators reflected in the geographical treatises cited above must have contributed considerably to the composition of those prototypes of modern cartography, the oldest portulans.

By the big waterways of Mesopotamia the Persian Gulf was linked to Baghdad, the centre of the Islamic Empire. By this means the navigation of the Indian Ocean became the instrument of a world-trade. The great merchants of Baghdad obtained in this way the silks of China and the spices and aromatics of. India, different kinds of wood, coconuts, muscatnuts, and the tin of Kala. All these wares found their way from Islamic countries into Europe, then deprived of all direct traffic with those countries.

A part of this sea-trade did not enter the Persian Gulf, but brought the products to Aden and the Red-Sea ports of Jedda and al-Qulzum (the ancient Clysma near Suez), and, in the crusading times, to 'Aidhab, an ancient port for pilgrim caravans which lay about opposite Jedda. From here the occidental part of the Islamic world was supplied. By the same way came also the African products, such as ivory; these were shipped from the Ethiopian seaport of Zaila f, opposite Aden. More typical than navigation of the traffic of Islam is the overland trade by the 'ship of the desert'.

Though, long before the appearance of Muhammad, trade caravans had crossed the steppes of Asia and Africa, we are accustomed to associate caravan trade with Islam. Even down to the last few years the Islamic peoples have not been surpassed by western civilization in the means of locomotion in the desert. The recently started motor traffic in the Syrian Desert, in Arabia, in Persia, and in the Sahara, some railways in Central Asia, and the recently established air services have begun to follow the immemorial tracks of the camel. In the centuries when the Islamic Empire flourished, caravan traffic was the most common means of travelling and trading between the different Islamic countries, especially the pilgrim caravans to Mecca.

At the same time there were some important overland routes that led out of the Empire, first those to India and China, secondly those to southern and central Russia and thirdly the African trade-roads. India and China could also be reached by sea; for this reason the caravan trade was not so important on this side as in other directions. The land-route to India was moreover hampered by the difficult roads in the mountains of Afghanistan. To trade with China it was necessary to pass through the regions occupied by Turkish peoples; the chief Chinese product, silk, was produced, moreover, in Persia at an early period.

After the fall of the Samanid Empire, in the eleventh century, political conditions became still more unfavourable for the Chinese overland trade. The great revival of the Asian trade routes in the thirteenth century was not the work of Islam, but of the Mongols. For our knowledge of the extension of Islamic trade influence in a northerly direction we can rely not only on written sources, but also on the enormous number of Muhammadan coins which have been found in different parts of Russia, Finland, Sweden, and Norway, not to mention some isolated finds in the British Isles and in Iceland.

On the middle course of the Volga, in the province of Kazan, great quantities of these coins have been found, but these are far surpassed in number by the Arabic coins found in the Baltic provinces. In Scandinavia the chief finds are on the south-western coast of Sweden and the southern point of Norway. The coins belong to the period from the end of the seventh to the beginning of the eleventh century. It is very unlikely that the Islamic merchants themselves advanced so far to the north as these places, for it appears from the written Arabic sources that the country of the Volga Bulgars, on the middle course of that river, was the final goal of their trade expeditions and their embassies; the faith of Islam, too, penetrated as far as those regions at an early date.

The route generally followed by trade went from Transoxania to the Delta region of Khwarizm (Khiva) at the mouth of the Oxus; the way up the Volga from its mouth was less usual. The fact, however, that the coins are found over so wide an area is a symptom of cultural influence, and proves that the Muhammadans purchased in the Bulgarian markets a good many wares from the peoples living in the north-west. Amongst these the Scandinavian Russians were the most important. We know from geographical works, principally from al-Maqdisi, what were the wares that the Islamic merchants acquired in this way: 'sables, miniver, ermines, the fur of foxes, beavers, spotted hares, and goats; also wax, arrows, birch bark, high fur caps, fish glue, fish teeth, castoreum, amber, prepared horse hides, honey, hazel nuts, falcons, swords, armour, maple wood, slaves, small and big cattle'.

Most of the slaves came from the Slavonic peoples, whose name still bears witness to the role they played in the civilized world and especially the Islamic countries. Another way by which slaves were imported was Spain, whence they came to the Maghrib and Egypt. This last category were chiefly eunuchs destined for the Islamic harems. It is well known that the slaves of different races so imported have contributed not a little to the spreading of Islamic cultural acquisitions in Europe. Apart from this far-reaching Islamic-Bulgarian trade of which traces have been found also in Germany there were also commercial relations with the empire of the Khazars, by the Caspian Sea and the mouths of the Volga, where was situated Itil or Atil, the capital of the Khazars.

This trade was less important for the exchange of merchandise, but the Khazar Empire, constituting a kind of buffer-state between Islam and the Byzantine Empire, furthered the transmission of many Islamic and oriental products which found their way into Christian countries. The African overland trade was divided into an eastern and a western area; on both sides the chief import was gold. In the country of the Buja, to the east of Aswan, beyond Islamic territory, lay al-f Allaqi, the big trade-centre of the region of the gold mines, famous since ancient Egyptian times. In western Africa an active trade went on with the gold country of Ghana, the capital of which must have been on the Niger.

The Muhammadan merchants from Morocco, Algeria, and Tunisia travelled several months' journey to the south and passed generally through Awdaghosht, an oasis situated fourteen days' journey to the north of Ghana. As a proof of the importance of trade in those regions the geographer Ibn Hauqal (c. 975) alleges that he saw in Awdaghosht an I.O.U. (the Arabic word is sakk, from which the modern word cheque has been derived), for an amount of 42,000 dinars, addressed to a merchant in the town of Sijilmasa in southern Morocco.

It is even said that in the preceding century the volume of trade had been still greater, as there existed then a straight road connexion between the western regions and Egypt, which road had been given up on account of its insecurity. In later centuries, also, Africa remained a domain where Muhammadan enterprise and missionary zeal could display their activity without competition. The author Ibn Sa'id, in the thirteenth century, is very well acquainted, through the travels of Ibn Fatima, with the Atlantic coast as far as the Senegal (which was thought to be connected with the Niger and even to belong to the same fluvial system as the Nile), and with the negro peoples living round Lake Chad; on the other hand, the Muhammadans never knew the sources of the Nile, for they only repeat the tradition of Ptolemy on this point.

Still the Europe of the Renaissance had no information except from Muhammadan sources about the interior of the Dark Continent, for the description of Africa by the Christianized Muslim Leo Africanus in 1526 was then, and for long afterwards, almost the only source of knowledge. The value attributed to Idrlsi in the first half of the nineteenth century has already been pointed out. The trade between Islam and Christian Europe showed at first a sharp contrast with the large commercial development previously described. There was as good as no direct commercial intercourse.

What trade there was lay in the hands of Jewish

merchants. At that time the Jews were almost exclusively a commercial people and only they could trade freely in both areas of civilization. Ibn Khurradadhbeh relates that Jewish merchants from the south of France crossed the sea to Egypt, traversed on foot the Isthmus of Suez, and travelled by ship to India; others went overland from Ceuta to Egypt, and from Syria to the Indus. They often visited Constantinople also. In this way the Islamic countries received from Europe slaves of whom mention has already been made silks (from the Byzantine Empire), furs, and arms, all of which came also by way of Russia. The same traders brought to Europe musk, aloes, camphor, cinnamon, and similar products; the names betray their oriental origin.

Other routes by which oriental products could enter Europe were the Empire of the Khazars, between the Caspian region and Byzantium, and the half-barbaric peoples of Russia, that kept up a lively trade with central Europe. On the Byzantine frontier the town of Trebizond was in the tenth century an important emporium for the Islamic-Greek trade. A number of Muhammadan merchants lived there, and the Byzantine government profited largely by the levying of customs. There was also some direct trade on the Spanish border.

So we may speak, in a way, of a state of mutual commercial isolation between the Christian and the Muhammadan world. It is true that since the eighth century Muslim travellers and traders are to be found in Italian towns and in Constantinople, but these relations were only the germ of the lively commercial intercourse that began to develop in the eleventh century, to be interrupted only for a short time in the first period of the Crusades. After the barrier of former ages had broken down, trade itself subsequently became one of the strongest factors in promoting the transmission of cultural values to the European peoples, who, aided by their rulers (as Roger of Sicily) were eagerly seeking to benefit by them.

The manifold ways in which commercial relations led to close cooperation between Muslims and Christians e.g.

in the form of joint partnerships and of commercial treaties cannot be treated here in detail. The great riches of material culture, which the Islamic world had gathered for nearly five centuries, were poured down upon Europe. These riches consisted not only of Chinese, Indian, and African products, which the enterprising spirit of Islam had fetched from far-distant lands; they were in the first place represented by what the Muhammadan countries themselves yielded of natural and industrial products.

Industrial production in Muhammadan countries had developed in a particular way; it was chiefly characterized by being completely under the control of the rulers, by its lack of capital, and by its organization of the craftsmen in guilds. This peculiar form of industrial development proved a great disadvantage to Islam when it came, in later times, into economic competition with European industry; but at the time of Islamic prosperity it had made possible a development of industrial skill which brought the artistic value of the products to an unequalled height.

In the first place should be mentioned the products of the textile industry; a number of names, now commonly in use, shows which textiles were originally imported from Islamic countries: muslin (from Mosul), damask (from Damascus), baldachin (originally a stuff made in Baghdad), and other woven stuffs, which bear Arabic or Persian names, like gauze, cotton, satin, andc. The import of oriental rugs is likewise as old as the Middle Ages.

It is curious to note, too, that the state robes of the medieval German Emperors bore Arabic inscriptions; they were ordered and executed probably in Sicily, where Islamic art and industry continued for a long time after the Christian reconquest. Natural products, which, by their name, betray their original importation from Muhammadan countries, are fruits like the orange, lemon, and apricot, vegetables such as spinach and artichokes, further saffron, and the now so important aniline. Likewise names of precious stones (lapis lazuli) and of musical instruments, though it cannot be proved that the borrowing of these terms goes back directly to commercial intercourse.

The same is to be said about so important a material as paper, the fabrication of which Europe learnt from the Muhammadan peoples in the twelfth century. Finally, our commercial vocabulary itself has preserved some very eloquent proofs of the fact that there was a time when Islamic trade and trade customs exercised a deep influence on the commercial development in Christian countries. In the word 'sterling', for example, is contained the ancient Greek word 'stater', but it has reached the English language only through the medium of Arabic. The word 'traffic' itself probably is to be derived from the Arabic tafriq, which means distribution, and such a well-known word as 'tariff' is nothing but the good Arabic ta'rif, meaning announcement.

To the same origin belong the words 'risk', 'tare', 'calibre', and the everyday word 'magazine', from Arabic makbazin, meaning stores (the French 'magasin' is still the common word for shop). The 'cheque 5 has already been mentioned in the description of the African trade, and the German and Dutch words for the same thing (Wechsel, wissel) are equally Arabic. So is also the term 'aval'.

Next to the knowledge of the bill of exchange the conception of the joint- stock company was acquired by the partnership of Muslim and Christian Italian merchants. Muhammadan mercantile law was based only theoretically on the Sacred Law, derived from the Quran and the sacred tradition; practically it was governed by a developed system of trade customs, to which the instances cited above bear witness. One of these trade forms was also the feigned bargain called 'mohatra', which word has also passed from Arabic into European languages. A largely used word like 'douane' is a reminder of the time when regular commercial intercourse had developed in different ports of the Mediterranean.

It is well known that this intercourse has also reacted largely on the commercial organization of western nations. The treaties which they concluded with Muhammadan rulers, and the institution of consular representatives in eastern ports, have been important stages in the development of the rules that nowadays govern international trade. As may be seen from the previous observations, the cultural gain, which Europe has acquired from the Islamic world in the domain of geography and commerce, is not the fruit of one moment, but is based on the mutual relations that have gone on since the beginning of the eleventh century and were especially lively during the Mongol period in the thirteenth century.

Also the fact that Islamic civilization with its accretions has been continued by States such as Turkey, Persia, and Muhammadan peoples in India and the East Indies, has caused many Islamic views and customs to become known and even practised in European countries. But no period shows so clearly the once enormous superiority of the Islamic peoples over the Christian world as the tenth century, when Islam was at the summit of its prosperity and Christian Europe had come to a seemingly hopeless standstill.

8

Islamic Minor Arts and Architecture

When Islam began that dramatic career which, in its Western course, was destined to plant a new form of art in cities overlooking the Atlantic, it set out from regions where art was in a primitive and backward state. Such art as existed in Arabia was either a sterile survival from the remote past, or merely imitative in nature, a reflection from abroad that flickered in places precariously affected by alien progress. Not even in the fertile spots where a settled population prospered, under conditions very different from those that kept the nomads of the desert in stagnant isolation, does any outstanding native art seem ever to have arisen. Islamic art derived its spiritual complexion from Arabia; but its material texture was fashioned elsewhere, in lands where art was a vital force.

In Syria and Egypt Christianity had wrought profound changes in the pagan art current at its inception. Various factors, rooted in the soil or brought in and developed by foreign domination, had been reanimated by a new spirit, and combined to produce a coherent and impressively beautiful art. Beyond the Euphrates and the Tigris another order of things prevailed. Some centuries had elapsed since the Persians, rising against their Parthian overlords, had set up the native Sasanian dynasty and entered upon a brilliant national revival. Their art, an ancient stock upon which Greek elements current since Alexander's invasion, and later importations from Inner Asia, had been grafted by Iranian genius, was now a vigorous growth characterized by most splendid magnificence.

It was amidst these two cultures, mutually hostile and both equally repugnant to the Muslims, that Tslamic art came gradually into being. In the Middle Ages art was first and foremost a religious expression. We instinctively identify the great orders of medieval art with the creeds that shaped them, for however clearly certain elements in their composition and technical procedure may unite them in common ancestry, they were moulded into distinct entities by religious influences. Christian art was essentially a vehicle for religious edification; its mission was always plainly apparent, clearly expounded with all the subtle resources of picture and symbol in ways as intelligible to the unlettered as to the scholar.

But its superb iconography seemed sheer idolatry to the Arabs, who, lacking any artistic tradition, regarded art with suspicion, associating it, like all primitive people, with magic. Moreover, in the first flush of puritanical zeal, luxury was to them specially reprehensible; an outcome of effete infidel levity, it was a snare of the Devil with which the true believer could have no truck. The splendour of Persian art, the very quality that Persian craftsmen were presently to impress so deeply upon Islamic art, was at first as offensive as the heathen abominations it so patently displayed. Islamic art had its beginnings in the mosque. Here it was born in the full light of day, and bred openly under public tutelage.

The first mosques were bare structures without any architectural pretensions, planned solely for prayer and exhortation. Their furniture, when it appeared for at first there was none was as simple as could be, and every innovation was subject to rigorous criticism. It is said that the first pulpit set up in Egypt was destroyed by order of the

Caliph when the scandal reached his ears, for it raised the preacher in unseemly dignity above his brethren. The first recessed niche built to mark the direction of Mecca was sharply questioned because it recalled too closely the Christian apse, from which, indeed, it was undoubtedly derived. But soon a more sophisticated generation arose to contrast the poverty of the mosque with the richness of the infidel church.

In due course the minbar and the mihrab became the chief ornaments in buildings that for skill in design and no Islamic Minor Arts and diversity of decoration count amongst the triumphs of architectural art. As Islam spread farther afield, contact with alien races enlarged its artistic vision, and, within the restriction permanently imposed" By the creed, produced fresh aspects of the ideal type. Moreover, as it acquired a wider outlook, a new cultural element purely secular in nature began to assert itself at the expense of spiritual supremacy. When alien customs began to infect rulers who were not conspicuous pillars of the faith, the odour of sanctity waxed faint in the palace.

Kinds of art not strictly orthodox crept in when cultured sovereigns began to indulge refined tastes for beautiful books, richly figured stuffs, and other such things, fit, perhaps, for a king, but not for a successor to the Prophet. When the ruler's connoisseurship found imitators amongst the nobility and those who aped the manners of their betters a distinct 'Court art' arose, a development not without profit to the craftsman, but grievous to the devout. Aristocratic seclusion was impossible under the early Caliphs, who enforced social equality as an inviolable principle, holding that every one at his need might seek the presence of the ruler, whose way of life, whose house and its appointments, should be above reproach.

It was not until an easy-living governing class began to detach itself from public business that the palace became a place apart, where a new standard of conduct prevailed. It is not our purpose to follow the growth of Islamic art step by step, but to sketch briefly some of its mature developments; and, concentrating upon certain important products, to trace how they affected contemporary and subsequent progress in Christian Europe. Moreover, we are concerned solely with the minor arts, the work of those craftsmen who, when a building was erected, were called in to furnish it down to the last detail with all the necessities and amenities dictated by the purpose which it was to serve.

The Muslims soon became great builders. Although mural painting seems to have existed from early times, the painting now known is restricted to so-called 'miniature' work, small pictures, illustrations in manuscripts and the like, which, whilst they display masterly technical ability and keen sense of colour, lack certain qualities conspicuous in the best work done under similar conditions in medieval Europe. Master builders of great ability abounded, but we seek in vain for their peers in sculpture and painting.

If, however, with the single exception of architecture, the Muslims failed to equal Western achievement in the fine arts, their success in the arts in which their genius had free play was unparalleled in medieval times. Islam was the direct heir to many ancient craft traditions unknown in the West. In much the same way that Muslim scholars transmitted to posterity a large fund of ancient learning, Muslim artisans preserved, developed, and spread abroad the traditional 'workshop practice' of arts current in the Orient, which had either never penetrated into Europe, or, if known there in former times, had decayed during the period of storm and stress that ushered in the Middle Ages.

In developing anew this ancient skill Islamic art acquired a characteristic so obvious that it may easily be taken as a matter of course and overlooked. Everything, whether made for common or ceremonial use, is lavishly enlivened with ornament, so justly planned and expressed that the patterns seem to be natural growths, like the figuring with which

Nature endows living creatures, rather than artificial embellishments. The forms taken by the designs, although definitely exotic, are not so far removed from European tradition as to be inconsistent with it. Their strangeness is attractive and romantic. So dexterously are their component elements unfolded that we are beguiled almost into the belief that beyond their material structure lies some elusive vitality. Such enrichment is no mere space-serving artifice for masking bare forms, but an essential part of fine craftsmanship, without which a work is incomplete.

To the contemplative Oriental eye the rhythmic dance of a pattern is as much a recreative necessity as is melody to the Western ear. Ornamental composition had such fascination for Oriental craftsmen that they continually devoted intensive study to its problems, systematizing its practice on lines which modern workers still pursue. The most casual survey of Islamic art will show that ornamental design must be ranked as the outstanding minor art evolved by Muslim genius. Although religious tenets absolutely forbade Muslim designers to introduce into their work human figures or living creatures, such representations are, as a matter of fact, very commonly found in Islamic ornament.

But they are not tolerated by any particular sect, as is sometimes supposed, nor are they under any circumstances allowed in the mosane. Their occurrence at once stamps the objects they decorate as made for secular use. Offences breaking the bounds of a discipline too exacting for universal sufferance, they were passed over by the broadminded, but were always vexatious to strict spirits, who might at any moment rise in angry protest. In our museums and art collections are many things showing how blatant lapses have been purged by a swift blow or scrape, sure evidence that at some time or other the fervour of rectitude has impelled the hand of reproof.

Another notable feature in Islamic ornament is the use of Arabic inscriptions. A passage from the Quran, an apt verse from a poet, or a phrase of greeting or blessing often runs round a border or frieze, or fills a shaped cartouche. Now and again the name and grandiose titles of a noble owner enrich some valued possession, giving a welcome clue to its date and provenance; facts which are sometimes exactly stated when the master craftsman has added to his work his signature, the name of the city where it was made, and the year of its completion. Arabic script, the sole Arab contribution to Islamic art, is a universal mark of Muslim dominance or influence wherever it spread.

The script in which the Quran was written, it was held sacred throughout Islam, whose scribes vied with one another in perfecting its beautiful characters. Generations of expert calligraphers worked with such success and approval that riot only was a fine book a priceless treasure, but the merest scrap of a great master's writing a collector's prize. European craftsmen gradually became familiar with the semblance of Arabic script, even if they could not read it. Early evidence of this knowledge and ignorance is afforded by a gold coin struck by Offa, king of Mercia (757-96), now in the British Museum.

This closely resembles a Muslim dinar, but has the words 'OFFA REX' inserted upside down in the middle of an Arabic legend, which is so accurately rendered that the date of the original piece and the Muhammadan religious formula it recited are both clearly legible in the copy. This coin had no successor similar in type, but it records how widely the sound currency then being issued from Muslim mints was circulating. In neither case can the workers have realized the significance of the strange writing they copied or adopted, for inscriptions so flagrantly Muhammadan could hardly have been set knowingly upon the coinage of a Christian king, or inserted on a sacred emblem.

From this time onward scraps of Arabic lettering, often so crudely rendered as to be illegible scribbles, and ornamental details derived from Muslim sources become increasingly numerous in craftwork wrought in Christian Europe. Pious attraction to the Holy Places, thirst after the learning inherited solely by Islam, commercial enterprise and other such interests, drew many travellers to Muslim lands, whence they returned with trophies of Muslim skill to bear out their tales of Saracenic magnificence. Amongst the things brought back by wandering scholars who sought in Muslim seats of learning knowledge unknown in their own countries, the astrolabe was a most important acquisition.

An astronomical instrument of ancient Greek invention, improved by the Alexandrian geographer Ptolemy, and perfected by the Muslims, the astrolabe came to Europe some time in the tenth century. Its principal use in the East was to determine the hour of prayer and the position of Mecca. But it also served other purposes, like that described in The Story told by the Tailor, where the glib barber delays his exasperated victim whilst he finds with his astrolabe the precise moment auspicious for shaving. Association with astrology gave the astrolabe and those versed in its use a sinister reputation throughout the Middle Ages, when in popular belief astronomy and astrology were synonymous terms.

The great tenth-century scholar Gerbert of Auvergne, who became Pope under the name of Sylvester II in 999, was held, from his astronomical learning, to have had dealings with the Devil during his sojourn in Cordoba. In recounting how Gerbert, who 'surpassed Ptolemy in the use of the astrolabe', revived the legitimate mathematical sciences in Gaul, where they had long been in abeyance, William of Malmesbury gives a dark hint of his necromantic skill. An interesting relic of late tenth-century science is preserved at Florence, an astrolabe made for the latitude of Rome, which is thought by some authorities to have belonged to Pope Sylvester.

The earliest dated astrolabe known is at Oxford. Made in 984, it was the joint work of two masters, Ahmad and

Mahmud, sons of Ibrahim the astrologist, of Ispahan. Amongst those in the British Museum is an English example dated 1260. Merton College Library possesses the instrument traditionally associated with Chaucer, who wrote a treatise on the astrolabe for his little son. To mariners the astrolabe was invaluable.

Its use for nautical observations continued in the West until the seventeenth century, when it was superseded by new inventions. A fine astrolabe is a beautiful work of art, made and engraved with amazing care and skill in a form that persisted for centuries without material change. One made under the superintendence of Ibrahim ibn Sa f id at Toledo in 1066-7, may be compared with another, similar in shape but covered with delicate ornament, the work of a celebrated Persian master, 'Abdu'l-Hamid, in 1715.

Amongst the many specimens of early Islamic metal-work that have come down to us is a casket in the Cathedral of Gerona, made of wood sheathed with silver-gilt plating heavily patterned in repousse with scrolling foliation. The casket bears an inscription stating that it was the work of two craftsmen, Badr and Tarif, and was made for a courtier of al-Hakam II (961-76) to give to the heir-apparent, Hisham, who succeeded his father as Caliph at Cordoba.

This is one of the few pieces of silver-work which have survived to our times; but, despite religious objection to the use in this world of the precious metals reserved for the blessed in Paradise, gold and silver plate was by no means prohibited in the Caliphs' palaces. Egyptian records describe in some detail the gold and silver treasure accumulated by the Fatimid Caliphs in Cairo, the bulk of which was dispersed by tumultuous Turkish mercenaries during a rising in 1067.

An inventory of the heirlooms hoarded in the palaces since their foundation, transcribed by the historian al-Maqrizi from early archives still existing in his time, helps us to picture some of the curious luxuries that the court goldsmiths were then contriving. It is a lengthy document, describing with business-like precision items such as gold and silver inkstands, chessmen, parasol-handles, vases for narcissus flowers and violets, golden birds, and trees set with precious stones, in such amazing numbers, that, even if we discount a few hundreds or so from the round thousands freely enumerated by the enthusiastic surveyors, the sceptical cannot remain wholly unimpressed.

Moreover, the reputed wealth of the Fatimids is amply borne out by a contemporary witness, the Persian traveller Nasir-i-Khusrau, who, in 1047, by favour of a palace official, made a tour of the State apartments. He traversed in succession eleven chambers, each, mo re splendid than the last, before entering the twelfth, in which was the throne, a stupendous work made of gold and decorated with scenes of the chase, interspersed with finely wrought inscriptions. Before the throne, which was raised upon three silver steps, was set a wonderful golden trellis of Early Islamic gold-and silver-work has practically disappeared.

It is mainly in what survives of the bronze, brass, and copper furniture and utensils used by wealthy Muslims that Islamic metal-work can now be studied. The great bronze griffin that stands in the Campo Santo at Pisa is a monumental example of a type more usually represented by small birds and beasts, often parts of fountains, or portable water-vessels, from some of which the later European so-called aquamaniles derived their fantastic shapes. The body of this engaging monster he has all the self-satisfied assurance of a pampered pet is completely covered with engraved patterns.

On the neck and wings in represented a scale-like feathering, and the back bears the semblance of a close-fitting cloth decorated with roundels and edged with an inscription in Kufic characters, which is continued on a band round the chest. On the haunches are pointed panels engraved with lions and falcons within borders of running spirals. The inscription, a verse showering adulation on the possessor, gives no clue to the date or origin of this remarkable piece of bronze-casting, but in all probability it is a relic brought from some Fatimid palace of the eleventh century. Other ways of decorating metal besides raising patterns in relief or engraving them were practised by Muslim craftsmen.

They excelled in the art of inlaying designs in gold and silver in bronze or brass; a process performed in several ways, known generally as damascening, a term derived from European association of the work with Damascus, where it was certainly practised, although it did not originate there. In the finest and most ancient kind the patterns were incised in the metal ground and the grooves filled in with gold or silver, both sometimes being used on the same object. The brilliance of the design was often heightened by filling other interstices with a black bastion- position, and in some cases this was the sole method of enrichment. Muslim inlaid metal-work reached perfection about the middle of the twelfth century, and persisted in great excellence for two hundred years.

A typical specimen, one of the finest extant, is a brass ewer in the British Museum, entirely covered with designs inlaid in silver. The ten-sided body and neck are divided horizontally into zones diversified with variously shaped panels, and every part of the surface is heavily enriched with figure subjects, geometric or floral patterns, and inscriptions. At the base a valance of knotted-work, finishing in tassel-like pendants, completes the design. The little inlaid silver plates that express the figures are exquisitely shaped, and have details such as features of faces, hands, and folded draperies, engraved upon them with minute care.

An inscription running round the neck states that the ewer was made by Shuja ibn Hanfar at Mosul in the year 1232. This ewer is representative of a school supposed to have been centred at Mosul, a city in close touch with ancient and prolific copper-mines, and filled with craftsmen who were renowned for all sorts of artistic products; particularly, as a thirteenth-century writer quoted by M. Reinaud explicitly declares, for the manufacture of copper vessels for table service. But the same technique and similar decoration occur on work earlier in date made in regions to the north and east of Mosul, showing the school to have had Armenian and Persian connexions, which are not yet clearly defined.

As the technical processes and some elements in the decoration of the later pieces go back to Hellenistic traditions of the second century, it is not probable that Islamic developments originated in a local art current in these regions from remote times. The influence of this school spread rapidly through Syria to Egypt, a migration accelerated by the Mongol invasion, which laid the cities of Mesopotamia in ruins and dispersed their craftsmen. The capture of Baghdad by Hulagu, grandson of Chingiz Khan, and the death of the Caliph Musta'sim brought the Abbasid dynasty to an end in 1258.

The medallions placed at intervals in the ornamental bands acquired delicate floral borders, and the inscriptions, from being more or less subsidiary, became the most important features. These two examples must suffice to give some idea of the many lovely pieces that have come down to us, often in marvelous preservation. At the end of the fourteenth century the art of inlaying was already in decline. The Mongol irruption into Syria and the sack of Damascus by Timur in 1401 wrought havoc in busy centres, and the Ottoman conquest of Egypt in 1517 scattered the few remaining Cairo masters. But whilst it was decaying in its original home, the art was receiving increased attention in Europe, where it was destined to enjoy a brilliant rebirth. In the fifteenth century the Oriental trade established by Italian cities during the Crusades flourished exceedingly.

Eastern products became popular in the splendid pageantry of the petty Italian princes, whose workmen adopted them as models and began to emulate their triumphs. In Venice Muslim metal-work inspired native craftsmen so profoundly that a distinct Venetian-Oriental school arose in which Muslim technique and designs were adapted to

Italian Renaissance taste. It is inlaid in silver with an Islamic interlaced knot-pattern that recalls the bold Cairo ornament of earlier times, and has as a central feature a silver shield enamelled with the arms of the Occhi di Cane, a noble Veronese family.

Other pieces were modelled upon contemporary Persian work, which was then actually being made in Venice itself by Persian craftsmen settled in that city. During the thirteenth and fourteenth centuries metal-working had followed in Persia a course similar to that taken by the Mosul school with which it was intimately connected, but its progress was marked by increasing refinement in the shapes of the vessels and certain modifications in their decoration. At the beginning of the second national revival of Persian art, which dates from the rise of the Safavid dynasty in the opening years of the sixteenth century, these changes were fully developed into a new style, in which the inlays were generally reduced to linear patterns or inscriptions, set on grounds covered with minutely chased scrolling patterns.

As used by medieval Muslim craftsmen, gold and silver inlaying was in some measure an Oriental counterpart of the enamelled metal-work produced by contemporary European workers, whose champlevé process inlaid designs in coloured glass-pastes upon many objects which it was customary for the Muslims to enrich with precious metals by a similar method. Enamelling on metal was certainly practised in the Orient, but examples definitely Islamic are rare. Gold plaques enamelled in colours are mentioned in al-Maqrizi's inventory of the Fatimid treasures, and a metal disk with foliated ornament and an inscription enamelled in cloisonne, recovered from the rubbish heaps of Fustat and now in the Museum of Arab Art at Cairo, is apparently a relic of this period.

But the most important specimen of Muslim enameled metal-work known is a copper bowl in the Museum Ferdinandeum at Innsbruck, which is decorated in champlevé with a central medallion containing a representation of the Ascent of Alexander, surrounded by others filled with mythical beasts, set upon a ground enriched with palm-trees and standing figures. Although Byzantine in style, this bowl bears an inscription showing that it was made for an Ortuqid prince of Mesopotamia, who reigned towards the middle of the twelfth century. Judging from the few specimens that have come down to us, it would seem that enameling did not find favour with Muslim metal-workers.

It was not until the fifteenth century, when richly enamelled sword-furniture was made in Spain, that the art reappears in Islam; and t4welding their acquisitions from abroad into a distinct tradition, in of a jar of so-called Gabri ware, a kind of pottery supposed to have been made by Fire-worshippers, who in certain parts of Persia clung obstinately to their ancient religion long after the Arab conquest. In this the decoration is roughly but expressively drawn by cutting through the thin white clay 'slip', with which the surface is coated, to the brick-red body beneath.

The whole is then covered with a transparent glaze, tinted yellow, green, purple, or warm brown, colours in some cases distributed in irresponsible splashes in a way that recalls a contemporary Chinese practice. From the prevalence of Sasanian motives such as mounted huntsmen, mythical monsters, and characteristic foliated work Gabri ware was formerly assigned to the beginning of the Muhammadan era, but as examples have been found inscribed with Kufic letters of eleventh- or twelfth-century style, most of it is now dated from this period. The incised method of drawing, known as graffito work, was in common use in China, but did not necessarily originate there, as it also occurs in pre-Islamic Egypt.

Pieces dating from the tenth century have been discovered in the Near East, North Africa, and Spain, showing by their wide diffusion how the ware was esteemed throughout Islam, but leaving its place of origin in doubt. Whether it was first made in Egypt or Persia is still a moot point upon which authorities are somewhat hotly divided. Ray was a great centre of ceramic industry, where several characteristic types originated. Its ruins are a mine of lovely specimens. Definitely associated with this city are certain vases and dishes painted in opaque colours blue, green, red-brown, and purple, touched here and there with gold-leaf upon white or tinted grounds with figure subjects and formal decoration remarkable for their delicate workmanship, which resemble so closely the paintings in contemporary manuscripts that it would seem that the artists were inspired by them.

A pot so shaped was known to the Italians as an albarello, a term perhaps derived from the Arabic al-barnlya denoting a drug-jar. The name shows the purpose that such vessels served in the Orient and the use to which they continued to be put in Italy, In the fifteenth century Italian apothecaries' shops displayed many such pots, filled with drugs and preserves imported from the East. This trade brought westwards the prototypes of the Italian drug-jars in much the same way that Chinese ginger-jars still come to us.

The Italians obtained drug- jars painted in lustre from Valencia, the Islamic centre of this ware in the West, where examples that rank amongst the finest ever made were manufactured, sometimes to the order of foreign purchasers, whose arms were painted upon them. Renaissance designs with its unfading broke definitely with tradition.

In contrast to this design the second, is purely naturalistic, being made up of parallel waved stems bearing alternately vine-leaves and grapes, and almond-blossom. Both these motives, one formal and the other realistic, are combined in the third pattern, which adds a network of slender acanthus leaves punctuated with acanthus rosettes. Such elaboration of simple themes into complex designs in which apparently incongruous motives are skilfully played off against one another is characteristic of this school, and incidentally we see how methodically Islamic designers were experimenting with decorative ideas.

It is a fine example of Damascus work in the subdued blue, green, and purple scheme that distinguishes Syrian from Turkish wares. Turkish and Syrian potters used the same technique as in their tiles, and similar kinds of decoration, in beautiful dishes, bowls, vases, and other vessels of various forms. The red touches that enliven the colour scheme show Turkish origin. Red is not always present on pieces made in Asia Minor, but it is never found in Syrian work. The most striking decorative elements used in this kind of pottery are undoubtedly the floral forms, such as those displayed so profusely upon the Damascus panel, where tulips, roses, hyacinths, irises, and almond-blossom issue from two elegant vases in a splendid riot of vigorous growth.

The flowers are always drawn with consummate skill, and with such just decorative sense that their naturalism never sinks into mere pictorial representation. It was from Persia that the designers gathered their floral elements and learned how to draw them with such exquisite grace. From Persia, largely through Turkish and Syrian channels, Western art obtained certain flowers now commonly cultivated in our gardens, but once known in Europe only from representations of them seen on pottery and porcelain imported from the Islamic East.

The tulip was first brought to the West by Busbecq, imperial ambassador to Constantinople, about the middle of the sixteenth century. In Syria, where excellent native material for glass-manufacture had been exploited in ancient times, the Muslims developed a characteristic style of glass-decoration, seen upon numerous bottles, beakers, vases, and other objects painted with figure subjects and formal ornaments in coloured enamels, and often heightened with gold. Some examples enriched in ways that recall certain kinds of Persian and Mesopotamian pottery are assumed from technical reasons to be the earliest in date.

They were, perhaps, the work of Mesopotamian craftsmen who migrated to Syria during the first Mongol invasion, and established there the workshops that flourished so brilliantly throughout the fourteenth century, only to suffer extinction when Timur overran Syria in 1401. From Venice the art spread to other European centres, and developed new styles. The gaily enamelled spirit-bottles common in the seventeenth and eighteenth centuries are debased descendants of medieval Muslim skill.

Interesting as are the imitations they never rivalled their Oriental prototypes in either beauty of form or spontaneous directness in their ornamentation. The bowl has a similar design, enamelled in green, blue, red, and white, and is gilt in places. This fine piece, of uncommon shape, bears no name, but is inscribed 'Glory to our Lord the Sultan!' The most splendid achievements of the Syrian glass-workers were the lamps or rather lamp-shades, fitted internally with small oil-vessels hooked by wires to the rim which, suspended by three or more silver or brass chains attached to loops contrived on the body of the lamp, illuminated the gloom of many great mosques with jewel-like radiance.

They are generally ornamented with band-work filled with medallions and inscriptions, enlivened with conventional foliage; but in some the whole surface is covered with floral patterning, like a brocaded silk. Another, is treated in the same way, but bears a shield with the blazon/of the donor who dedicated it to some unknown mosque. Muslim nobles, following an ancient Oriental tradition, often set devices of heraldic character upon their belongings. Their use of such figures influenced the development of Western heraldry which, during the Crusades, evolved into a systematic science with a peculiar nomenclature of its own. In this the technical term for blue, azure, is derived from the Persian word denoting the blue stone called lapis lazuli.

There are other interesting links between European and Oriental heraldry, such as that curious figure the double-headed eagle which makes its first appearance in remote antiquity on Hittite monuments. It became the badge of the

Seljuk Sultans early in the twelfth century, and in the fourteenth was adopted as the blazon of the Holy Roman Emperors. Besides symbolical birds and beasts such as the eagle, which was fairly common, and the lion, borne by the Mamluk Sultan Baybars there were other devices of a different nature, attached to certain court functionaries the cup-bearer, the polo-master, and various military secretaries of state by virtue of their offices.

The significance of the chalice-like cup and the polo-sticks is obvious, but the meaning of the last figure in the series was long a perplexing question. The pointed shield on the tall bottle shows how a personal device an eagle sometimes accompanied an official badge. Muslim blazons were always brightly coloured if the means by which they were expressed rendered this possible, for a noble's colours were an important part of his arms. In Persia, Syria, and Egypt the sumptuous textile arts to which we shall now turn were already highly developed when the Arabs conquered those countries.

In the adjoining provinces of the Byzantine Empire important weaving centres were manufacturing silk fabrics of wonderful richness, and incorporating in their patterns many Sasanian elements taken over when Christian workers began to emulate their neighbours' skill. Although silken garments had been specifically prohibited by the Prophet, the Muslims not only encouraged existing silk factories but established new ones wherever they went. So shameless and unrestrained was their interest in the forbidden luxury that they rapidly and surely gained a dominating position as leading silk-mercers in the medieval world.

This is shown by the names by which many fabrics were known in the Middle Ages, trade terms that in some cases have persisted down to our own times, recording the distant places where certain materials were originally made, or the markets where they were procured. Thus the cloth known in Chaucer's time as 'fustian' came from Fustat, the first Muslim capital of Egypt. The stuffs we still call 'damasks' took their name from Damascus, that great trade-centre to which the West referred many things not exclusively made there. Our 'muslin' is the mussolina imported by Italian merchants from Mosul.

Baghdad, Italianized as 'Baldacco', gave its name to the rich silk fabrics brought thence and also to the silken canopy suspended over the altar in many churches, the 'baldacchino'. In later times dress fabrics from Granada were known as 'grenadines' in European shops, where ladies also bought Persian tdftah under the name of 'taffeta'. The 'Attabiyah quarter of Baghdad, where dwelt the descendants of 'Attab, great-grandson of a companion of the Prophet, was in the twelfth century renowned for a special fabric which, imitated in Spain, was known there as attabi silk. France and Italy adopted it as tabis, and by this trade name it became popular throughout Europe.

In 1661, on October 13 (Lord's Day), Mr. Pepys put on his 'false taby waste coate with gold lace', all unconscious of the word's ancient history; and in 1786 Miss Burney attended a royal birthday celebration at Windsor attired in a gown of 'lilac tabby', a tint known in Persia as llldq and brought westwards with the flowering shrub of that name. These beautiful watered silks are now out of fashion; but a brown and yellow attabi pattern is still worn by our familiar friend the tabby cat.

Although there is in Berlin a scrap that bears the magic name of Harun al-Rashid, silks associated with Baghdad are extremely rare. A fragment preserved in the Colegiata de San Isidore at Leon bears an inscription definitely stating that it was woven at Baghdad, perhaps by a master called Abu Nasr, a name that appears in the mutilated lettering in a place where the maker's signature might well be put. Woven in red, yellow, black, and white, the design is a characteristic early Islamic pattern of about the end of the tenth century in date, showing birds, beasts, and foliated ornaments inherited from an older tradition set in and around large circular panels.

A prominent element, the elephant, probably came from India. This beast occurs on a somewhat earlier Persian silk discovered a few years ago in a village church near Calais, a piece which is now one of the treasures of the Louvre. It is also found on several Byzantine imitations of Persian fabrics, notably on the magnificent silk preserved in the tomb of Charlemagne at Aachen. In Europe the demand for rich silk textiles increased rapidly as the Oriental trade developed. Finely wrought stuffs came from Muslim countries in such quantity that Western enterprise saw in this lucrative industry a potential source of wealth, and, setting up looms in various centres, began seriously to compete with the Eastern and Spanish factories.

It was largely from Sicily, where Muslim invaders had established in the royal palace at Palermo a famous weaving-house which continued to flourish when the island reverted to Christian rule under the Normans that the first Italian workers gained their technical knowledge and models for their designs. During the Norman occupation the Sicilian school was reinforced by contact with Byzantine traditions brought in when a number of Greek weavers, captured in a raid into the Aegean seas in 1 147, were installed in the palace work- shops. At the beginning of the thirteenth century silk-weaving was already the chief industry in several opulent Italian cities, where fabrics, hard to distinguish from the Sicilian stuffs they imitated, were produced and exported in profusion.

In the fourteenth century Italian silks reflected new influences which were then affecting Muslim art. In the blue and white silk fabric brocaded with gold are seen not only the lions, palmettes, and foliated work, Arabic inscriptions, and other Oriental elements usual in Italian work of this period, but also characteristic Chinese birds. Their appearance in Europe was largely due to events that had brought about great changes in the Far East. In 1280 the nomad Mongols under Kublai Khan, brother of Hulagu, who had overthrown the Abbasids in 1258, invaded China, and set up the Yuan dynasty which lasted until 1367.

As a result of these conquests a wide stretch of Asia, extending from Persia to the Pacific, was for nearly a century ruled by members of the same Mongol house, a circumstance that led to a remarkable interchange of artistic traditions between eastern and western Asia. In China an imposing Muhammadan population had sprung from colonies planted there during the T'ang dynasty, using, as happened wherever Islam spread, the Arabic language. It included many craftsmen, among whom were silk-weavers, who, working with the skill hereditary in the ancient home of silk-culture, produced at unknown centres fabrics that were prized throughout Islam. Their beautiful stuffs so appealed to their Western brethren that they affected everywhere the development of Muslim textile design, and, through this channel, the textiles of Western Europe.

Some superb examples of medieval Chinese workmanship have survived; the most remarkable is, perhaps, a piece preserved at Danzig which must have been specially made for the Mamluk Sultan al-Nasir Muhammad ibn Qala'un, whose name is woven into the design. Not only in the Middle Ages but also in later times Oriental silks were often made up into church vestments. The chasuble was cut from a Persian fabric of late sixteenth- or early seventeenth-century make, with a pattern by no means suitable for the purpose to which it was put, and one that most certainly would not have been tolerated in a mosque.

Its main elements are rows of standing youths attired in court dress, holding cups and wine-bottles. They are set amidst slender trailing stems bearing foliage and flowers of the kind that the Turkish potters were then closely copying; in the interspaces are lively birds posed and drawn in a manner that points to a Chinese origin. The design belongs to a group of similar gay patterns fashionable upon such brocades during the Safavid period. Elaborate examples were even more pictorial in character, showing episodes from romantic histories, such as the meeting of Khusrau and Shlrin or the woeful story of Laila and Majnun, and sometimes enriched with veritable landscapes of flowering trees and shrubs wherein roam all sorts of kindly or ferocious beasts, drawn and coloured with irresistible spirit and brilliance.

The pattern on the silk strip used for the orphrey introduces an interesting series of textile designs produced during a period when Turkish and Italian weavers were so actively and successfully imitating each others' stuffs that experts often find it difficult to distinguish fabrics as definitely of European or of Oriental origin. Although late in date and European in appearance, this piece has a Turkish pattern of a type that arose in Asia Minor some time in the fifteenth century. In their simplest forms these patterns are composed of plain or decorated bands running vertically in opposed curves which, uniting at intervals, cover the field with a net-like design. Some examples have more or less elaborated formal ornaments set within the meshes of the net, as in the pattern on the orphrey; whilst in others similar elements spring from the bands at their junctions.

Within the interspaces left by the main system secondary netting is contrived, from which spring roses, tulip century buds, pinks, and narcissus flowers. From flower-knops, such as the main element in this design, the Italians evolved the floral elements, and the very similar one used in the late fifteenth-century velvet. During the sixteenth century European and Turkish weavers, each alternately outdoing their rivals, worked out many intricate variations of the net and knop theme, and gave the rich velvets so fashionable at this period the special type of pattern that became traditionally associated with them.

It was a pattern of this kind that William Morris designed for the sumptuous brocaded velvet woven in blue, orange, white, and gold which was his sole attempt to revive these costly fabrics. The carpet, now a universal necessity, came into Europe from the Orient as a luxury reserved for wealthy connoisseurs, who at first regarded it more as a treasure than as a thing of use. Carpets, both with smooth faces like tapestries, and with loose threads knotted into the fabric so as to produce a velvet-like 'pile' surface, are of great antiquity in the East, where they served as sleeping-mats and hangings, as well as coverings for floors. From representations of Oriental rugs in Italian pictures it is known that they came to Europe at least as early as the fourteenth century.

In the sixteenth they were regular articles of commerce. It is recorded that in 1521 Cardinal Wolsey, through the good offices of the Venetian ambassador, secured sixty Oriental rugs for his palace at Hampton Court. They probably resembled examples seen in pictures by Holbein, which can be matched by existing carpets made in Asia Minor at that time. At Boughton House, in Northamptonshire, are preserved three pile carpets specially made for Sir Edward Montagu, with his arms and the date, 1584, woven in the border. Of a type known then, as now, as 'Turkey' carpets, they are decorated with shaped ornaments, coloured blue and enlivened with detail in yellow, set upon a red ground.

In the sixteenth century Persian craftsmen carried carpet-weaving to heights never attained before or since, producing with miraculous skill designs unparalleled in beauty. One of these masterpieces, brought from Ardabll where it lay for centuries in the mosque of Shaykh Safi the venerated ancestor of the Safavid Shahs is now in the Victoria and Albert Museum. In the centre is a large medallion with serrated edges, surrounded by pointed oval panels, all enriched with foliated work in glowing colours. A quarter of the central element is repeated in each corner of the rectangular field, which is of deep blue covered with gay flowers issuing from meandering stems, amidst which two lamps, represented as if suspended in mid-air, form secondary centres in the design.

The diversity of style to which we are accustomed in European relief work, where sculpturesque and pictorial influences unknown in Muslim countries have become traditional, is absent in Islamic carving and modelling, in which repeating patterns similar to or precisely the same as those used in weaving, inlaying, or painting are generally found. Such patterns were adapted to decorative purposes in ways wholly foreign to European usage. A design that served to enrich the title-page of an illuminated manuscript, or as the pattern of a silk fabric, would be deemed equally suitable for carving in stone upon the exterior of a dome, or the walls of a mosque. The white marble fountain-basin inscribed with the name of Muhammad II, Sultan of Hama uncle of Abu-1-Fida the historian shows how the carver adapted a type of design common to several crafts to his special needs.

The scheme is essentially a repeating pattern; its elements might be extended indefinitely either laterally as a border or frieze, or both laterally and vertically as an 'all-over' design. Similar ornament is carved on the long frieze and in the panels of the wooden casing from the tomb of a Shaikh who died in 1216. One side of this remarkably rich example is at South Kensington, and the rest at Cairo. In carvings of the Fatimid period the ground was often sunk very deeply, with almost the effect of pierced work, a panel in the Museum of Arab Art at Cairo. Although made in Sicily, the carved wooden ceiling is Fatimid in style. Besides showing how effective are such deeply cut panels, it has amongst the leafage in its ornament numerous birds and beasts, features often seen in Fatimid work designed for court or secular decoration, in which human figures were also freely used.

This ceiling follows the characteristic method of construction adopted by Islamic carpenters, a system which arose from considerations both practical and decorative. Climatic conditions that rendered wood very liable to shrink and warp, and scarcity of suitable timber, led to panels being reduced to the smallest possible dimensions, and to a corresponding increase in the supporting framework. To secure stability and variety of interest in the designs, a strangely elaborate method of assembling small panels was gradually evolved, a scheme that actually expressed by structural means pattern-schemes in which the Muslims took particular delight.

Designs made up of various polygonal shapes radiating from, stars form a type of ornament that is, perhaps, the most characteristic Islamic contribution to decorative art. In woodwork, which played a great part in developing the type, it finds its most complete expression, but such patterns were used by many craftsmen working in different arts. The designing of them exercised ingenious spirits everywhere throughout Islam, and if in later times they tended to become irritatingly intricate and to degenerate into over-conscious spectacular geometry, their simpler forms were always singularly effective vehicles for displaying the rich colour-schemes in which Muslim genius was so adept.

In the original the geometrical setting-out, shown by thin lines in the diagram, is scratched with a pointed tool upon the paper, and the pattern is drawn in ink upon this basis. The method used is instructive, as it probably records an ancient workshop tradition, showing how Oriental designers set about a task which may be tackled in many different ways as the very considerable literature devoted to these patterns testifies. In 'one of them the panels are carved with foliated ornament cut in sharp relief, and in the other they are inlaid with geometrical patterns. The Muslims produced many beautiful things made partly or wholly of ivory, a substance which they decorated with carved, inlaid, or painted ornament. In the tenth century a school of ivory-carvers centred at Cordoba was working in a style that already proclaims mature experience.

Amongst the extant examples of their work is the cylindrical casket, from the cathedral of Zamora, which is now exhibited in the Museo Arquelogico at Madrid. Around the domed lid runs an inscription stating that it was made in the year 964 for the Caliph al-Hakam II, as a gift to his wife, the mother of prince 'Abd-al-Rahman. The finest example of a group that includes several similar objects made in Cordoba at about the same date, it is entirely covered with palmette leafage, peacocks and other birds, and beasts. Other specimens now in London, Paris, and elsewhere, although similar in shape and workmanship, have different ornament, being carved with interlaced lobed circles enclosing figure subjects.

This piece is the work of several craftsmen, the names of two of them Khayr and 'Ubayda being legible upon panels they carved. It was made in 1005 for a court functionary whose name and titles are prominently inscribed upon the lid. This is representative of a series thought to have been made in Cairo in the fourteenth century. Dating from the thirteenth century, and rather vaguely described as 'Siculo-Arabic', are a number of plain cylindrical and rectangular ivory boxes painted in colours and gold, with circles filled with knot-work or with figures, beasts and birds, flowers and trees, in a style that recalls illuminated manuscripts.

Ivory caskets, painted, carved, or pierced, were used as jewel-cases, perfume or sweetmeat boxes, and for other similar purposes. They were often, as the inscriptions testify, made specially as gifts. The earliest are amongst the most valuable records of Islamic art in its beginnings. Many have come down to us in wonderful completeness, but judging from the traces of colour still visible on some specimens, it is probable that the carved caskets in their original state were resplendent with colour and gold.

Some still retain their metal hinges and clasps, fittings which are interesting examples of a minor branch of the metalworker's art. This superb work is historically important, for it bears the name of al-'Aziz, the second Fatimid Caliph of Egypt, and may well be one of the crystal ewers mentioned in al-Maqrizi's inventory of the treasures dispersed in 1067, because they had this Caliph's name engraved on them. In workmanship and design it is a worthy memorial of a period that marks an epoch in Islamic art.

Amongst the things in everyday use that owe something of their substance, technique, or design to Islam, our printed books are, perhaps, the most widespread. Although at first sight their connexion with the Orient may appear remote, modern methods of book-production have gained much from medieval Muslim enterprise and skill. It was only in recent times that Islamic literature began to be reproduced by mechanical means, either from type or by lithography, the latter process being specially favoured, as it faithfully preserved the actual work of the scribe, the most honoured of all craftsmen. But although printing was perfected in Europe long before it spread to Muslim countries, it is to the Orient that we owe a substance that was a great, if not the chief, factor in its development.

Paper, an ancient Chinese invention, became known to the Muslims when they captured Samarqand in 704, and learned how to make it from Chinese workmen. Its use spread westwards throughout Islam. A considerable number of Arabic manuscripts written on paper date from the ninth century, but it was not imported into Christian Europe until the twelfth, and was still uncommon there in the thirteenth.

The first European paper factories were established by the Muslims in Spain and Sicily, whence the manufacture passed into Italy. When in the fifteenth century book-production was commercialized by the introduction of mechanical apparatus, paper became an essential material in the manufacture of machine-made books, without which printing could hardly have progressed as it did. It is not, however, solely for paper that the modern publisher is indebted to the Muslims. During the fifteenth century, when Venice was so actively absorbing and scattering abroad Islamic fashions in art, books bound in Italian workshops assumed a very Oriental appearance. At this period some volumes took on a peculiarity common in Muslim bindings, the flap that folds over to protect the front edges.

This feature still persists in certain bindings made for accountants such as our bankers' 'passbooks' and is a memorial of their Oriental descent. Another innovation inspired by Muslim work was a new method of decorating leather covers. In the Middle Ages European binders often enriched leather covers by impressing devices upon them by means of metal dies, a process that developed effective schemes as the stamps became larger and more elaborate in design, and cleverly devised units giving a wide range of repeating surface patterns and borders came more generally into use. But ornament produced by 'blind tooling', as it is termed, was expressed only in relief until Oriental workers began to enrich stamped designs by filling the sunk parts with gold paint, a practice introduced into Europe by Muslim binders settled in Venice.

Towards the end of the fifteenth century this method was supplemented by a new process, in which the gold was permanently fixed by re-impressing the heated tool through gold-leaf. This new departure appears to have originated at Cordoba. In the sixteenth century it was universally used by both Christian and Islamic binders, although the older Oriental way of using gold was never entirely superseded. The result obtained by the Oriental use of gold is seen in the superb patterns worked on the late fourteenth or early fifteenth century binding.

It is a marvel of clear, delicate design, patiently executed by making an infinite number of impressions with a few simple tools. The crimson leather cover has a central device stamped and enriched with gold; above and beneath it, and in each corner, are shaped panels sunk below the surface and decorated with lace-like ornament cut out of thin white leather and pasted on a black ground. A formal landscape, with trees, birds, and beasts amongst which is a dragon from the Far East is painted in gold upon the plain field.

The Venetian sixteenth-century cover has similar sunk panels and painted decorations obviously imitated from a

Persian model. The Egyptian binding has a central pointed oval panel, which is quartered in each corner, and the Persian cover is decorated with a variant of the same scheme, a plan, as we have already seen, common to many crafts. A similar design, with central and corner devices of Muslim origin and linear work of Oriental inspiration, is tooled in gold upon a Venetian cover, dated 1546, the same arrangement appears in a later German example, although the details are now being modified in accordance with contemporary European fashions.

These four bindings trace roughly the development of certain technical processes that, originating in Muslim lands, found their way into European workshops and brought with them schemes of design and ornamental elements which, with slight changes, have become firmly incorporated in modern practice. The gold tooling and lettering now universal upon fine leather bindings are expressed by means that were perfected by Muslim workers; and when, in the nineteenth century, mechanically produced book-covers began to supplement ancient hand-work, machine-bound books to a great extent merely stereotyped ways of working that hark back to Islamic origins.

The gaily decorated 'marbled' patterns so common upon end-papers., paper covers, and edges of books bound in European workshops during the eighteenth century, were directly derived from Oriental sources. Delicate examples of such patterns occur on strips of paper pasted round the margins of Muslim drawings and specimens of calligraphy mounted during the sixteenth century for connoisseurs whose fastidious taste required elaborately contrived settings for their treasures. Marbled papers were known in England in Bacon's time; he tells us that 'the Turkes have a pretty art of chamoletting of paper, which is not with us in use.

They take divers oyled colours, and put them severally (in drops) upon water; and stirre the water lightly, and then wet their paper, (being of some thicknesse,) with it, and the paper will be waved, and veined, like Chamolet or Marble.' Books bound in the West towards the end of the sixteenth century are found with end-papers brought from the Orient, but it was not until about a century later that European binders began to make them themselves. Handmade marbled papers are now rarely used, but more or less clumsily reproduced imitations still serve various purposes.

For more than a thousand years Europe has looked upon Islamic art as a thing of wonder; at first largely because it was closely associated with lands deemed the Christian heritage, but later solely by reason of its own intrinsic beauty. Many of its rich products owe their preservation to medieval piety, for not a few have rested secure for ages in churches, where a casket that had served as a Caliph's jewel-case became the repository of sacred relics, perhaps brought in it from the Holy Land wrapped in a scrap of splendid silk cut from a Muslim robe of honour.

The awe with which such things were regarded found appropriate meanings for the strange figures and mysterious writings upon them, thought sometimes to be talismans and characters in the tradition of Solomon, or even to date from his time, for in the Middle Ages archaeology was nothing if not romantic. It was only in the last century that the cold light of research dared to throw doubts upon the associations which had long hallowed some remarkable treasures as gifts from Harun al-Rashid to Charlemagne, or as acquired by Saint Louis in the Orient. But whether such things were paraded under false colours or not, their magnificence was real enough.

Masterpieces that every craftsman revered, they were always an inspiration to those who devoted themselves to arts neglected in the West. Intercourse between Christians and Muslims began in times long prior to the Crusades. In Spain Islam was firmly established upon the very frontiers of Western Europe, and from the first exercised profound influence upon Christian culture. In Sicily the two religions occupied common ground, while North Africa was wholly ruled by the Muslims, whose ships swept the Mediterranean from end to end. With the Crusades a new era opened. The half-fabulous magnificence traditionally ascribed to the Saracens became a reality to astonished Christendom.

A host drawn from every part of Europe came suddenly into close contact with a social order that in every respect outranged the narrow limits of their experience. In every activity of life the reactions of this impact with alien progress soon became apparent, and in art its results were by no means the least far-reaching. As time went on Italian merchant's established direct traffic with Syrian ports, Oriental trade became regularly organized, and all kinds of rare things from Islamic workshops arrived in European markets. These imports met new-found needs, aroused emulation wherever they went, and opened up lines of development either immediately or in subtle ways destined to mature in the future.

During that critical period when the West was emerging from medieval conditions, forces aroused and fostered by religious enthusiasm entered upon another phase of energy centred wholly in commercial activities. In the fifteenth century European craftsmen, impelled by Muslim success in the sumptuous and lucrative arts that had become essential to Renaissance splendour, turned with renewed interest to the Orient. Moved by deeper study of Islamic methods, they reviewed and enlarged their own technical procedure, and in so doing were no longer content to absorb such ornamental elements as came by the way. They began to explore intently Muslim canons of design, and to adapt them in a new spirit to work that was purely European in conception.

Not only humble craftsmen, but also outstanding figures like Leonardo da Vinci, experimented with Oriental pattern-work, developed from a rough sketch in one of his note-books, records his interest in such studies. These innovations were not always results of direct observation, for early in the sixteenth century a new method of spreading the inspiration came into being, the 'pattern-book', an immediate product of the printing-press. By means of such collections specimens of master designers' researches in the new style became known to those to whom access to original sources was difficult.

One of the most interesting pattern-books is the rare volume by Francesco di Pellegrino, whose examples are wholly derived from Islamic models. From this and contemporary pattern-books of the same kind such as those by Peter Flotner, Virgil Solis, Martinus Petrus, and others it is instructive to turn to the designs by Holbein, in whose drawings for silver- smiths and workers in other crafts Muslim inspirations are skilfully welded into an original style.

In the seventeenth and eighteenth centuries Dutch and English enterprise was reaping the fruits of Vasco da Gama's adventure into the Indies. A new stream of trade flowed in ever increasing volume directly from the Orient, and influenced crafts closely connected with everyday life, which, attracting an increasing demand, were now being organized in ways that fore-shadowed modern industrial developments. From Muhammadan Asia came many seemingly insignificant things which, becoming necessities, have found not only European favour but spread throughout the civilized world.

Cargoes of cottons and 'chintzes' printed with gaily coloured patterns brought a new vogue in textiles, which, developed in the 'persiennes' of Paris, gave ladies in the time of Queen Anne pretty dress fabrics, and, later, brought wealth to Manchester. New 'shawls', as their name tells us, came from Persia. Certain forms of tea and coffee pots, imitated perhaps from Moghul ewers brought back from India by opulent nabobs, were still common on Victorian breakfast tables, and have persisted in modified shapes until today.

Ever since the beginnings of Islam, Western piety, learning, commerce, and curiosity have found each something to its taste in the products of Muslim skill; but in knowledge of their technical excellence and their beauty master craftsmen such as Odericus of Rome, who in 1286 wrought Islamic patterns upon the inlaid marble pavement of the Presbytery of Westminster Abbey, and William Morris, who wove another into his velvet in 1884, together with a host of others before, since, and between them, have time and again refreshed Western art from a fund which has been to us rather an annuity than a legacy.

There is no evidence of any Muhammadan paintings having been brought to Europe before the seventeenth century, and Rembrandt is believed to have been the first painter in the West who was sufficiently interested in Oriental art to make copies of some pictures that had reached Holland from the far East portraits of members of the imperial family of Delhi. Any direct influence of the pictorial art of the Muslim world upon any individual artist in Europe is therefore excluded; still less is there evidence that any great movement in the art of painting in Europe has been stimulated by influences from the Muslim East; it is impossible, for example, to trace to Islam any new direction in pictorial art similar to that which manifested itself in Italian painting in the fifteenth and sixteenth centuries as the result of the revived interest in classical art.

Such Muhammadan influences as are traceable, tend, therefore, to be superficial; but they make their appearance in Europe at quite an early period of the Arab domination in the waters of the Mediterranean. From Oriental fabrics were copied several representations of animals, such as appear in the eleventh-century manuscript of the commentary on the Apocalypse by Beatus in the Bibliotheque Nationale, and in several other manuscripts, especially those of the school of Limoges during the early Middle Ages; but the effect of the direct contact of the Christian world with Muhammadan culture and of the importation of objects of Oriental art, was never so marked in painting as it was in sculpture, architecture, or metal-work.

It exhibits itself chiefly in the adaptation of Oriental motifs for ornamental purposes and is for the most part confined to sub-ordinate details. These decorative motifs, though brought to the notice of western artists by the importation of Muhammadan silks and other objects of Muhammadan manufacture, were not confined to such characteristic features as were devised by the followers of Islam themselves, but included also those which Muhammadans had taken over from their predecessors; and among such artistic heritages from the past are several conventional designs of great antiquity, such as the Chaldean sacred tree, which passed on, through Sasanian art, into the Muslim period.

This tree of life, in accordance with the primitive type, was often flanked by two beasts facing each other, but the Christian artists often omitted the central feature of the design, the sacred tree; among other primitive, pre-Muslim designs are the two animals, one the prey of the other, and animals with two heads and a single body. They occur more frequently in sculpture than in painting, and in the latter case were possibly often copied from similar carvings on capitals and bas-reliefs in churches. Of the presence of Muslim artists working for Christian patrons on the continent of Europe during the early Middle Ages, such as those who decorated the Palatine Chapel at Palermo for Roger II (1101-54), there appears to be no evidence.

During the period of the Crusades more frequent intercourse with the Muslim East facilitated the importation of objects bearing specifically Muhammadan decorative motifs, and in the country of those centres of commercial communication with the East Genoa, Pisa, and Venice these motifs became introduced into paintings. Consequently, an interest in the Oriental world, stimulated largely by curiosity and the fascination of the unfamiliar, manifests itself in the early products of the Sienese school of painting, and becomes more prominent in Tuscan art.

Turbaned figures and Oriental physiognomies make their appearance in such Italian pictures as early as the second half of the fourteenth century; such foreign personages generally take a subordinate place in the representation of a sacred scene, and it is in the accessories that Oriental influence make themselves especially felt, e.g. in the copying of Persian and other carpets, the clothing of even the more important persons in Oriental stuffs, and the introduction of exotic animals, such as leopards, apes, and parrots. In details of landscape, also, it is possible to recognize details of trees and foliage that appear to be deliberate imitations of Oriental designs.

A borrowing of a particularly Oriental character occurs in the frequent adaptation of Arabic letters for decorative purposes. This is one of the first examples of the direct influence of Muslim art on Christian workmen to attract the attention of European scholars, and since Adrien de Longperier published his article, 'De 1'emploi des caracteres arabes dans Pornementation, chez les peuples Chretiens de Poccident', in the Revue arcbeologique, in 1846, an increasing number of instances have been collected, the richest collection of which is to be found in the learned articles of Mr. A. H. Christie in the Burlington Magazine.

Such an ornamental use of Arabic characters appears in Italian painting as early as Giotto (e.g. on the right shoulder of the figure of Christ in the Resurrection of Lazarus, in the Arena Chapel, Padua). Fra Angelico and Fra Lippo Lippi were especially fond of this kind of decoration, and employed it even for the sleeves of the Virgin and the borders of her robe obviously entirely in ignorance of the origin of such shapes. The source of their knowledge of this script must be sought in the many pieces of silk and other fabrics brought into Europe from the East, or in lamps and other brass vessels.

Architecture

A Generation hence it may be possible to estimate with some confidence the legacy of the Islamic world to architecture; but in the present state of scholarship so much doubt exists as to several important aspects of Muhammadan architecture that only a violent partisan can feel sure of his ground. It is unfortunate that much recent research, which should have thrown light on uncertain points, has been presented to us in the form of polemical arguments. These are not mainly concerned with the nature of Muslim architecture in its maturer periods, still less with its effect on the evolution of architecture in our Western world, but rather with its origins and its earlier buildings.

Nevertheless, they have a direct bearing on the question of its legacy to mankind, for we cannot fairly recognize a bequest from Islam unless there is some proof that Islam possessed the original f title. In other words, so many things in Muhammadan architecture are said to have been stolen from non-Islamic peoples that some scholars actually hold that the Muslims were mere borrowers of the architectonic forms and had no architecture of their own worth the name. To reach a conclusion on this fundamental point, it is necessary in the first instance to attempt a brief outline of the origins and nature of Muhammadan architecture in general.

The Arabs, who within a half-century swept like a desert whirlwind from the Hijaz to the Pillars of Hercules in the West and to the confines of India in the East, conquered countries already civilized. Their dominions extended over an area wider than that of the Roman Empire at its greatest extent, and embraced many nations whose architecture differed from that of Rome and in some cases was far older. Whatever position one may assume in the bitter controversy between those who believe in the mainly Roman origin of our Western medieval architecture, and those who attribute everything to Iran or Armenia, it is becoming clear that the latter school of thought demands our serious attention.

A series of remarkable discoveries in Armenia, Mesopotamia, and Turkistan, though revealed to us in a bellicose way, has shaken our confidence in the ultra-Roman point of view. It may be that the Church has fostered for centuries a belief that our 'Romanesque' and Gothic buildings rose from the ashes of Imperial Rome, or that pedantic humanists of the Renaissance are to blame for our misconceptions. But whatever the cause, it is evident that now we must look eastwards with an impartial mind, at the outset getting rid of the habit of regarding 'the East' as a single entity. Hardly any one seriously doubts the fact of our debt to Rome; the time has come, however, to reconsider the extent of our obligation.

Of the territory subdued by the Arab conquerors, Syria, part of Armenia, and the habitable part of North Africa including Egypt were taken from the East Roman Empire; Spain was captured from the Visigoths, but had previously been a Roman province; and the lands from Mesopotamia to Turkistan and Afghanistan constituted the former Sasanian kingdom of Chosroes II. Christianity had penetrated the whole of this vast area up to the eastern frontier of Armenia and Syria, and there was a sixth-century cathedral as far south as San'a' in Yemen (southern Arabia).

The conquerors therefore found, ready to hand, skilled builders in every one of the subject provinces, and a great number of buildings which they, like the Coptic and Visigothic Christians before them, freely used as stone-quarries. Much has been made of this undeniable fact, but one must remember also that the Arabs found native craftsmen in the eastern provinces of their dominions who built in a style quite foreign to that of the Romans, and who, if we are to believe certain authorities, taught the Byzantine architects everything that makes Byzantine work differ from that of Rome.

There is no need to dispute the view commonly and justifiably held that the first Arab conquerors had no architectural skill or taste. In the nature of things it must have been so. Such a conquest was only possible to a race of soldiers inspired by religious enthusiasm, whose time was necessarily occupied mainly in fighting and praying. Moreover, they were not a town-dwelling people but nomads; and even when they forsook fighting to take up the task of government, they inevitably relied for technical skill in the building arts on craftsmen they found on the spot, or (and this is important) on craftsmen brought from one conquered country to another.

Thus it is known that Armenian masons were employed not only in Egypt but in Spain, and perhaps at the ninth-century church of Germigny-des-Pres in France, which has several Muhammadan features. But in spite of the Arabs' probable ignorance of architecture in the early years of conquest, the remarkable and incontrovertible fact about Muslim architecture is that in all countries and in all cent unmistakable individuality of its own., although its origin so diverse.

There was something about it that differentiated it from the work of all the local schools of craftsmanship which were technically instrumental in bringing it into being. The factor that transmuted and welded a host of varying modes of building into one style possessing individual characteristics was presumably tile faith of Islam; for the buildings erected by the Arabs in their early years were chiefly mosques and palaces a most of the important architectural works of subsequent centuries continued to be mosques or other religious buildings, such as madrasahs and convents, containing mosques.

The mosque was the typical and principal Arab building varying to some extent in form with different localities, but always retaining its main features. The annual pilgrimage to Mecca from all parts of the Islamic world doubtless contributed to the standardization or the mosque form, for in each town that the pilgrim passed through on his long journey he would make his prayers in the local mosque, and it he happened to be a building craftsman or an architect he would notice its design. The primitive mosque at Madmah, built by Muhammad in 22, was the prototype of all others, it was a square enclosure surrounded by walls of brick and stone. The roots were probably made of palm branches covered with mud and resting on palm-trunks.

The congregation Knelt facing north, the direction of the holy city of Jerusalem, and this direction (qiblah) was marked in some way. In 624 the direction for prayer was changed from Jerusalem to Mecca; that is (in the case of Madmah) from north to south, there was no need to borrow architectural features from anywhere tor no architectural features were required.

This short list includes all the chief ritual requirements of the mosque in all periods. None of the buildings mentioned retains its original structure and even their plans have been lost in successive alterations. But the plan is all that matters, for the primitive mosque was barely a building and certainly not a work of architecture as we understand it. But such conjecture seems hardly necessary or appropriate: it is not until the Arabs begin to translate this religious enclosure and shelter into architecture that the question of origins arises. The transition from bare necessity to attempts at dignity and splendour was very rapid surprisingly so when one considers the austerity of the Islamic cult and the severity of the campaigning life led by so many of its votaries.

Within twenty years of Muhammad's death, his own mosque at Madman was rebuilt with walls and piers of dressed stone. The Dome of the Rock wasn't elaborate stone building, strictly speaking a mashhad ('place of witness') where pilgrims circumambulated the Rock, the spot whence Muhammad was believed to have ascended to Heaven. Moreover, it remained unique; and for four centuries at least there was no important attempt at departure from the normal square congregational mosque with its open court. It has therefore been assumed, far too plausibility, in this view, but it must not be pressed too far.

In evolving this new type of building, an aisled rotunda, the Arabs had a definite purpose in mind. They wished to glorify and shelter the Sacred Rock of Jerusalem, already in ancient object of devotion to Muslims as well as Jews; and they desired to erect a building which should rival and surpass the famous Christian church of the Holy Sepulcher near by. The new Mashhad was placed in the middle of a spacious rock plateau, known as the Haram al-Sharif, or 'Koly Sanctuary', on a great terrace or podium.

In adopting the dome, or more precisely the 'annular rotunda', for the distinctive feature of their shrine, the Arabs showed sound judgement; and it is true that the dome had been used in this way, as the culminating and controlling element of a building designed to shelter a tomb or other venerated place, by both Romans and Byzantines before them. But these were not the only dome-builders on earth; and Strzygowski, the protagonist of Iranian inspiration, argues that the Eastern dome originated in Asia Minor or farther east, passed through Armenia to Byzantium and thence to the Balkans and Russia under the patronage of the Greek Church.

Thus, though the Arabs here used a dome for the first time, they were adopting a feature which was not exclusively Christian or even exclusively Roman, and were probably copied from the famous 'Anastasias' dome, adjoining it and of almost identical size. For the rest, the walls are of solid stone, the arches of the internal arcade and of the window-openings are semicircular, and the whole of the columns used in the two arcades are antiques, taken from old buildings, pagan or Christian. Hence neither the shafts nor "the capitals of these columns are uniform in style.

Across the springing of the arches are massive timber ties, probably introduced to resist the shocks of earthquakes prevalent in the locality, or perhaps because the builders were nervous of trusting the arch alone; similar precautions are to be found in Byzantine buildings. The dome itself is double and constructed entirely of timber, covered externally with lead and internally "with modelled "arid, painted plaster, but it is not the original structure. Much of the mosaic work is original, but most of the remaining decorations are of later date.

Hence we find that, at the Dome of the Rock, the innovations are the domical plan, the use of semicircular arches, timber ties, and perhaps mosaic. The semicircular arch was decidedly not an Arab invention, the origin of timber ties is doubtful, and the earliest use of mosaic is pre-Islamic. After the Dome of the Rock, the next important Muslim building in chronological order is the Great Mosque at Damascus, erected in the first years of the eighth century. The principal lawn or sanctuary is a lofty apartment with doors or screens in the arches separating it from the sahn. Arcaded porticoes also surround the remaining three sides of the sahn. The new features in this mosque are numerous. The principal lawn has three aisles, crossed by a central transept, over the middle of which is a dome.

The aralias surrounding the central court are carried partly on piers and partly on columns, and the arches are of the 'horseshoe' form which was destined to become characteristic of Western Muslim architecture, for some not very apparent reason. A horseshoe may be round or pointed at the top, but in either case its curve is carried down below the 'springing line'. At Damascus the round horseshoe arch is used. Above the main arcade, all round the sahn is a range of semicircular-headed windows, two to each arch. Of the four Roman towers that once stood at the angles of the terminus within which the mosque was built, and which were used by the Arabs as minarets, only one (at the south-west angle) now remains, the other minarets being later in date.

The horseshoe arch has been found in pre-Islamic buildings, carved in the rock, but its occurrence at Damascus is one of the earliest cases where it has a true structural function. The first instance of a tower being utilized for this purpose seems to have been at Damascus. The earliest surviving minaret is that of the Great Mosque at Qayrawan near Tunis, and is recorded to have been built during the caliphate of Hisham (724-43). It is a huge and massive square tower, tapering slightly upwards, crowned with battlement is, and surmounted by two stages, one built at a later date.

Even if it is true that the four square towers at Damascus were the first minarets adapted to that end, it does not seem that a perfectly plain structure, such as that at Qayrawan, need be ascribed to Syria or any other special place of origin. It is an instance of ritual requirement met in the simplest and most straightforward way. Otherwise, the mosque at Qayrawan is of the congregational type, frequently altered, but retaining in the main the form in which it was rebuilt at the end of the ninth century.

The mosque of Zaytunah at Tunis, founded in 732, is another early and interesting example of the congregational type, with arcades formed of unpleasantly stilted arches supported on antique columns. Over the capitals of the arches are wooden blocks or abaci, connected by wooden tie-beams. This device mars the effect of many early Muslim buildings. The Great Mosque at Cordoba in Spain, begun in 786, continues the succession. Its area was more than doubled in the tenth century, but its original form may still be recalled by a careful study of the existing structure. It was a congregational mosque with a very deep sanctuary, containing eleven aisles separated by arcades, each with twenty columns.

These columns, as in other cases already mentioned, were taken from older Roman buildings. The enormous size of the sanctuary made it desirable to have a proportionately lofty ceiling, much loftier in fact than the height of the available columns with ordinary horseshoe arches above them. So a second range of arches was built at a higher level, creating a complicated and restless effect that is far from pleasing. Thus we find that the use of readymade antique columns dictated the whole design of the arcade, both at Qayrawan and Cordoba, whereas the introduction of brick or stone piers, or of taller columns specially made for the building, would have enabled the architect to dispense with such regrettable subterfuges.

The whole of the mosque at Cordoba was surrounded by a high buttressed wall, and there were arcades all round the sahn. We must now retrace our steps to Mesopotamia, where a series of mosques built in the brick style traditional to that country connects the prototype at Madinah with the famous mosque of Ibn Tulun at Cairo. Of these intermediate examples the most noteworthy are at Ukhaidir, Raqqah, Abu Dulaf, and Samarra. The first two of these are now ascribed to the late eighth century, and the other two are of the mid-ninth century. They all carry on the tradition of Sasanian architecture and all have the 'congregational' plan.

The mosque at Ukhaidir, so admirably described in the late Gertrude Bell's monograph, is of vital interest to us because one finds there in embryo the pointed arch which afterwards became the distinctive feature of Western Gothic architecture. The characteristic Sasanian arch is semicircular, but occasionally one meets with isolated early examples of pointed arches. Horseshoe arches were probably used in Mesopotamia before this; there are several in Syrian churches, and actually a Hellenistic example at Chiusi in Italy.

At Ukhaidir the arches are pointed ovoid and slightly stilted, as at Mashatta. But in the Baghdad Gate at Raqqah and at Abu Dulaf near Samarra the arch had assumed the curve typical of later Muslim architecture, and by the end of the eighth century it was replacing all other arch-forms in Mesopotamia. The much earlier pointed arches found occasionally in India are cut out of solid rock, so are not really arches at all. It consists of a sahn with a deep sanctuary on the Mecca side and fairly deep porticoes round the remaining sides of the John. The great brick enclosing-wall has circular towers at each angle and semicircular towers intermediately.

In the south wall of the sanctuary there is a row of small window-openings with cusped or multifold heads. This remarkable feature, also found at Cordoba, may have originated in Buddhist India as Havell suggests; otherwise it must be credited, with all its implications in Western art, to the Muslims. Still more important is the substitution of brick piers to carry the arcades, in place of the antique columns used at Cordoba and elsewhere. These piers are octagonal in form on a square base, and have four circular or octagonal marble shafts to each pier. The shafts were jointed with metal dowels and had bell-shaped capitals. Here we have another feature that passed into Western architecture.

The curious spiral minarets used at Samarra, and later at the mosque of Ibn Tulun, led to no subsequent advance. The mosque of Ibn Tulun at Cairo, commenced in 876, has been described at great length and by many writers but its importance in the history of Muhammadan architecture has been diminished to some extent since we have realized that some of its most distinctive features were anticipated in rather older buildings in Mesopotamia. It is a large congregational mosque, nearly square in plan, with a sahn surrounded on sides by arcaded porticoes, the sanctuary lawn being much deeper than the others. Outside the main walls is an over enclosing court feature that we have not met with before.

Bibliography

Armstrong, Karen. Islam: A Short History. New York: Modern Library, revised ed., 2002.

Awde, Nicholas, trans. and ed. Women in Islam: An Anthology from the Qur'an and Hadîths. New York: Palgrave Macmillan, 2000.

Booth, E. Aristotelian Aporetic Ontology in Islamic and Christian Thinkers. Cambridge, 1983.

Bowker, John. What Muslims Believe. Oxford, UK: Onewworld, 1999.

Burrell, D. Freedom and Creation in Three Traditions. Notre Dame, 1993.

Burrell, D. Knowing the Unknowable God: Ibn Sina, Maimonides, Aquinas (Notre Dame: 1986).

Cook, Michael. The Koran: A Very Short Introduction. Oxford, UK: Oxford University Press, 2000.

Corbin, H. History of Islamic Philosophy, trans. L. Sherrard. London, 1993.

Denny, Frederick Mathewson. An Introduction to Islam. New York: Macmillan, 1994.

Elias, Jamal J. Islam. Upper Saddle River, NJ: Prentice Hall, 1999.

Encyclopedia of Islam , 2nd ed., 11 vols. Leiden, 1960-2002.

Endress, Gerhard. Islam: An Historical Introduction. New York: Columbia University Press, 2nd ed., 2002.

Esposito, John L. and John Obert Voll. Makers of Contemporary Islam. UK, Oxford University Press, 2001.

Fakhry, M. A History of Islamic Philosophy , 2nd ed. New York, 1983.

Gilsenan, Michael. Recognising Islam: an anthropologist's introduction. London: Croom Helm, 1982.

Hodgson, Marshall G.S. The Venture of Islam, 3 Vols. Chicago, IL: University of Chicago Press, 1974.

Keller, Nuh Ha Mim, trans. Al-Nawawi's Manual of Islam. Cambridge, UK: The Islamic Texts Society, 1996.

Lewis, Bernard, ed. The World of Islam: Faith, People, Culture. New York: Thames and Hudson, 1992.

Morewedge, P. (ed.), Neoplatonism and Islamic Thought. Albany, 1992.

Murata, Sachiko and William C. Chittick. The Vision of Islam. New York: Paragon House, 1994.

Nasr, Seyyed Hossein. Islamic Spirituality II: Manifestations. New York: Crossroad, 1991.

Nasr, Seyyed Hossein. The Heart of Islam: Enduring Values for Humanity. San Francisco, CA, Harper San Francisco, 2002.

Qadir , C.A. Philosophy and Science in the Islamic World. London, 1990.

Renard, John, ed. Windows on the House of Islam: Muslim Sources on Spirituality. Berkeley, CA: University of California Press, 1998.

Rippin, Andrew and Jan Knappert, eds. Textual Sources for the Study of Islam. Chicago, IL: University of Chicago Press, 1986.

Rippin, Andrew. Muslims: Their Religious Beliefs and Practices. London: Routledge, 2nd ed., 2001.

Rosenthal, F. Greek Philosophy in the Arab World.

Aldershot, 1990.

Ruthven, Malise. Islam in the World. New York: Oxford University Press, 2nd ed., 2000.

Savory, R.M., ed. Introduction to Islamic Civilization. Cambridge, UK: Cambridge University Press, 1976.

Schimmel, Annemarie. Islam: An Introduction. Albany, NY: State University of New York Press, 1992.

Schulze, Reinhard. A Modern History of the Islamic World. Washington Square, NY: New York University Press, 2000.

Waines, David. An Introduction to Islam. Cambridge, UK: Cambridge University Press, 1995.

Watt, M.W. Islamic Philosophy and Theology. Edinburgh, 1962, revised ed. 1985.

Watt, William Montgomery. The Formative Period of Islamic Thought. Oxford, UK: Oneworld,1998.

Watt, William Montgomery. What is Islam? London: Longman, 1970.

Williams, John Alden, ed. The Word of Islam. Austin, TX: University of Texas Press, 1994.

Wolfson, H.A. Studies in the History of Philosophy and Religion , ed. I. Twersky, G.H. Williams, in 2 vols. Cambridge, MA, 1973, 1977.

Wolfson, H.A. The Philosophy of the Kalam. Cambridge, MA, 1976.

Ziai, H. "Islamic Philosophy," in The Oxford Companion to Philosophy, ed. T. Honderich. Oxford , 1955.

Index

A

B

C

E

F

I

L

M